Learning About Learning

GEMS Teacher's Guide

Grades 6–8

Skills
Observing, Comparing, Communicating, Using Simulations, Measuring, Recording and Interpreting Data, Graphing, Organizing, Noticing Patterns, Making Inferences, Drawing Conclusions

Concepts
How individuals learn, How the scientific community learns, Health and Safety, Product Testing, Animal Behavior, Nature of Science, Ethics of Experimentation, Human Nervous System, Neurons, Learning and the Brain

Themes
Systems and Interactions, Models and Simulations, Patterns of Change, Scale and Structure, Evolution, Unity and Diversity

Math Strands
Number, Function, Pattern, Measurement, Logic and Language

Nature of Science and Mathematics
Scientific Community, Cooperative Efforts, Creativity and Constraints, Theory-Based and Testable, Changing Nature of Facts and Theories, Science and Technology, Objectivity and Ethics, Real-Life Applications

Time
Ten or more 45–60 minute sessions

by
Jacqueline Barber
Katharine Barrett
Kevin Beals
Lincoln Bergman
Marian C. Diamond

LHS GEMS

Great Explorations in Math and Science
Lawrence Hall of Science
University of California at Berkeley

Cover Design
Carol Bevilacqua

Illustrations
Lisa Haderlie Baker
Carol Bevilacqua
Rose Craig
Lisa Klofkorn

Photographs
Richard Hoyt
Laurence Bradley

LHS★

Lawrence Hall of Science,
University of California,
Berkeley, CA 94720

Initial support for the origination and publication of the GEMS series was provided by the A.W. Mellon Foundation and the Carnegie Corporation of New York. Under a grant from the National Science Foundation, GEMS Leader's Workshops have been held across the country. GEMS has also received support from: the McDonnell-Douglas Foundation and the McDonnell-Douglas Employees Community Fund; the Hewlett Packard Company; Join Hands, the Health and Safety Educational Alliance; and the people at Chevron USA. GEMS also gratefully acknowledges the contribution of word processing equipment from Apple Computer, Inc. This support does not imply responsibility for statements or views expressed in publications of the GEMS program. For further information on GEMS leadership opportunities, or to receive a catalog and the *GEMS Network News*, please contact GEMS at the address and phone number below. We also welcome letters to the *GEMS Network News*.

The development, testing, and publication of *Learning About Learning* was sponsored by a grant from Join Hands, the Health and Safety Educational Alliance. The GEMS Program and the Lawrence Hall of Science greatly appreciate this support.

International Standard Book Number: 0-924886-42-0

COMMENTS WELCOME!

Great Explorations in Math and Science (GEMS) is an ongoing curriculum development project. GEMS guides are revised periodically, to incorporate teacher comments and new approaches. We welcome your criticisms, suggestions, helpful hints, and any anecdotes about your experience presenting GEMS activities. Your suggestions will be reviewed each time a GEMS guide is revised. Please send your comments to:

GEMS Revisions,
c/o Lawrence Hall of Science,
University of California,
Berkeley, CA 94720-5200.
The phone number is (510) 642-7771.
The fax number is (510) 643-0309.
Our e-mail is GEMS@uclink4.berkeley.edu

Great Explorations in Math and Science (GEMS) Program

The Lawrence Hall of Science (LHS) is a public science center on the University of California at Berkeley campus. LHS offers a full program of activities for the public, including workshops and classes, exhibits, films, lectures, and special events. LHS is also a center for teacher education and curriculum research and development.

Over the years, LHS staff have developed a multitude of activities, assembly programs, classes, and interactive exhibits. These programs have proven to be successful at the Hall and should be useful to schools, other science centers, museums, and community groups. A number of these guided-discovery activities have been published under the Great Explorations in Math and Science (GEMS) title, after an extensive refinement and adaptation process that includes classroom testing of trial versions, modifications to ensure the use of easy-to-obtain materials, with carefully written and edited step-by-step instructions and background information to allow presentation by teachers without special background in mathematics or science.

Staff

Glenn T. Seaborg, **Principal Investigator**
Jacqueline Barber, **Director**
Kimi Hosoume, **Assistant Director**
Cary Sneider, **Science Curriculum Specialist**
Jaine Kopp, **Mathematics Curriculum Specialist**
Carolyn Willard, **GEMS Sites and Centers Coordinator**
Laura Tucker, **GEMS Workshop Coordinator**
Katharine Barrett, Kevin Beals, Ellen Blinderman, Beatrice Boffen, Gigi Dornfest, John Erickson, Stan Fukunaga, Cathy Larripa, Linda Lipner, Laura Lowell, Stephen Rutherford, Debra Sutter, Rebecca Tilley, **Staff Development Specialists**
Cynthia Eaton, **Administrative Coordinator**
Karen Milligan, **Distribution Coordinator**
Terry Cort, **Workshop Administrator**
Felicia Roston, **Shipping Coordinator**
Bryan Burd, George Kasarjian, **Shipping Assistants**
Stephanie Van Meter, **Trial Testing Coordinator**
Lisa Haderlie Baker, **Art Director**
Carol Bevilacqua, Rose Craig, Lisa Klofkorn, **Designers**
Gerri Ginsburg, **Public Information Representative**
Lincoln Bergman, **Principal Editor**
Carl Babcock, **Senior Editor**
Florence Stone, **Assistant Editor**
Kay Fairwell, **Principal Publications Coordinator**
Larry Gates, Nancy Lin, Karla Penuelas, Alisa Sramala, **Staff Assistants**

Contributing Authors

Jacqueline Barber
Katharine Barrett
Kevin Beals
Lincoln Bergman
Beverly Braxton
Kevin Cuff
Celia Cuomo
Linda De Lucchi
Gigi Dornfest
Jean Echols
Philip Gonsalves
Jan M. Goodman
Alan Gould
Kimi Hosoume
Susan Jagoda
Jaine Kopp
Linda Lipner
Laura Lowell
Larry Malone
Cary I. Sneider
Craig Strang
Debra Sutter
Rebecca Tilley
Jennifer Meux White
Carolyn Willard

Reviewers

We would like to thank the following educators who reviewed, tested, or coordinated the reviewing of *this series* of GEMS materials in manuscript and draft form (including the GEMS guides *Learning About Learning* and *Secret Formulas*). Their critical comments and recommendations, based on classroom presentation of these activities nationwide, contributed significantly to these GEMS publications. Their participation in the review process does not necessarily imply endorsement of the GEMS program or responsibility for statements or views expressed. This role is an invaluable one; feedback is carefully recorded and integrated as appropriate into the publications. **THANK YOU!**

ALASKA

Iditarod Elementary School, Wasilla
Tacy Carr
Cynthia Dolmas Curran*
Carol Lowery
Bonnie Tesar

ARIZONA

Hualapai Elementary School, Kingman
Nora Brown
Catherine Ann Claes*
Traci A. D'Arcy
Rhonda Gilbert
Lisa Julle*
Barbara McLarty
Stephanie L. Murillo
Rose Roberts

Northern Arizona University, Flagstaff
Lynda Hatch**

CALIFORNIA

Albany Middle School, Albany
Jenny Anderson
Chiyo Masuda
Kay Sorg*
Janet Teel

Beacon Day School, Oakland
Deborah Ellis

Claremont Middle School, Oakland
Susan Cristancho*
Malia Dinell-Schwartz
Sheila Lucia
Mike Predovic

Dover Middle School, Fairfield
Rebecca Hammond
Sarah Yourd

Fairmont Elementary School, El Cerrito
Nancy Buckingham
Carrie Cook*
Karen DeTore
Sandi Healy
Linda Lambie*
Katy Miles
Laura Peck
Nancy Rutter-Spriggs

Foshay Learning Center, Los Angeles
Stephanie Hoffman*

Golden State Middle School, West Sacramento
Natasha Lowrie

Jefferson Elementary School, Berkeley
Mary Ann Furuichi
Linda Mengel*
Fern Stroud
Gaye Ying

Malcolm X Intermediate School, Berkeley
Arden Clute
DeEtte LaRue
Mahalia Ryba*

Marina Middle School, Los Angeles
Leticia Escajeda

Markham Elementary School, Oakland
Eleanor Feuille
Sharon Kerr*
Ruth Quezada
Audry Taylor
Margaret Wright

Nelson Elementary School, Pinedale
Julia Hollenbeck
Vicki Jackson
Erla Stanley
Phyllis Todd*

Nobel Middle School, Northridge
Margie Hickman

Oxford School, Berkeley
Anita Baker*
Mary Barrett
Joe Brulenski
Barbara Edwards
Judy Kono

Park Day School, Oakland
Aggie Brenneman
Karen Corzan*
Michelle McAfee Krueger
Suzie McLean-Balderston

Parker Elementary School, Oakland
Lorynne Dupree
Linda Rogers*
Zepita Sharp
Marian Wilson

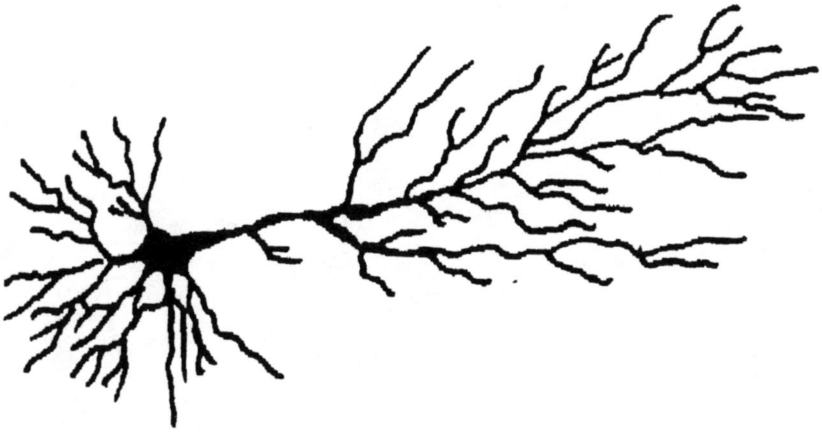

Washington Irving Middle School, Los Angeles
Mary Lu Camacho
Bernadette J. Cullen
Joe Kevany
Thomas Yee*

Westside Science Center, Los Angeles
Nonnie Korten**

Willard Junior High School, Berkeley
Kathy Evan
Clydine James

COLORADO

Franklin Elementary School, Sterling
Vickie Baseggio
Marty Belknap
Barbara Nelson
Shelly Stumpf*

DISTRICT OF COLUMBIA

Anne Beers Elementary School, Washington, D.C.
Elizabeth Dortch
Fredric Hutchinson
Gloria McKenzie-Freeman
Connie Parker*
Gregory Taylor
Gloria Warren Tucker**

MAINE

Coastal Ridge Elementary School, York
Nancy Annis
Rick Comeau**
Julie Crafts
Patricia Gray
Carol A. Moody

York Middle School, York
Andrew Berenson
Deborah J. Bradburn
Rick Comeau**
Jean Dominguez
Susan E. Miller
Robert G. Vincent

MICHIGAN

Marine City Middle School, Marine City
Peggy Brooks*
Gina Day
Laura Newton
Alan Starkey

NORTH CAROLINA

C. W. Stanford Middle School, Hillsborough
Leslie Kay Jones*
Tom Kuntzleman
Christopher Longwill
Dawn M. Wills

Grady Brown Elementary School, Hillsborough
Lisa A. Crocker
Audrey T. Johnson
Sandra Kosik
Sandra L. McKee*
Tonya L. Price
Karen Sexton

* On-Site Coordinator
** Regional Coordinator

Contents

Acknowledgments

For many years, the Biology Education Program at the Lawrence Hall of Science has been developing and teaching activities about learning and the human brain. Many staff members contributed to the development of a wide range of innovative activities and exhibits, including Katharine Barrett, Dr. Susan Brady, Richard Rainbolt, Alysia Galo, Heidi Schnabel, and Dr. Jennifer White. In 1990, Dr. Marian Diamond, a leading brain researcher, became Director of the Lawrence Hall of Science. While Dr. Diamond had collaborated with LHS staff for many years, her leadership of the Hall brought with it new enthusiasm and interest in continuing to develop opportunities for students and their parents to learn about how they learn, and this most precious resource that each and everyone of us possesses—our brain!

Learning About Learning builds on this early work as well as on a great deal of subsequent curriculum development conducted by the authors. The result is a broadening of the scope of this teacher's guide to include a perspective on how learning is essential to our survival (as individuals and as a species), how learning causes humans to thrive, and how this thriving enhances our very survival. This overall message is embodied in Marian Diamond's lifelong study of the brain.

We greatly appreciate the time taken by wolf researcher Dr. Elizabeth Coscia in her careful review and comments on the wolf role-play activities and background information. Dr. Michael S. Taekman, a neurosurgeon with offices in Berkeley and Oakland, was kind enough to review the background information, particularly as it relates to medical issues, neuropathy, the case of Genie, and related subjects. Jennifer Seiler of the Chemistry Education Program at LHS provided extremely helpful assistance in the development and refinement of the Hexacarbon Solvent Mystery.

In addition to the dozens of classroom teachers who carefully helped us craft this guide through their diligent trial testing of early versions, and who are listed at the front of the guide, we would like to give special thanks to Kay Sorg and Malia Dinnell Schwartz, two trial teachers who put in a great deal of extra effort and creativity, substantially influencing the activities in this unit, and to all the teachers who helped us further refine the hexacarbon mystery by teaching it in their classrooms.

We are also grateful to Natasha Lowrie at Golden State Middle School in West Sacramento, California, who allowed one of the co-authors, Kevin Beals, to present a late revision of Activity 4, The Hexacarbon Solvent Mystery, to her group of eager sixth graders.

Margey Race and Flori Ramos of LHS made helpful comments on the "Learning About Learning" play in Activity 10.

We would particularly like to acknowledge the careful review of this guide, many constructive suggestions made, and contributions to the "Behind the Scenes" section by representatives of Join Hands, the Health and Safety Educational Alliance, whose grant sponsored this guide, especially its Executive Director Paul Ford and Board Member Kay Puryear.

Multiplication
Place Value
Capitalization Rules
Ms. Kerr's
THINK
Learning About Learning
Estudiando a Estudiando

Introduction

Learning About Learning is a unique unit of study. It allows students to investigate the topic of learning from several different perspectives. How, as individual humans, do we learn? How can we help or hinder that learning process? Do animals learn in a similar way? How, as a community of humans, do we learn things that are important to our survival? How do our brains get information? Does the actual structure of our brains change with learning?

Students consider these and other questions as they delve into the study of the human organism, animal behavior, health and safety, product testing, the ethics of experimentation, and what scientists do. In addition to providing a compelling way to study these important content areas, this unit enables students to learn more effectively themselves as they continually reflect on their own learning process. They are truly learning about learning!

Activities 1 through 3 of the guide focus on how **individual** humans and animals learn. Students learn that learning relies on information from the world that we perceive through our senses. This learning is important to our very survival.

In Activity 1, they begin by making tactile mazes using sticker strips, and then test those mazes on a blindfolded partner. They time how long it takes their partner to run the maze several different times. This provides a measure of learning. They discuss how limiting sensory information (by wearing a blindfold) makes learning more challenging.

In Activity 2, students again learn each others' mazes, this time, coaching each other. As a class, they focus on the things which both help and interfere with their learning. They discuss the learning differences that humans have and how becoming more conscious of these differences and of the different learning strengths that people have can help us take these differences into account, as well as assist us in learning (and teaching!) more effectively.

In Activity 3, students continue to explore how humans and animals learn using sensory information from their environment. Students pretend to be lost wolf pups and use their sense of smell to learn who the members of their pack are, and where their home den is. They discuss the importance of learning and sensory information to survival.

Activities 4 and 5 of the guide focus on how, **as a community of humans,** we learn things that are important for our survival. Students see how our more greatly developed capacities to think and learn from experience distinguish us from animals. The issues of health and safety, product testing, and the ethics of experimentation are raised in the context of several real-life stories.

In Activity 4, students attempt to solve two health-related mysteries that are based on the true stories of how scientists discovered that a certain chemical solvent used in a fabric printing plant was dangerous, and how scientists learned of the severe nerve damage that can be caused by sniffing glue or other solvents. Students follow two trails of clues, learning firsthand how scientists learn. They become the researchers as they ask questions and evaluate evidence, make inferences, and discover that the two mysteries are intertwined. They are also introduced to some of the methods scientists use to test product safety and improve environmental and occupational health and safety.

In Activity 5, students investigate how animals and humans learn what is safe to eat and why there is a need for regulations applying to foods, drugs, cosmetics and their safety. In class, students again pretend to be wolves. This time they are hungry wolves, investigating unknown "food" items. They reflect on how the wolves learned what was "safe" to eat and how, as humans, we have evolved other ways of ensuring that our foods are safe without having to rely on first-hand sensory information. For homework, students read an historic health and safety story. This tragic story involved an untested eyelash and eyebrow dye and led to the development of the Federal Food, Drug, and Cosmetic Act of 1938, enabling the Food and Drug Administration (FDA) finally to begin to protect people by regulating these substances.

Activities 6, 7, and 8 continue to focus on **how the scientific community learns.** Students test the hypothesis that learning changes the actual structure of the brain as they investigate the effects of environment on learning. They see that learning is not just important for our survival—it causes us to thrive. Again, the context of real-life stories and research makes these topics relevant and interesting to students.

In Activity 6, students read and discuss the story of "Genie," a true story about a girl raised in isolation. They learn how a team of scientists tried to determine what effect this "impoverished" environment had on Genie's capacity to learn and on the structure of her developing brain. They discuss the ethics of learning by conducting research on humans.

In Activity 7, students conduct "brain research" themselves as they measure and compare diagrams of brain cells from rats raised in "impoverished" environments and those raised in "enriched" environments. This simulation is based on the work of a leading brain researcher, Dr. Marian Diamond, and her quest to see if learning changes the physical structure of the brain.

In Activity 8, students complete their "brain research" as they draw conclusions from their experimental data. Among other findings, students conclude that not only do "enriched" environments result in *increased growth* of rat brain cells, "impoverished" environments result in *decreased growth* of rat brain cells. They then discuss the implications of this research for humans.

The last two activities provide closure to the unit, enabling the students to reflect on what they have learned.

In Activity 9, students engage in dialogue about the benefits and costs of learning by conducting research with humans, animals, or *in vitro* (with cell and tissue cultures). This discussion of ethics provides a wonderful setting to follow up, in a formal way, on the many ethical issues that get raised through the activities in this unit.

In Activity 10, students read aloud Common Sense: The GEMS Learning About Learning Play, in dramatic style. The fun interaction of characters summarizes some of the main ideas of the unit in a light-hearted and memorable way.

Certain subjects are difficult to access in a hands-on way. For instance, in astronomy, the objects of study are so distant that they can't be interacted with directly. In this case, scientists learn much of what they know from models, simulations, observations made from a distance, and inferences. Likewise, the topics of how we learn and what happens in our brains are less tangible than other topics. In this case, distance is not the issue—ethics and practicality are.

Issues of ethics and practicality, as well as gaps in current knowledge and technology, limit the ways in which researchers can study the human brain and the learning process directly. In the classroom, it is also a challenge to find ways to focus on the brain and on learning itself. In this unit, we have sought to do this through the use of diverse learning formats. Thus, the activities in this unit will engage your students in some direct hands-on learning, quite a few simulations (where they play the role of animals or scientists), putting on a play, reading and hearing accounts of true, compelling stories, and finally, providing opportunities to reflect on what they've learned in small groups and as a class. We hope that you and your students will enjoy this more interactive approach to what has traditionally been communicated through a chapter in a textbook.

We bring the issue of the ethics of experimentation right into the unit for students to understand more about and grapple with at whatever level of complexity is appropriate. Addressing some of the important issues of health and safety in this unit seemed a natural, necessary, and fitting accompaniment to the ethical issues—there are compelling reasons why we need to learn certain things, and these reasons are related to our own survival as well as the health of the planet.

The rich variety of homework articles, stories, and activities that present and simulate **the actual work and processes used by real scientists** is a strong facet of this unit. This kind of information is often glossed over or completely omitted, leading to the spread of many misconceptions about what scientists do and how they do it, as well as "setting up" scientists and mathematicians as "authorities" and "experts," rather than as constant seekers and lifelong learners. Learning about how the scientific community really learns conveys fascinating information while providing a much more connected understanding of the important processes we call "science" and of the women and men who "do" science. In a time when there is an urgent need for young people of all backgrounds to gain knowledge and skills in scientific, mathematical, and technological fields, it can be of great value for students to understand more about what these careers involve.

Some teachers enjoy bringing more specific brain anatomy and physiology into this unit. We have provided Activity-by-Activity background with specific information about the brain and additional scientific information, as it relates to each activity, in the "Behind the Scenes" section. We want to emphasize, however, that no pre-teaching is necessary. The unit, as it is designed, serves as a wonderful *introduction* to the topic of learning and the human brain. The additional background information is provided in case you choose to build upon the opportunity provided by your students' curiosity to delve further into these fascinating and important areas of interest.

"Summary Outlines" are provided to help you guide your students through these activities. This guide is spiral bound for your convenience in duplicating student sheets. Selected student outcomes are also included, accompanied by assessment suggestions. These assessment suggestions include descriptions of the many assessment opportunities that are built into these activities, along with additional assessment ideas. Books that make strong literature connections to the activities featured in this guide are summarized under "Literature Connections." Many helpful resources and references are provided in the "Resources" section.

Finally, we hope that you and your students will enjoy your voyage of learning about learning. As you will discover, you and your students' learning will result in an increased number of dendrites in every one of your brains! We grew more than a few in developing and writing this unit!

Research on the brain proceeds at a rapid pace. Every week brings new discoveries that may contribute to treatment of diseases such as Alzheimer's and Parkinson's, and shed much light on learning, memory, and aging. ***The 1990s have been called "the decade of the brain," and, as we enter the next century, there can be no doubt that this amazing pace will continue.*** *You and your students may want to find out more about current research. An article in the January 4, 2000* New York Times *by Sandra Blakeslee, entitled "A Decade of Discovery Yields a Shock About the Brain," reports on increasing evidence that* ***the brain develops and maintains itself throughout our lives by adding new brain cells.*** *For many decades, scientists thought people were born with all the brain cells they would ever have. It was agreed the brain could add many new connections, such as dendrites and synapses, but thought impossible for the brain to grow new neurons, or brain cells. But new technology has enabled scientists to study the brain more closely and many studies now indicate growth of new cells. While there is still controversy, the article quotes a Norwegian neurobiologist, Dr. Morten Raastad, who compares resistance to this new idea to the way geologists for years rejected the idea of plate tectonics and continental drift!*

Time Frame

Activity 1: Learning a Maze
Preparation...30 minutes
Class Activity............one or two 45–60 minute sessions

Activity 2: Good Teachers, Good Learners
Preparation...10 minutes
Class Activity..........................one 45–60 minute session

Activity 3: Silent Smell Tracking
Preparation...30 minutes
Class Activity..........................one 45–60 minute session

Activity 4: The Hexacarbon Solvent Mystery
Preparation...30 minutes
Class Activity..........two or three 45–60 minute sessions

Activity 5: Learning What is Safe
Preparation...60 minutes
Class Activity..........................one 45–60 minute session
(optional additional session to discuss homework article)......................15–30 minutes

Activity 6: The Story of Genie
Preparation..10–20 minutes
Class Activity........................one 45–60 minute session

Activity 7: Learning and Environment (Part I)
Preparation..30–45 minutes
Class Activity.......................one 45–60 minute session

Activity 8: Learning and Environment (Part II)
Preparation...10 minutes
Class Activity..........................one 45–60 minute session

Activity 9: Ethics of Learning
Preparation...0 minutes
Class Activity..........................one 30–60 minute session

Activity 10: The Learning About Learning Play
Preparation...20 minutes
Class Activity.......................one 30–45 minute session

Note: Preparation times are an average and do not include obtaining the materials or reading the teacher's guide.

ON
NEURON

Activity 1: Learning a Maze

In this activity, students use stick-on mailing label strips to create mazes on construction paper that can be learned by their blindfolded partners. Students time how long it takes their partners to run a maze, using only their fingertips to feel the pathways. The time it takes to complete a maze tends to improve each time a student does it, providing one way to measure the learning that occurs.

At the conclusion of the activity students discuss what the learning experience was like for them. They share their thoughts about how they knew they were learning, what they learned well, where improvement was still needed, and whether timing was a good way to measure their learning. Finally, they discuss what it was like not being able to see and how learning relies on information from the world that we perceive through our senses.

There are several fine books that describe the experience of a person who is newly blind, and how he learns to cope in the world without vision. One such book, called The Cay, *is written by Theodore Taylor. It describes the struggles of an 11-year-old boy to re-learn many things. Several teachers commented on how reading this book while doing the activities in* Learning About Learning, *especially Activities 1 and 2, helped the unit come alive for their students. (See the "Literature Connections" for other suggestions.)*

What You Need

For the class:

- ❏ 4–5 sheets of stick-on mailing labels, 30 labels per page (1" x 2 5/8" labels). See "Getting Ready" section.
- ❏ paper cutter
- ❏ an overhead transparency of the Make A Maze student sheet (master on page 16)
- ❏ an extra blank overhead transparency on which to model the maze-making
- ❏ 2 small stickers (one of a different shape/size/texture from the other). See "Getting Ready" section.
- ❏ 1 transparency pen
- ❏ overhead projector
- ❏ chalkboard and chalk
- ❏ clock with a second hand

For each pair of students:

- ❏ 1 manila folder (or tall book) to create a visual barrier
- ❏ 2 Make A Maze student sheets (master on page 16)
- ❏ 2 sheets of construction paper (8 ½" x 11"). See "Getting Ready" section.
- ❏ 4 small stickers (two of a different shape/size/texture from the other two). See "Getting Ready" section.
- ❏ 2 pencils
- ❏ (*optional*) 2 envelopes to hold the strips and stickers

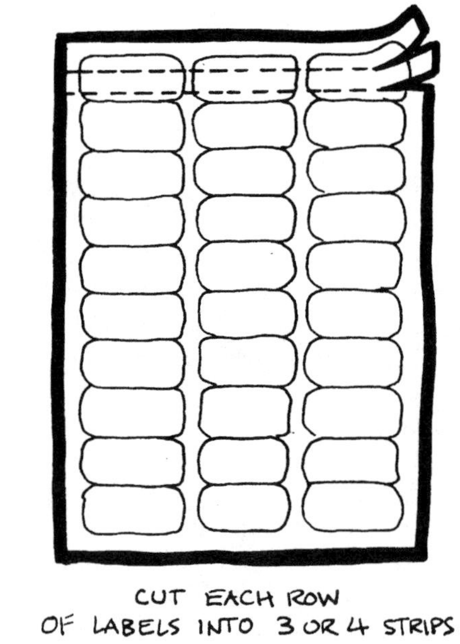

One teacher used self-adhesive stars for one type of sticker. She used the outsides border of the sticker stars for the second type of sticker.

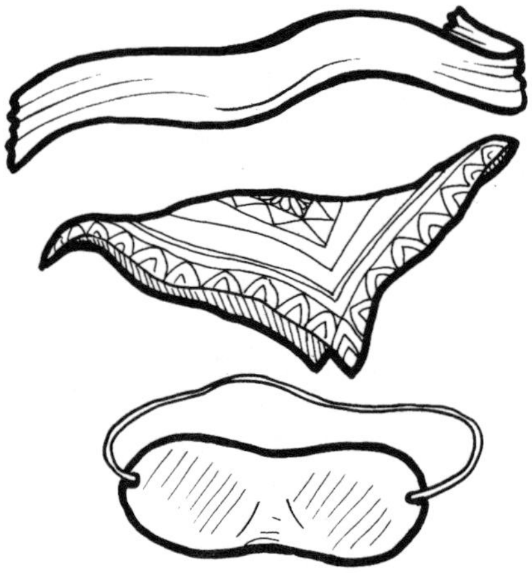

One teacher had students make makeshift blindfolds out of safety goggles.

- ❑ (*optional*) 1 blindfold (bandanna, strip of fabric, or eye mask without eye holes). See "Getting Ready" section.

Getting Ready

Several Days Before the Activity

1. Acquire the materials needed for this session.

Stick-on Mailing Labels: The mailing labels that come three columns to a page of 30 labels in a standard, 8 ½" x 11" format work well. Each label is 1" x 2 ⅝". While the exact size is not critical (since you will be cutting them into strips), it is important to get mailing labels that have slightly rounded edges. This rounded edge makes these labels far easier to peel from their backing. One box of labels will be enough for several teachers and their classes. *Note*: this is an excellent material to get parents to donate as mailing labels are readily available in many office situations.

Construction Paper: Students will build their mazes on construction paper using stick-on strips made from the mailing labels. Construction paper feels substantially different from the smooth mailing labels and therefore is important to the success of this activity.

Stickers: You will need two different small stickers for each student to use—one at the beginning of the maze and one at the end. The stickers need to feel different from each other (different size, shape, and/or texture) so students can distinguish the beginning of the maze from the end while blindfolded. Stickers that feel too similar will be frustrating to the students. Stick-on dots, circle reinforcements, and stars are inexpensive suggestions.

Blindfolds: We strongly recommend getting blindfolds because it relieves the tremendous temptation students have to peek during this sightless activity. However, if getting this many blindfolds (one for each pair of students) proves difficult, you can have your students close their eyes during the activity instead.

2. Duplicate one copy of the Make A Maze student sheet for each student (master on page 16). Make an overhead transparency of this student sheet for modeling and demonstration.

3. Make a class set of stick-on strips for students to use in making their tactile mazes. You will need 4–5 sheets of stick-on mailing labels per class. Using a paper cutter, cut each row of labels into three or four thin strips, about ¼" x 8 ½". Each strip will then have three separate pieces that may be peeled from the backing to make the maze pathway. Each student will need four of these thin strips to make a pathway of 12 sections. Make some extras in case students "mess up."

EACH STUDENT GETS 4 OF THESE STRIPS

4. (*Optional*) Place 12 sections of stick-on label (four of the strips you cut) and two small stickers in an envelope for each student for easy distribution. Alternatively, you can place the stickers and stick-on strips in a central location and have students get them themselves.

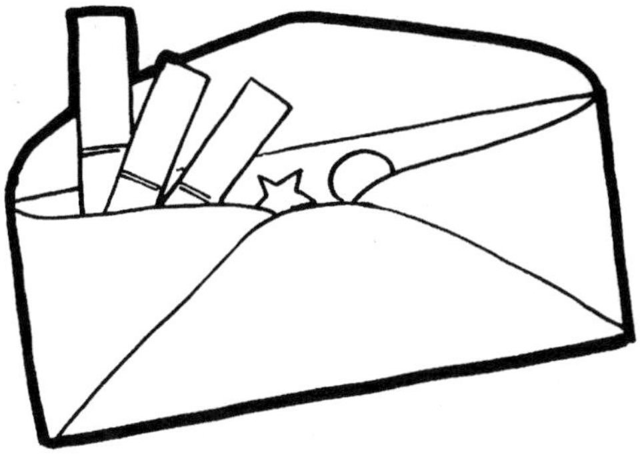

The Day of the Activity

1. Set up an overhead projector. Place the overhead transparency of the Make A Maze student sheet, the extra blank transparency, transparency pen, a set of 12 stick-on strips, two small stickers, and a blindfold nearby for the demonstration.

2. Have the student sheets, construction paper, envelopes containing strips and stickers, the rest of the blindfolds, and the manila folders handy.

3. If many of your students do not have watches, set up a clock with a second hand in a central location.

Learning About Learning

1. Begin by asking students, "How do you think we learn?" Spend just a few minutes hearing students' ideas. Accept all responses at this time—these are your students initial thoughts. They will be refined throughout the course of this unit. You may want to record their ideas on the chalkboard.

2. Tell them that this is the first session of a unit called *Learning About Learning*. Explain to your students that they will be doing just that—learning about learning! They will learn:

- how to measure their learning;
- how, as individual humans, we go about learning;
- how, as a community of humans, we learn;

- how learning is key to our survival;
- what conditions are best for learning;
- how our brains change as a result of learning; and
- how learning can change your brain no matter how old you are.

Introducing the Tactile Maze Activity

1. Tell your students that in this activity each one of them will be challenged to learn a maze, without using the sense of sight. First, they will design secret mazes for each other. These will be tactile mazes that allow them to feel the pathways with their fingers, since they will be blindfolded when they do the maze.

2. Second, they will work in pairs to learn each other's mazes. They will take turns. First, one person will do the other person's maze several times (blindfolded, of course). Her partner will time how long it takes to do the maze each time. As the student learns the maze, the time it takes to do it is likely to get shorter and shorter. By timing the maze runs, we can *measure your learning*. After one person has a chance to learn the other's maze, they will switch roles.

3. Model how to make a tactile maze on the overhead using a blank overhead transparency and stick-on strips and stickers.

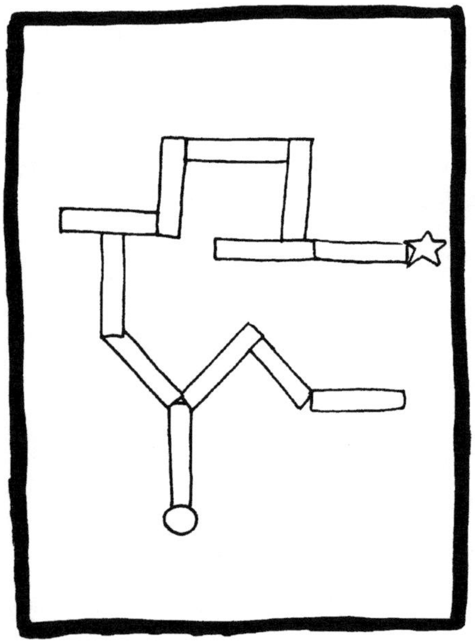

a. Begin by explaining that you have 12 stick-on sections to use in making the maze. You also have one sticker to mark the beginning of the maze; another sticker to mark the end of the maze.

b. Go ahead and actually create a maze on the overhead transparency. Talk about your decisions as you make them. For example, "I think I'll put a Y right near the beginning; I'll make a dead end here; this will be my end point;" etc.

c. Tell students that when *they* design their mazes, they should set up a barrier so their partner can't see their maze ahead of time. Show how this can be done with a manila folder or tall book.

4. Model how to conduct the maze-learning trials by inviting a volunteer to be your partner. Blindfold the

volunteer. Point out that when *they* learn each others' mazes, they will not have seen what it looks like first.

One teacher had her students tie their bandanna blindfolds leaving an overhanging flap so there was no peeking.

a. Ask someone in the class to be your timer. Begin by placing the blindfolded volunteer's finger on the sticker that indicates the start of the maze and saying, "GO!" As the volunteer moves along the maze, point out to the class how she is *feeling* her way. When the volunteer reaches the sticker at the end of the maze, tell your timer, "STOP TIMING."

b. Find out from your timer how long it took. Record this time on the overhead of the Make A Maze student sheet. (You might want to point out that when they do this as partners, they will be their own timers.)

c. Repeat this process, having the volunteer run the maze a second time, and record the time it took.

d. Ask the students to compare the time trials to see if it took less time for the volunteer to run the maze the second time. Ask how long they predict the next trial will take. The one after that?

e. Tell students they will conduct *three* timed trials of each maze.

5. Spend just a few minutes addressing the issue of competition and judging each other. Point out that it is impossible to determine who is the best or fastest learner, because each maze is different. It might take one person longer to run a maze because that maze is more complicated or trickier. Remind them that the main goal is **not** to do the maze as quickly as possible, but rather to see **how** they learn the maze and whether they can **measure** that process.

Making Mazes and Measuring Learning

1. When students understand what they are to do, assign partners. Distribute student sheets, construction paper, stick-on strips, stickers, and manila folders and have them begin making their mazes.

2. Circulate around the room as students are working, encouraging students as you go. **Make sure that they finish making their mazes within about ten minutes,** so they will have time to learn each maze.

3. When each pair of students finishes making their mazes, have them begin the maze-learning trials. Fifteen minutes should be enough for pairs of students to conduct three timed trials on each other's mazes. Help them pace themselves by reminding them how much time is remaining.

4. Ten minutes before the end of class, ask students to stop what they are doing and to focus their attention with you.

Some teachers have found that their students become very involved in designing mazes and want more time. Many of these teachers decided to spend an extra session on this activity—one on making mazes, and one on measuring learning. If you decide to do this, keep in mind that students will revisit their mazes in Activity 2.

Note: While the following wrap-up discussion is best conducted immediately after this activity, if you run out of time, this is a good break point. You might be able to conduct the wrap-up discussion at the beginning of the next session and still have enough time to conduct Activity 2.

Reflecting on the Experience

1. Conduct a brief discussion about the experience of learning mazes. Could they tell they were learning? What evidence indicated that they were learning? Did it get easier each time? Were they able to improve the time it took to learn the maze? What was the hardest part? Did they notice that there were areas of the maze that they had learned well and others that still seemed unknown? Spend several minutes having several students share what it was like for them.

2. Ask if they think timing the trials was a good way to measure learning. Invite them to discuss how effective the time trials were as a measure of learning. Ask if it is possible to be learning more about the maze without improving your time.

3. Remind them that they learned the maze without their sense of sight. Were they aware of using any other sense than touch? Was it harder without seeing? Would it have been even harder if they could not see *and* not hear?

4. Conclude by pointing out that when we learn, we rely on information from the world that we perceive through our senses. The more multi-sensory information we receive, the easier the learning is.

5. Students will need their mazes and their student sheets for the next session. Either collect them or have students put them in a safe place.

Going Further

1. Have students try doing a maze they have already learned, but this time change the maze's orientation so, for instance, the construction paper is sideways on the desk instead of "longways." Does the orientation of the maze affect a person's ability to do it?

2. Set aside 10 minutes of class time during which students are blindfolded. Then present 10 minutes of class time during which communication between you and the students is limited to visually transmitted information (chalkboard notes, sign language, written notes, posters, mime). Have students write about their experiences.

3. Suggest that students try watching a video in class or their favorite TV program at home for 10–15 minutes with the sound turned down. Without their sense of hearing, were they able to follow the story? What cues did they use?

4. Invite a sightless person to class to tell of his or her experiences living in the world. What does he or she think students should know/learn about being blind? Ask the visitor to explain how he or she compensates for lack of vision and finds ways to navigate through daily life. What helps and what hinders the ability of a blind or seriously visually impaired person to be fully involved at all levels of community life? Have newer laws, such as the Americans with Disabilities Act, along with increasing community consciousness of the need to ensure access to transportation, events, and facilities, led to real improvement in society's relation to the blind?

5. Samples of Braille writing are often available for free or on loan from libraries and from community organizations that work with the blind. Obtain materials in Braille and invite your students to learn this tactile alphabet. (See "Resources" section for possible sources of Braille materials.)

6. Read a passage of a book about a blind person. (See the "Literature Connections" and "Resources" sections for ideas.)

7. Read passages of books that have rich descriptions of tactile experiences.

MAKE A MAZE

Name: ____________________

1. Design your own maze by connecting sticker strips on a piece of construction paper.
2. See how long it takes for someone else to learn your maze while blindfolded.

Subject #1 ______________

Trial	Time (mins/secs)
1	
2	
3	

Subject #2 ______________

Trial	Time (mins/secs)
1	
2	
3	

Subject #3 ______________

Trial	Time (mins/secs)
1	
2	
3	

STUDENT RESOURCE BOOK
Mathematics
UNLIMITED

Activity 2: Good Teachers, Good Learners

In this activity, students again work with partners to learn tactile mazes. However this time, one partner plays the role of coach with the goal of actively helping the other partner learn the maze. After this teaching and learning experience, students generate lists of things that help and hinder learning. The teacher helps students articulate what helps them learn best, drawing ideas from students' life experiences as learners. The class concludes with a discussion of individual learning differences.

The focus of this session encourages students to widen their maze learning experiences to include other kinds of learning and to consider the different combinations of strengths that different individuals bring to the "learning table." Many teachers, for example, as noted on page 22, take this opportunity to introduce students to intriguing ideas about "multiple intelligences" derived from the concepts of Howard Gardner.

The reflection on learning in this activity also encourages students to start developing a more conscious picture of their own individual learning processes. In this sense, it is an important bridge to the intense learning about many new things they are about to experience in the rest of the unit. This process of self understanding is also an important and concrete step toward students "taking responsibility for their own learning."

What You Need

For the class:

- ❑ student mazes and Make A Maze student sheets from Activity 1
- ❑ 2 large sheets of butcher paper
- ❑ a marker
- ❑ masking tape
- ❑ clock with a second hand

Getting Ready

The Day of the Activity

1. If you collected the students' mazes and student sheets, have them handy.

2. Write "Helps Learning" and "Hinders Learning" on the top of the two large pieces of paper and post them at the front of the room. Have a marker nearby.

3. If many of your students do not have watches, set up a clock with a second hand in a central location.

Learn How You Learn

1. Tell the class that their job as students is to learn. In a sense, they are professional learners—and will be for many more years! Because of that, it is really important for them to be aware of how they learn best. There are certain ways that all humans learn best. However, there are also individual differences in how each of us learn. Knowing our personal learning styles is a powerful way to become a better learner.

2. Today, they will be learning tactile mazes again, but this time they will focus on things that **help their learning** and things that **interfere with (get in the way of or hinder) their learning.**

Coaching Each Other

You might want to talk about learning in sports and how coaches can help or sometimes hinder that process. Students often have recent experiences in this arena—both positive and negative.

1. Explain that students will be working with new partners who don't already know their mazes. As in the last session, they will take turns learning each other's mazes. But this time, in addition to timing your partner as she learns your maze, you will be her teacher or coach. As a good teacher, **your goal is to help your partner learn the maze.**

2. Ask the class for several suggestions of good teaching techniques that might be used. [Encouragement, praise, providing an overview of the maze—for instance telling that there are two main paths.]

Some teachers like to model good and bad coaching techniques for the class. This can be done as a humorous role play and effectively illustrates the role of a coach.

3. Ask the students, "Is it okay to just tell your partner how to run the maze or to physically put her finger right at the end?" Emphasize that the goal is not that they complete the maze quickly, but that they LEARN the maze. Tell the students that they, as teachers, are responsible for teaching their students, in this case their partner.

4. You might want to set up some parameters for them to follow as they coach each other, such as:

- no touching your partner's hand while he does the maze, and;
- no telling specific ways to go (for instance: go left, go right).

Some teachers like to ask students for several suggestions of good coaching techniques that they might use in helping their partner learn the maze.

5. Tell them that they will have about 15 minutes to coach each other in learning their new mazes. Remind them that they will conduct three timed trials for each maze and record their results on the student sheet.

6. After your students understand what they are to do, have them take out (or hand out) their mazes and student sheets, choose a new partner, come get a blindfold, and begin.

7. Circulate as students teach and learn the mazes. Remind the coaches that their role is to help their partners learn, not to tell the answer. Help students articulate what strategies they are using by pointing them out as you see them. "I like the way you are providing encouragement." "I see you are letting her make mistakes. That's important in learning." "How did you feel when he teased you?"

8. Help students stay on task by reminding them of the time parameter. When most students have finished, give them a minute or two to refocus their attention on you.

What Helps and Hinders Learning

1. Tell your students that you are going to make two lists: things they discovered that helped their learning, and things that hindered (or interfered with) their learning. Invite them to give examples of something they or their coach did today that helped or hindered their learning of the maze.

2. As you call on students, help them articulate their specific experiences as general statements. For instance, a student might say: "The first thing I did was use my whole hand to feel the whole maze. That gave me an idea of how big it was, how many branches there were, and where the end was. Then it was easier to figure out the path." You might generalize this by writing: "See the big picture first. Then figure out the details."

Some teachers have found it valuable to have students again find a new partner and learn each other's mazes. This time, students can be challenged to: 1) use some of the best learning strategies that were mentioned to see if doing so results in students learning faster; 2) try being a "bad" teacher. One teacher had her students conduct controlled experiments, comparing maze trials in which a single coaching method was used to those in which no coaching was given. One class created graphs of average time to run a maze for coached and uncoached maze runs. If you have time and if your students are still interested, doing these kinds of extensions will provide more valuable firsthand experience.

Howard Gardner has originated and popularized a theory referred to as "multiple intelligences." According to his theory, "intelligence" has seven main domains: linguistic, musical, spatial, logical-mathematical, body-kinesthetic, interpersonal, and intrapersonal. All humans possess these different domains of intelligence, though certain domains may be more or less dominant in specific individuals. Knowing where one's strengths are has many implications for learning. There has been a great deal written about Gardner's ideas, some of it specifically for use by the classroom teacher. Several books focus on how his work has been very successfully applied in the classroom and in assessment. See the "Resources" section for sources of materials and "Behind the Scenes" for more about Howard Gardner's theory of multiple intelligences.

Note: This task can be hard for students. If your students are having difficulty generating ideas of what helped and hindered learning, go ahead and add things you saw students doing.

3. To draw more ideas out of your students, ask them to think beyond today's experience with the maze to their general experience as learners. Remind them that they have had many teachers over the years, with many different styles of teaching, and that they have been involved in learning many different things.

4. You may want to add some things to the list yourself. For instance:

- **Take notes.** Taking notes in class is valuable not just because you then have a record of what was said, but the process of writing the information helps us to remember that information.

- **Get your hands on it.** People learn best when they have an opportunity to find out firsthand rather than hearing or reading about something.

- **Use a highlighter.** Highlighting portions of notes or of reading assignments is a very visual way of pulling out the main ideas.

- **Devise memory tricks.** There are many different memory tricks that you can devise to help remember or learn things.

- **Teach somebody else.** Many people believe that we never learn something as thoroughly as we do when we need to teach it to someone else.

5. Summarize by saying that these lists represent many good ideas about ways humans tend to learn best and things that interfere with learning. Remind the class that every learner is different. Some people are very visual learners; others learn best through their ears—they are auditory learners; still others are kinesthetic learners—they learn best by touching and through physical movement. All of us reflect different combinations of these ways of learning. So some of these ideas may be more helpful for some than others.

6. If your students are still engaged in the discussion, you might want to bring up the topic of learning differences. Ask them to imagine, for example, what if their brains couldn't:

- see letters and words in order;
- tell left from right;
- remember auditory instructions.

7. Ask them how these differences might affect their learning. What things could they do to compensate for these differences? Explain that many people encounter challenges in the ways they learn and most of us tend to learn best in a particular way or ways. This has nothing to do with intelligence, but does affect the kind of sensory information people need to learn most effectively.

"The discussion on learning differences fell on the day before my students received their report cards. It was great to be able to discuss students' different learning needs without de-valuing anyone. This was perfect timing! Next year I'll plan the timing so it happens like this again."
—Sixth grade teacher

Going Further

1. Have your students coach someone at home in learning their maze. Challenge them to apply some of the learning methods they discussed in class.

2. If you have a classroom pet, have students design mazes or playgrounds for the animal to explore. See if the animal can learn the pathway of a maze. What could be evidence that the animal learned? Have your students conduct activities from the GEMS guide *Mapping Animal Movements* to extend this rich experience.

3. Relating this session to Howard Gardner's theory of multiple intelligences is a good extension. (See the "Behind the Scenes" section for more information and the "Resources" section for books which address this area of learning theory.)

Understanding that people learn in different ways and that everyone has strengths and unique talents can also be a natural way for students to gain respect for and tolerance of many other kinds of differences and diversities. The idea of "multiple intelligences," which suggests that we all "shine" in different ways, and greatly widens our often too narrow definition of "intelligence," strikes powerfully against "put-downs" based on test scores, tracking systems, race, sex, class background, ethnicity, religion, culture, language, accent, height, weight, etc., because it celebrates the unique contributions that ***each and every*** *individual can make. And that's a wonderful thing to* ***learn!***

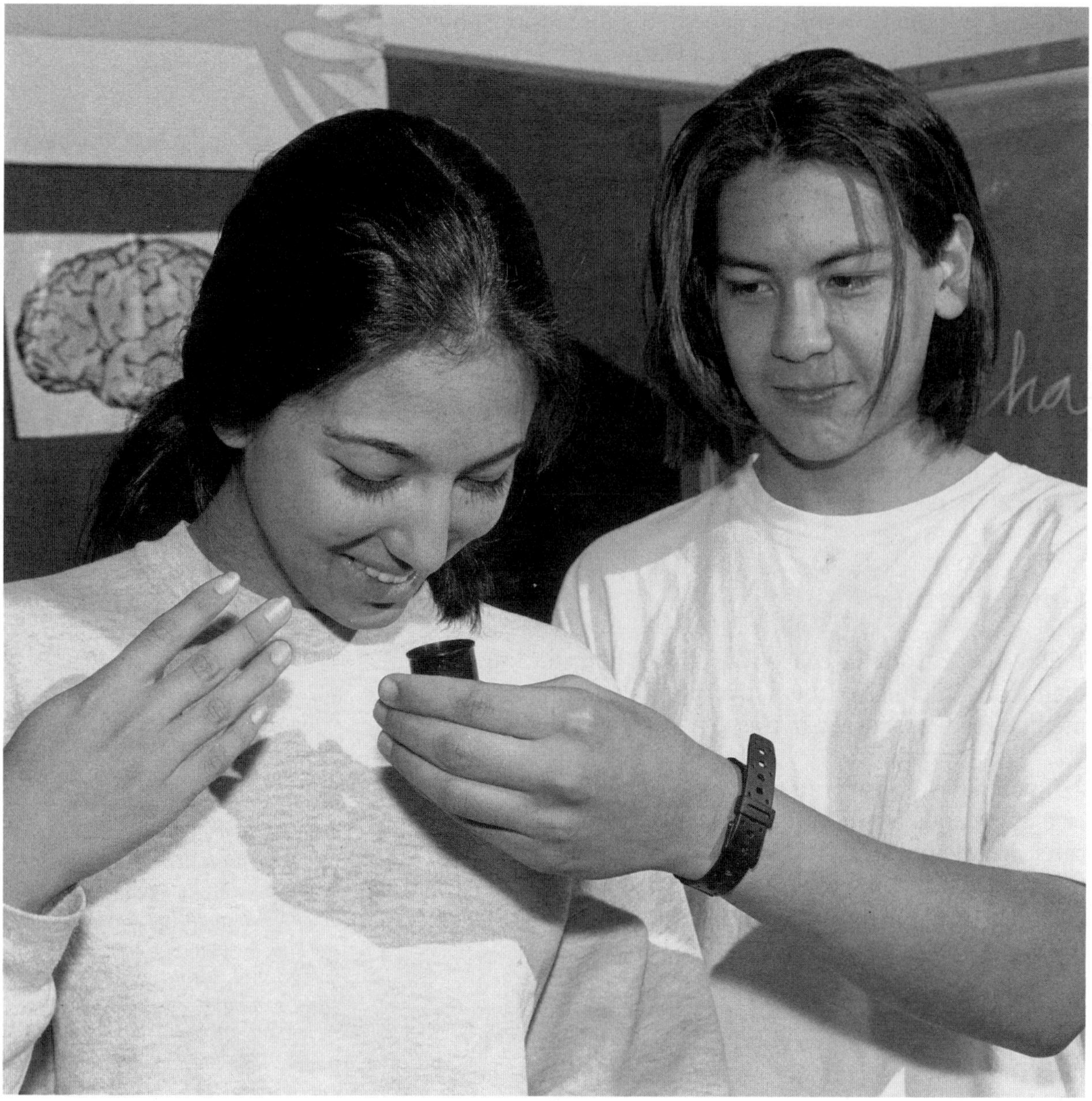

Activity 3: Silent Smell Tracking

In this activity, students enact a simulation of lost wolf pups searching for other wolves from their pack and their home den. Each pair of students receives a "secret scent" in a plastic film canister. This is the scent of their wolf pack. Students move around the classroom silently searching—first for other wolves that have a similar scent and then, as a group, for their den.

Students reflect on how sensory information is important for both animals and humans to learn. They see how learning is key to survival, whether you are a wolf or a human. At the end of this activity, they are introduced to a diagram of the human nervous system.

See the special note on page 29 about wolf vocalization. If you wish to make this a non-silent activity, that is fine. Some teachers have allowed the students to make sounds (within reason of course), but not to talk.

Sophisticated middle school students sometimes scoff at the idea of role-playing wolf pups. We have found that while they may say otherwise, this experience is one that makes a big impression and is something they talk about with their friends and families.

What You Need

For the class:

- ❑ 4–6 food extracts (Lemon, vanilla, maple, licorice, cherry, coconut, almond, and cinnamon work well. Clove is not recommended because it is very strong and can desensitize the nose to other smells.)
- ❑ 4–6 film canisters (to prepare home den smell sources)
- ❑ 4–6 cotton balls (to prepare home den smell sources)
- ❑ a bag or box large enough to hold about 20 film canisters
- ❑ overhead transparency of Nervous System Diagram (master on page 32)
- ❑ *(optional)* 4–6 labels (small enough to fit on the bottom of the film canister—stick-on dots work well)
- ❑ *(optional)* a fine-point marker
- ❑ *(optional)* extra cotton balls

You may want to accompany the learning in this unit with other anatomical and physiological charts and information for your students. See the "Behind the Scenes" and "Resources" sections for some suggestions.

For each pair of students:

- ❑ 1 film canister (to prepare individual smell sources)
- ❑ 1 cotton ball (to prepare individual smell sources)
- ❑ *(optional)* 1 label (small enough to fit on the bottom of the film canister—stick-on dots work well)

For each student:

- ❑ 1 copy of Nervous System Diagram (master on page 32)

Getting Ready

A Week Before the Activity

1. Gather used film canisters. These are often available for free at film developing stores. Obtain the food extracts.

2. Decide how many film canisters you will need for each extract, as described here:

    a. You will need one film canister for each extract to serve as the home den smell source. (For example, if you are using five different extracts, you will need five film canisters—one per extract.)

    b. Your students will work in pairs, trying to locate other pairs with the same extract. You will need to divide the total number of student pairs by the number of extracts you have, to figure out how many film canisters of each extract you will need. (For example, if you have 15 student pairs and five extracts, you will need to make three canisters for each extract. Fifteen pairs using five extracts = three pairs of students per extract = three canisters per extract).

    c. Add the numbers you calculated in a. and b. above to determine the total number of film canisters you will need for each extract. (For the above examples, this would be four canisters per extract.)

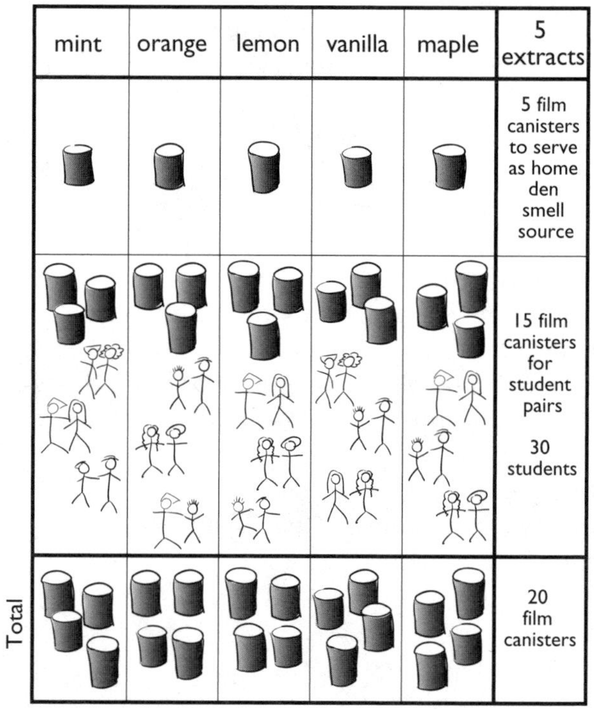

3. *(Optional)* Label each film canister with a secret code. First, assign a code to each extract. (This could be a color, a certain kind of marking, a geometric shape, or a number. The more subtle the better so students don't immediately match codes rather than smells.) Stick a label on the bottom of each film canister. Use a fine-point marker to put the appropriate code on each label.

Sometimes extracts "bleed" through the cotton after several hours, making the color of the extract visible. If you notice this happening, add an extra cotton ball on top of the first one.

Note: Some teachers prefer not to label the film canisters. This makes it so students have no way to "cheat" or figure out the "answer" except by using their sense of smell and conferring with each other. The drawback is that this makes it harder for you to re-sort the canisters at the end of the session.

4. Pour some extract on a cotton ball and place the wet side of the cotton at the bottom of the film canister. This will hide the color of the extract from students when they open the canister to smell the flavor. Seal the canisters and place in a bag or box until needed.

5. Duplicate one copy of the Nervous System Diagram for each student (master on page 32). Also make one overhead transparency of this illustration for use in the next activity.

Immediately Before the Activity

Decide where you want your students to do this activity:

Outside option. Some teachers like to conduct the active part of this session (when their students silently roam around trying to find others with the same smell) outside the classroom—either in the hallway or outdoors. Then, when the "wolf pups" from the same family have found each other, they return to the classroom and sit at the table or group of desks that represents their "home den" (it has a film canister matching their smell). If this is what you are planning to do, be prepared to set one film canister of each extract at a table or group of desks as the students are leaving the classroom to do the simulation. (Setting them out too soon, where the students are sitting, will be too tempting and/or confusing to some.) Designate one additional table or group of desks as an "orphan" area.

One teacher conducted this activity in the woods. The students really felt like wolves in this setting!

Classroom option. Other teachers, with more spacious classrooms, prefer to conduct the entire session in the classroom. In this case, the "home dens" become designated locations around the classroom. If this is what you are planning to do, then set out one film canister of each extract around the room in clearly visible locations. Designate one additional area as an "orphan" area. Open windows or doors to provide additional ventilation during the activity.

Introducing the Activity

1. Remind the class that during the last two activities they focused on how humans learn. Ask the students to think now about wolves. "What are situations in which wolves need to learn in order to survive?" [to stay away from cars and trucks; to find prey; that gunshots mean trouble; that ranchers sometimes leave out poison bait, etc.]

2. Say that wolves, like people, rely on information they perceive through their senses for their learning. Point out that wolves have a very sensitive sense of smell. Wolves can smell prey more than a mile away! They rely on their sense of smell much more than humans do.

3. Tell the class they are going to enact a simulation of lost wolf pups. Ask students to imagine that they are all lost wolf pups. Explain that each pair of lost "wolf pups" will receive a "secret scent" in a film canister. Several other "wolf pups" will receive the same "secret scent." This is the scent of their wolf pack. Their challenge is to find all the other pups that are from their own pack, and then together to find their home den.

Even though humans have a relatively poor sense of smell compared with wolves, dogs, and cats, we can detect many chemicals more efficiently than sophisticated chemical analysis equipment. For example, wine tasters, perfume developers, and tea sniffers develop their sense of smell until they can discern subtle variations in flavors and odors.

4. Explain the procedure:

a. When they get their film canister, they should take the lid off for a quick whiff, then replace the lid. As they roam around the room looking for other wolf pups from their pack, they can compare smells with others, then replace the lid again.

b. When they have located all the pups from their pack, they should **together** look for and try to identify their home den. (Tell the students where you have set up the home dens. You may also want to tell them approximately how many wolf pups there are in each pack.)

c. Remind them that wolves cannot talk, so neither should they! This should be a **silent** smell tracking activity.

d. If they are unable to match their smell with that of others, tell them to come to the orphan area that you have set up. Point out where that is.

e. If you have labeled the bottoms of your film canisters with a code, you may want to mention to your students not to look at it. Explain that doing so would take the fun out of the simulation.

Some teachers found that it is too difficult to require their students to be silent during this simulation. Others enjoyed the relative quiet! One teacher had her students brainstorm various techniques of non-vocal communication to prepare the class for this challenge. If you think asking your students not to talk will be unrealistic, you might want to eliminate this aspect of the simulation. ***While the silence does help students focus on sense of smell and non-verbal communication (and helps maintain relative calm in the classroom!) it's also true that wolves are extremely vocal animals, making many different sounds to communicate with each other. Actual wolf pups engaged in this kind of activity would be far from silent! See "Behind the Scenes" for more information on wolf behavior.***

Lost Wolf Pups Simulation

1. When your students understand what they are to do, assign partners, distribute a film canister to each pair of students, and have them begin.

2. The simulation should take about 5–10 minutes. While it may seem chaotic at first to have so many students roaming the room at once, remember that it will be silent! Circulate as your students are doing the activity, reminding them not to speak. When groups of pups begin to form, remind them that they should seek out their den.

3. If there are orphans or students who are having a hard time matching their scent, you can use your human voice to instruct the silent wolves. Have others help by checking out the scent of the orphan wolf. (Lemon and orange smell quite similar to each other; some people find that vanilla and maple do, too. Having this ambiguity adds some interest to the simulation, especially for older students.)

Olfactory senses can tire after repeated exposure to scents, making it difficult to determine smells. One teacher made a cheesecloth pouch containing coffee beans. She found that sniffing the coffee beans refreshed students' ability to distinguish smells.

4. When everyone (or most everyone) has located his or her pack and den, collect the canisters and have the students sit down.

Reflect on the Wolf Simulation

Some teachers like conducting the simulation twice. It goes quickly, students enjoy it, and some students are better able to focus on the process the second time through. If you do this, students would of course need to trade in their scents for new ones.

1. Lead a discussion about what it was like to do the silent scent tracking activity. What was challenging about it? Were some of the extracts difficult to distinguish? Was it harder or easier to distinguish smells as time passed? If your students are curious, you might want to tell them what flavor extracts are in the film canisters.

2. Relate the simulation to reality by telling them that in real life, each wolf pack *does* have its own smell. The odor comes from glands located in various places on the wolves'

bodies (at the base of the tail, in the skin, and the feet). Wolves develop a pack scent by rubbing together and by smelling each other. (The body smell of wolves can also include scents from odor-bearing trees and plants found near their den or within their territory.)

In real life, the "orphan" pups (pups whose sense of smell was not good enough to enable them to identify their homes) would most often stay lost, be unable to benefit from the hunting success of the pack, and then die. Over time, this process of natural selection favored the survival of wolves with a strong sense of smell.

3. Close the discussion of wolves by saying that this is an example of how learning (in this case the smell of the pack) is crucial for wolves' survival.

Humans as Sensory Beings

1. Though we humans tend to rely more on our sense of sight than our sense of smell, we do use our sense of smell for our own protection. What we smell can sometimes give us an early warning against damage to our bodies and brains. For example, rotten meat often has a strong odor. This odor warns us not to eat the meat.

People who have lost their sense of smell for some reason, either temporarily or permanently, are at more of a safety risk than others. For instance, they may not be able to detect the smell of a burning building.

2. Ask the class to brainstorm other odors that tip us off to a potential danger. [rotten eggs, gasoline, dead animals, smoke, etc.] You may want to mention that natural gas had no odor, but an odor is added to it so people will smell when there is a gas leak.

3. Point out that not all things that smell bad are dangerous, but a bad smell *can* be a clue that a substance is in some way hazardous.

4. Distribute the Nervous System Diagram to the students. Point out the brain, the spinal cord, and the nerves. Show how information from our senses travels through our nerves to the brain.

You may want to point out that information from most of our body comes through peripheral nerves to the spinal cord. The nerves that relay information from the face and the senses that are located in our heads are called the cranial nerves.

5. Summarize by saying that our senses, the nerves that carry sensory information to the brain, and our brains are all involved in learning. Whether we are wolves or humans, learning is crucial for our very survival.

Going Further

1. Tell students that often our earliest and most powerful memories are associated with smells. The smell of lilacs, new-mown grass, the vinegar used in egg dying, burning hair, moth balls, rubbing alcohol—these are just some of the odors with which we may have strong positive or negative associations. Encourage the class to share some of these smell memories. Then ask them to write about a memory that relates to a particular smell. Encourage them to describe the emotions they felt at that time.

2. Suggest that students try a "Smell Test" at home on a friend or family member:

a. Cut small, one-quarter-inch cubes of apple and place them in a plastic bag. Then repeat the procedure with an onion. Seal the onion cubes in their own plastic bag.

b. Invite your subject to sit blindfolded while pinching his or her nose closed with thumb and forefinger. Use a spoon to put a piece of apple on the person's tongue. Have the person chew, then guess what the food is.

c. Repeat the procedure, using another spoon for the onion cube. Next have the person guess the foods while breathing freely. You may want to try other foods as well.

3. Have students read passages from Farley Mowat's *Never Cry Wolf* or see the excellent Disney movie based on this book. It contains many fascinating observations about wolf behavior, communicated in an interesting and humorous way. Students could also do their own research on an aspect of wolf behavior (in Activity 5 your students again pretend to be wolves).

One of the most famous descriptions of this phenomenon in world literature occurs in Remembrance of Things Past *by Marcel Proust, in which the smell of a* madeleine, *or small cake, brings back a rushing flood of childhood memories. There are many theories about the powerful relation between smell and memory.* A Natural History of the Senses *by Diane Ackerman contains an interesting chapter on the sense of smell.*

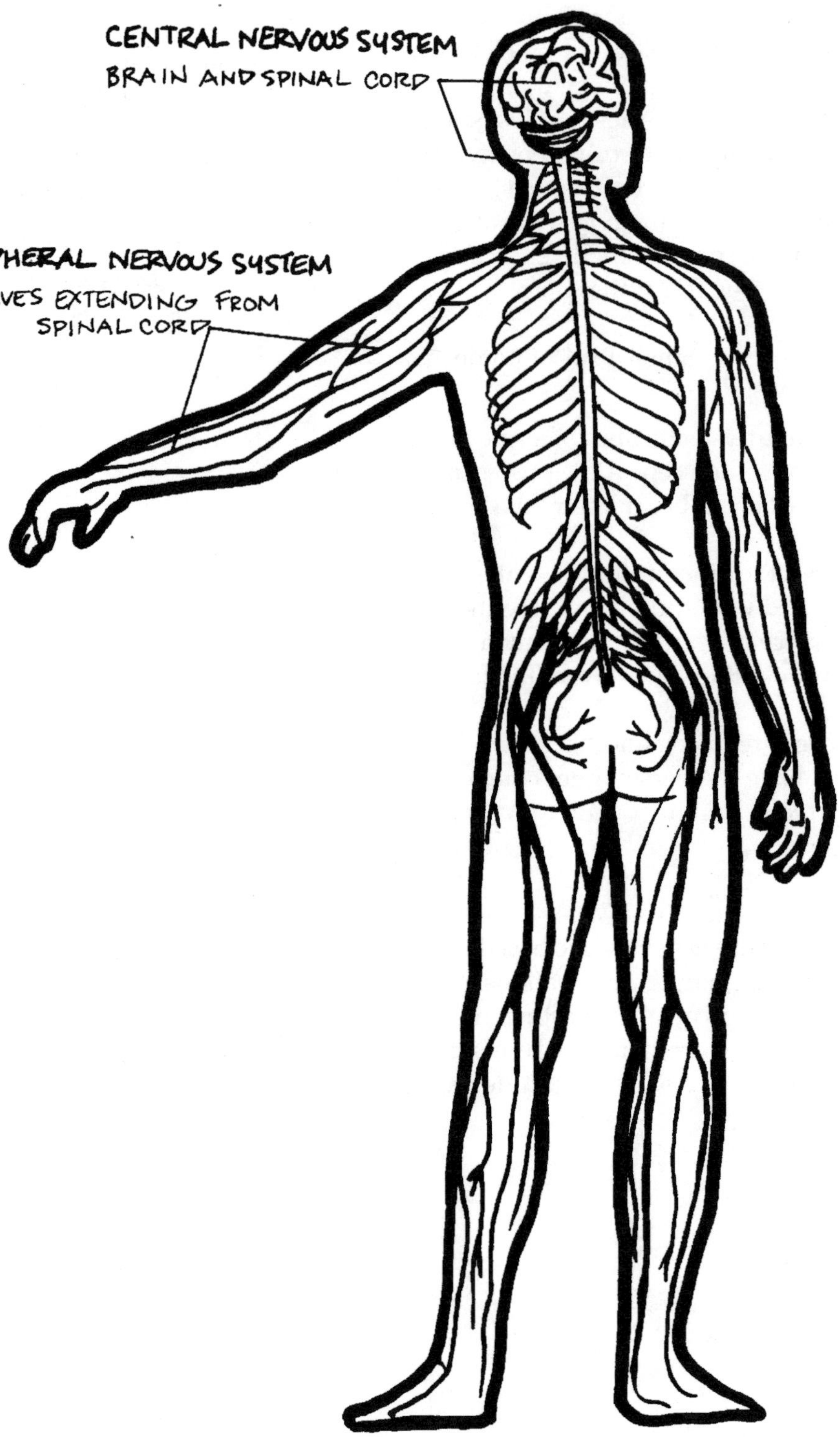

NERVOUS SYSTEM

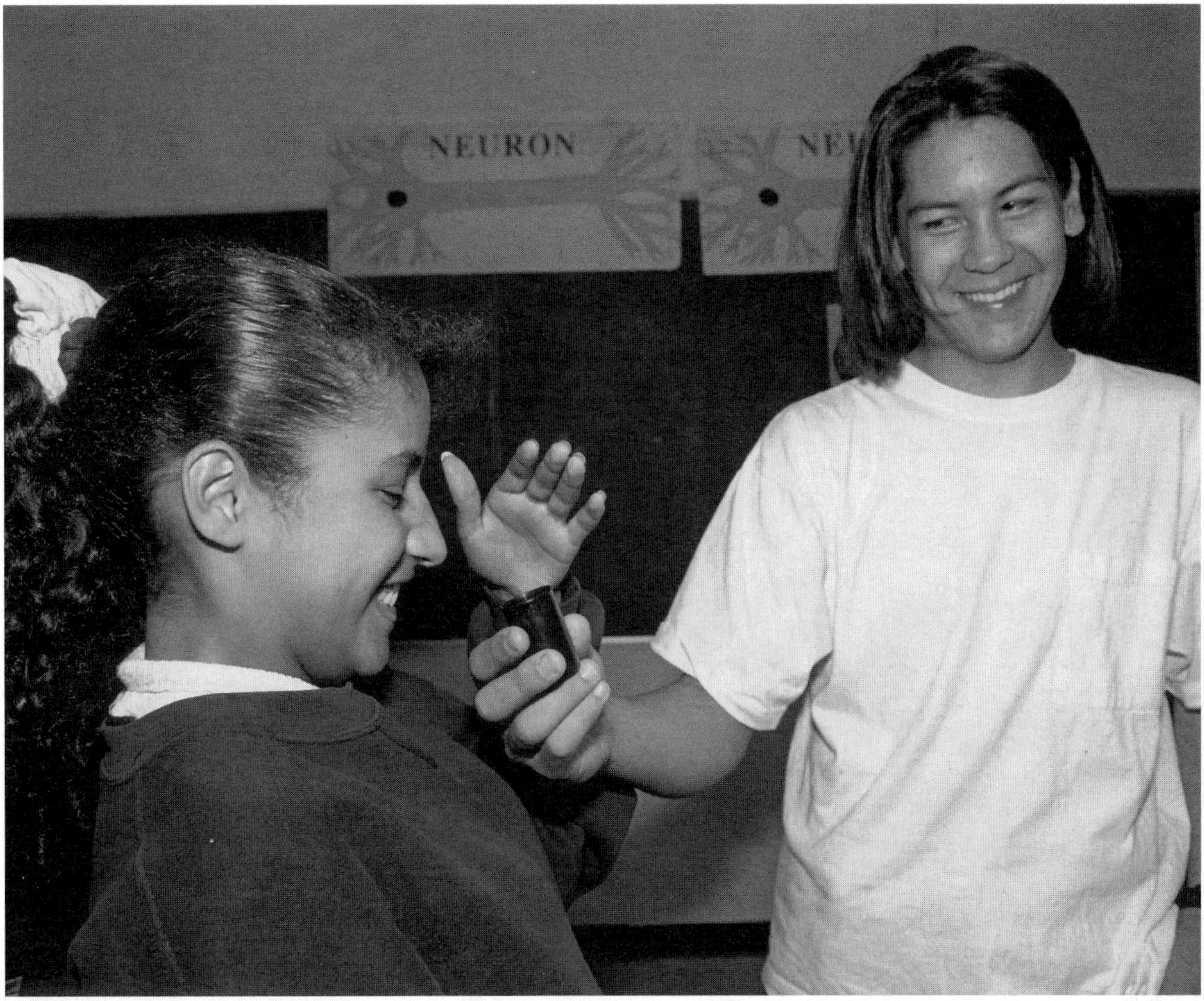
NEURON

NEURON
NEURON
MnBK
n-hexane
#3

Activity 4: The Hexacarbon Solvent Mystery

In this activity, students briefly revisit the nervous system, then attempt to solve two "real-life" neurological medical mysteries. The discussion of the nervous system helps set the stage for understanding the medical mysteries they are to investigate—both of which involve damage to the nervous system by toxic chemicals.

After a short series of fun activities on the nervous system, students hear the setting for the mysteries—two different groups of people, in different locations, begin experiencing serious damage to their nerves. One group works in a fabric printing factory; the other group is made up of seven young men aged 17–22 years.

These mysteries are based on two real situations: outbreaks of neuropathy at a fabric printing plant in Columbus, Ohio, in 1973 and in a group of young men who had all sniffed lacquer thinner (or "glue") in Tampa, Florida, in 1974. Some fictional details have been added and the sequencing of events altered in order to create scenarios to arouse the interest of students. However, the trail of clues, the accounts of scientific studies, and the final conclusions are faithful to the true accounts.

The students work in medical research teams of four to investigate the cause of the health problems. They begin by interviewing one victim from each of the two groups (the roles are played by the teacher). They go on to pore over lists of chemicals used in the factory, activities of the seven young men one week prior to experiencing symptoms, and similar evidence. As the teams notice patterns and come up with new discoveries and questions, they also gain access to new information.

Over the course of their research, the student medical research teams discover different pieces of the overall puzzle. Some may discover that many of the workers who fell ill at the factory in Mystery #1 worked in the print department. These workers were using a new solvent that was recently introduced to the printing process. In the second mystery, others may discover that the seven young men all sniffed "glue" (actually it is not glue, but a lacquer thinner). When students check the ingredients of the lacquer thinner, they may discover that it contains similar solvents to those used in the fabric printing factory.

Solvents are liquids that help dissolve other materials. Some types of solvents, such as certain ones in the hexacarbon chemical family, can cause nerve damage in people. This hazard was first discovered through these and other historic cases.

At the conclusion of their research, each medical research team shares its theories and inferences about what is suspected to be causing the problems. With the help of three student volunteers, each playing the role of a "chemical suspect," the teacher leads a dramatization of the results that the original medical researchers discovered in the 1970s when these real-life mysteries were solved. Through this drama the students see how two of the solvents, when inhaled or ingested, are metabolized by the body to form the same chemical—one that causes nerve damage. They also learn that one relatively harmless chemical becomes dangerous in the presence of another chemical. **This activity vividly illustrates that product testing is critical to ensuring human health and safety—even chemicals that were once tested and thought to be safe can turn out to be hazardous under new or different conditions of use.**

The activity ends with a class reading of What Really Happened providing an opportunity for students to realize that what they discovered was similar to what the "real" medical researchers determined. It also provides reflection on: 1) some of the methods used by scientists and medical researchers to confirm that these suspected chemicals were in fact causing the nerve damage; and 2) additional experiments that were conducted to further determine the safety of these chemical solvents.

Other important issues are raised that relate to the intersection of science and society, including occupational health and safety, and the serious problems caused by drug abuse. This activity enables students to see **how the community of scientists learns things that are important to our health and safety.**

Although every group has a chance to feel successful in solving a piece of the mystery, the dramatization reveals some additional "plot twists and conspiracies" providing an additional "surprise ending" element to the intertwined mysteries.

This activity has a variety of components. Expect it to take at least *one long class session. Be forewarned that student involvement and enthusiasm often cause the activity to spill over into two or even three sessions. To assist you in getting a handle on this activity, here are its main components:*

Revisiting the Nervous System
Introduce the Mysteries
Conduct the Interviews
Students Conduct Medical Research
Reveal the Suspects
Read What Really Happened

What You Need

For the class:

- ❑ 5 2 ½' lengths of string
- ❑ 5 half-sheets of 8 ½" x 11" card stock
- ❑ 1 single-hole paper punch
- ❑ 1 pad of large post-its (3" x 5")
- ❑ 1 large, dark-colored felt marker
- ❑ transparent tape
- ❑ colored copying paper
- ❑ 1 fairly new dollar bill
- ❑ chalk and chalkboard
- ❑ 2 copies of the Victim Name Tag sheet, one on white paper and one on colored paper (master on page 54)
- ❑ 1 copy of the Chemical Name Tag sheet (master on page 55)
- ❑ 1 copy of the Chemical Suspect Statements sheet (master on page 56)
- ❑ 1 copy of each of the two Victim Information sheets (masters on pages 57–58)
- ❑ 1 overhead transparency of the Nervous System Diagram (made during preparation for Activity 3)
- ❑ overhead projector

For each team of four students:

- ❑ 1 copy of each of the following student sheets on white paper (masters on pages 59–62)
    - Chemical List from the Fabric Printing Factory
    - List of Workers with Neuropathy
    - Map of the Fabric Printing Factory
    - Job Descriptions of Workers in Print Room
- ❑ 1 copy of each of the following student sheets on colored paper (masters on pages 63–70)
    - List of Activities of Seven Victims (7 pages)
    - Lacquer Thinner Ingredients
- ❑ 1 large manila envelope (for containing student sheets)
- ❑ 4 sheets of colored paper
- ❑ 4 copies of What Really Happened (master on pages 71–72)
- ❑ paper
- ❑ pencils

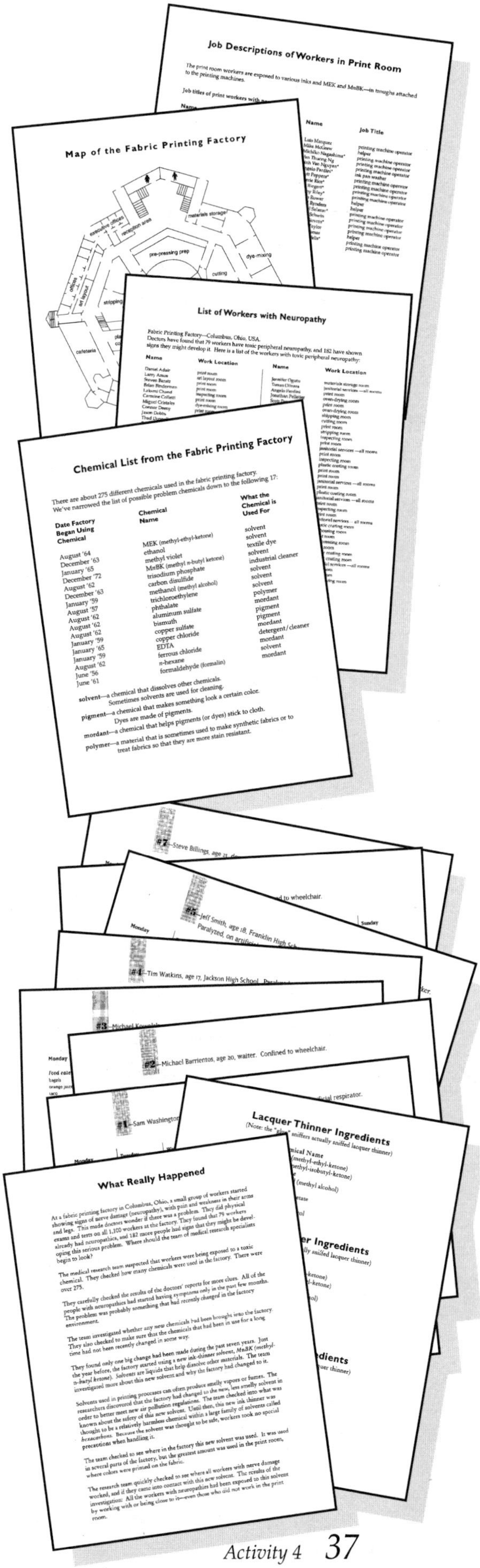

Getting Ready

Before the Day of the Activity

A. Prepare Medical Research Packets

1. Duplicate one copy of each of the following student sheets onto *white* paper for each team of four students (masters on pages 59–62):
    - Chemical List from the Fabric Printing Factory
    - List of Workers with Neuropathy
    - Map of the Fabric Printing Factory
    - Job Descriptions of Workers in Print Room

2. Duplicate one copy of each of the following student sheets onto *colored* paper for each team of four students (masters on pages 63–70):
    - List of Activities of Seven Victims (7 pages)
    - Lacquer Thinner Ingredients

3. Set the copies of two of the student sheets aside: Job Descriptions of Workers in Print Room and Lacquer Thinner Ingredients. Put the remaining student sheets (white and colored) in a manila envelope for each team of four students.

B. Prepare Chemical Suspect Statements

1. Duplicate one copy of the Chemical Suspect Statements sheet (master on page 56).

2. Cut out each of the three statements so that each of the three student "actors" will have their own piece of paper with their statement on it to read to the class.

C. Duplicate True Story

Duplicate one copy of What Really Happened (master on pages 71–72) for each student so they can read along as the story is read aloud.

D. Prepare Name Tags

1. Make five blank necklace-style name tags:
   - Use the half-sheets of card stock.
   - Punch holes in the upper two corners of each half-sheet.
   - Thread a piece of string through the holes and tie the two ends together.

Two of the name tags will be for the neuropathy victims. The other three name tags will be for the suspected chemicals.

2. First, make the victim name tags. Duplicate two copies of the Victim Name Tag sheet, one on *white* paper and one on *colored* paper (master on page 54).

- From the *white* sheet, cut out the label that says:

Mystery #1

Luis Marquez

and tape it to one of the name tags.

- From the *colored* sheet, cut out the label that says:

Mystery #2

Steve Billings

and tape it to one of the name tags.

3. Now, make the chemical name tags. Duplicate one copy of the Chemical Name Tag sheet onto white paper (master on page 55).

- Cut out the labels that say:

MEK

(methyl-ethyl-ketone)

2,5 HD
(2,5-hexanedione)

2,5 HD
(2,5-hexanedione)

M*n*BK
(methyl *n*-butyl ketone)

n-hexane
(normal hexane)

- Tape the labels that say MEK and 2,5 HD on the remaining three blank necklace-style name tags.

- Tape the labels that say M*n*BK and *n*-hexane to post-its, and stick them on the two name tags that say 2,5 HD so that they cover those words.

- Use the dark-colored felt marker to write the numbers #1, #2, and #3 on three post-its. Stick them on the three chemical name tags so that they cover the words:

    Put #1 on the name tag that says M*n*BK.
    Put #2 on the name tag that says *n*-hexane.
    Put #3 on the name tag that says MEK.

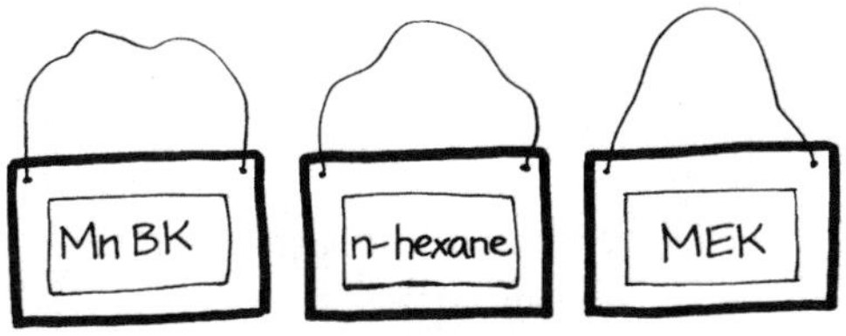

COVER 2,5HD NAME TAGS WITH POST-ITS

COVER ALL THREE NAME TAGS WITH POST-ITS

You may need to layer two or three blank post-its under the numbered post-its so that the labels underneath cannot be read through the post-its.

When you are finished, you should have two necklace-style name tags with the names of the victims, and three with only the numbers #1, #2, and #3 visible.

Optional: You may want to attach the three Chemical Suspect Statements to the back of the three chemical name tags, so student "actors" who play these roles will have their "lines" handy.

E. Prepare Yourself to Play the Role of the Two Neuropathy Victims

1. Duplicate one copy of each of the two Victim Information sheets (masters on pages 57–58). Duplicate the victim information for Luis Marquez on white paper and the

victim information for Steve Billings on colored paper. During the activity the teacher will take turns assuming the roles of two people whose nervous systems were damaged. This is not difficult to do and does not require acting ability. Students will ask you questions in two short interviews at the introduction of each mystery. As student medical research teams begin working on solving the mysteries, they will have other questions to ask. You respond to their questions. Read the Victim Information sheets ahead of time so you are familiar with the facts. You will also want to use them as "cheat sheets" during the interviews. Please see the Important Note About the Interviews on page 44.

"I was a bit nervous preparing for the interviews but it actually worked out extremely well! The students loved questioning me and felt like detectives. Their questions were easy to answer. It was fun for all."
—Eighth grade teacher

2. It is very likely that your students will ask some questions for which you will need to make up reasonable answers. That's fine! Keep in mind that other details about the victim's life are relatively unimportant, and whatever you choose to make up should work fine. **Also keep in mind that your responses can be very brief and there are things the individual being portrayed can realistically respond to by saying "I don't know," or "I can't remember."**

If you are uncomfortable with the idea of playing these roles in the interview, you may want to ask two mature students, perhaps from another class, to play the roles. They will need to be coached ahead of time and instructed not to divulge the most critical information, which you'll need to point out to them. They will need to be available throughout the activity to answer additional questions.

The Day of the Activity

1. Have the dollar bill, the two neuropathy victim name tags, and the Victim Information sheets with you for the introduction of the activity.

2. Have the medical research packets on hand for distribution at the beginning of the medical research time. Also have the two additional sheets (Job Descriptions of Workers in Print Room and Lacquer Thinner Ingredients) and a sheet of colored paper for each team available to distribute later in the session.

3. Place the three numbered chemical name tags and the chemical suspect statements together for use at the end of the activity. *(Optional)* You may want to attach the chemical suspect statements to the back of each of the appropriate chemical name tags.

4. Set up the overhead projector with the transparency of the Nervous System Diagram (the one you made in the previous activity).

Revisiting the Nervous System

1. Remind the students that in the last session you talked about the value of **learning,** for survival. Today they will learn about a true story that shows how scientists solved two mysteries that threatened the lives and well being of many people.

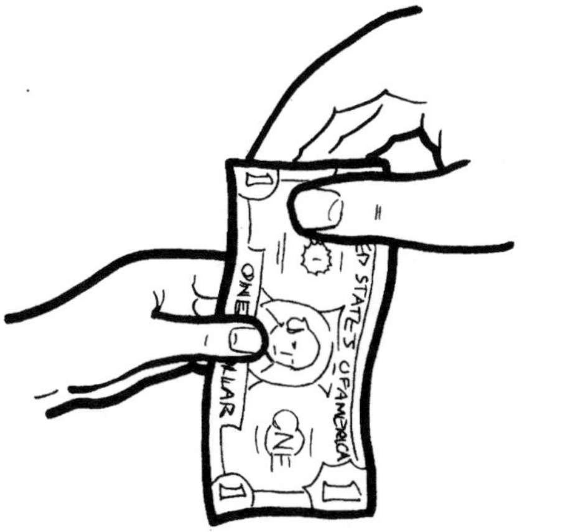

2. Hold up a dollar bill vertically, between your thumb and forefinger, and tell the students that they can have it if they can catch it as you drop it. (If you'd rather not make this offer, just present it as a challenge—whether or not they can catch it.) Tell students they will need to put their fingers on either side of the bill at the level of George Washington's face, ready to grab it. Demonstrate this yourself by dropping it with one hand and catching it with the other. (This should be very easy for you because your catching response can be triggered by your brain at the instance of release.) Tell them to watch your fingers, and as you drop the bill, to catch it with their fingers.

3. Invite a few volunteers to try, one at a time. Unless they start anticipating or grabbing randomly, they shouldn't be able to catch the dollar bill and it will fall to the floor. If you notice them anticipating or grabbing randomly, simply wait till they settle down before you let go.

4. Ask students why they think you could catch the bill and they couldn't. Explain to your students that their brains control their bodies. Their brains communicate with other parts of the body through the rest of the ***nervous system.***

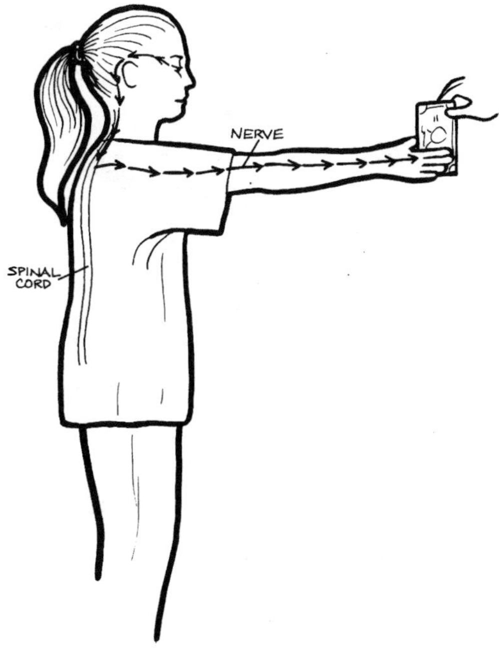

5. Show the overhead transparency of the diagram of the nervous system. Remind students that the nervous system is composed of the brain, the spinal cord, and all of the nerves that run to and from the brain and spinal cord to different parts of the body. The brain and spinal cord are referred to as the ***central nervous system (CNS).*** The cranial and spinal nerves make up the ***peripheral nervous system (PNS).***

6. As their eyes see your fingers let go of the dollar bill, their optic nerves send a message to the brain which then sends a message down the spinal cord, through the nerves in their arms, to the nerves in their fingers, instructing the muscles in their fingers to grab the bill. Let them know that the reason they couldn't catch the bill is that, although these messages travel very fast, they're not fast enough to

Nerve messages travel about 100 meters per second.

get there and tell their fingers to catch the bill before it drops. On the other hand, when you drop the dollar for yourself, your own brain can anticipate the release time and instantly send the catch response.

7. Next, tell all the students to stand up and balance on one foot. Let them know that this demonstrates that their nervous system is working. Their brains sent the message through the spinal cord and to the nerves in their limbs, stimulating their muscles so they could stand up and balance.

8. Tell your students to sit down. Have them circle their right foot in a clockwise direction on the floor. As they continue to do so, tell them to write the number 6 in the air with their right index finger. Most (if not all) will *not* be able to perform both motions at the same time. Explain that this difficulty is because this is not a task their brains are familiar with. Tell them that if they wanted to, they could train their brains to send appropriate messages, and then they'd be able to do it. Their brains have to *learn* and remember the patterns they send through their nerves in order to get each particular job done.

9. Make the comparison of learning to hit a ball with a bat. Tell them that, to perform that task, their brains have to learn what message to send. In the same way, when they stood up and balanced, their brains were sending a familiar message they had learned a long time ago.

The autonomic nervous system (ANS) is involved in messages and reactions that are involuntary.

10. Instruct your students to sneeze, then have them try to hiccup. While it is possible to "fake" a sneeze or a hiccup, explain that none of us can truly sneeze or hiccup on command, because although some "brain messages" are *voluntary,* others are *involuntary*—we have no control over them.

11. Tell them that when the nervous system is damaged, these messages, both voluntary and involuntary, get messed up. Sometimes a person may no longer be able to perform even simple tasks. At other times, damage to the nervous system may be more subtle, affecting only certain specific abilities.

12. Ask them to close their eyes, stretch out their right arm, then bring in the arm and with one finger, touch their noses. Tell them that is one test a doctor might use to test for **damage** to a part of a person's nervous system. If you were unable to do this simple motion, a doctor would

suspect damage to a particular area of your nervous system—in this case, damage to the ***cerebellum,*** a part of the brain.

Introduce the Mysteries

1. Tell your students that they're going to attempt to solve **two real medical mysteries** from the past about **damage to the nervous system.** Let them know that they'll be divided up into medical research teams of four, and that each team will be given much of the same kind of evidence that the real medical research teams collected. Mention that although these are real mysteries that actually happened, all of the people's names and some other details have been changed.

2. Explain that in each of the two mysteries, a number of people were discovered to have nerve damage—or what doctors call ***neuropathy*** (pronounced: nur-AHHH-pa-thee). The word means a disease of the ***nerves***—in this case the nerves most severely affected were the ***peripheral nerves*** (the ones that run to the arms, hands, and legs). These people could no longer do some of the activities you just did using your nervous system. Some had weakness and pain in the arms and legs and it was getting worse; some had so much nerve damage they were becoming paralyzed.

One teacher gathered props and visuals to use: several bottles of solvent, glue, a bottle of ink. She enlarged the map of the fabric printing factory and posted it on the wall.

3. Tell students that you, the teacher, will be playing the role of two neuropathy victims—one from each mystery. Their job is to be "medical detectives" or researchers and interview you to find out what is wrong with you and what might have caused the problem.

4. Explain that they will soon have access to lists and other information that contain some other important clues, but first they get a chance to interview one victim from each mystery. They should only ask questions related to the mystery, to try to figure out what's going on, what's the cause of the problem, and what could be done about it. Suggest that they may wish to take notes.

"My students really like the technical terms. I write them on the board when they occur."
—Eighth grade teacher

5. Remind them that you will be answering their questions **not** as yourself, but as the characters would probably answer. To be sure it's clear, mention again that they'll question you as one of the victims of Mystery #1 first, and then as a victim of Mystery #2.

6. Point out that the name tag and victim information sheet for Mystery #1 is on white paper, and Mystery #2 is on colored paper.

Conduct the Interviews

1. Put on the Luis Marquez name tag and assume his character. (You may want to write "Mystery #1" and his name on the chalkboard.) Using the appropriate Victim Information sheet, introduce yourself as a 22-year-old male worker in a fabric printing factory in Columbus, Ohio. It is June, 1973. Conduct the interview standing, to distinguish this character from the second one, who is wheelchair-bound. Let students know that they'll have to keep the interviews short—about two or three minutes for each. Tell students not to worry if they still have questions because there will be other chances to ask them later on.

Important Note About the Interviews: Your students will probably be very enthusiastic in their interviewing, but *be careful to keep critical answers vague enough so that you don't give away the "answer."* There still needs to be a worthwhile mystery to investigate when they finish the interviews! For example, if students ask questions about a chemical that has recently been introduced to Luis Marquez' factory, he can assure them that it has been tested, is safe, and that it replaced a dangerous one. If they ask Steve Billings if he does drugs, he can say yes, but should be evasive as to what kind of drug. **Don't volunteer information the students don't ask for.** Also, if a student asks about the chemicals in the print department, you don't need to reel off all the information given on the sheet that has to do with those chemicals. Be sketchy on these key points, and, in general, give concise responses.

Discovering the link between the two mysteries provides a wonderful "aha!" experience for your students. While you wouldn't want to tell them that the two mysteries are connected, make sure that the teams consider them together so they can discover the connection.

2. After you finish the Luis Marquez interview, put on the Steve Billings name tag and assume his character. You may want to write "Mystery #2" and his name on the chalkboard. Using the other Victim Information sheet, introduce yourself as one of seven white male patients, ages 17–22, who are experiencing similar symptoms between mid-February and late March, 1974. All live in the same area. Four are confined to wheelchairs, and three are completely paralyzed—unable to breathe without an artificial respirator. It is late April, 1974. Conduct the interview while sitting, to represent that you are confined to a wheelchair. Again, be fairly brief.

Students Conduct Medical Research

1. Show the students the contents of the packets that each medical research team will receive:

Mystery #1
- Chemical List from the Fabric Printing Factory
- List of Workers with Neuropathy
- Map of the Fabric Printing Factory

Mystery #2
- List of Activities of Seven Victims (for the week prior to their symptoms)

2. Remind students that any information having to do with Mystery #1 will be on white paper; information having to do with Mystery #2 will be on colored paper. (You may want to write "white" next to Mystery #1 and whatever color paper you've selected—for example, "yellow"—next to Mystery #2 on the chalkboard.)

3. Let students know that more information may become available later, as they pursue their investigations. (*Note*: More information for each mystery is on the two sheets you have not handed out yet: Job Descriptions of Workers in Print Room for Mystery #1 and Lacquer Thinner Ingredients for Mystery #2.)

4. Tell the students that they may continue to ask the victims (you!) any related questions they have as they are analyzing the written information and as you walk around the room. (If the questions become overwhelming to you, you may want to stage another whole-class interview session at some point during the research time either for the whole group or for those that still have more questions.)

"My students used dictionaries and chemistry books to help them with their research. I did not suggest this. They were so motivated in solving the mysteries that they sought all possible resources."
—Sixth grade teacher

5. Distribute the research packets and have the students begin. As the research teams work, move around the classroom carrying with you the two name tags, as well as your victim information sheets.

6. When students want to ask either Luis or Steve a question, put on the appropriate name tag to help make it clear which mystery you're talking about and who it is that is answering the questions. (This will help when students ask, for example, "Do you use drugs?" With the name tag on, you can repeat the question, for clarity of identity—"Do I, Steve Billings, use drugs?" "Well,...)

7. Be sure to spend some time with each team. As you circulate, you may want to ask questions that challenge the students' reasoning and logic, and/or drop hints to any group that is struggling.

8. After about ten minutes have passed, announce to the entire class that Tim Watkins, the 17-year-old on an artificial respirator, has unfortunately just died of asthmatic complications. This adds the element of urgency which is true to medical mysteries—the longer it takes to solve them, the more casualties there may be.

9. Pass out the two additional sheets to each group at appropriate times. For instance, if a group asks questions about the workers who work in the print room, give them the Job Descriptions of Workers in Print Room sheet. When a group discovers that all seven of the victims in Mystery #2 sniffed glue, give them the Lacquer Thinner Ingredients sheet. If a group is stuck on one mystery, that might be the time to give them that information sheet. **Make sure every group receives both of these sheets eventually.**

10. Let the research teams work until they come to some conclusion or until you sense that some number of the groups may soon begin to lose interest. Some groups race through in a relatively short amount of time. Others take longer. (Discussions can be quite intense, and each group has to figure out ways of analyzing the evidence, communicating their flashes of insight, and sharing/critiquing their theories and inferences with each other.)

11. Ask questions to further challenge the more rapid groups, and drop small hints to groups who are having difficulty. Some groups may arrive at the conclusion that "it's the lacquer thinner." Challenge them to look further by asking them what, in the lacquer thinner, do they think causes the problem.

If your students are very involved and taking a long time, you might want to let them continue the research for this whole session and even part of another session.

12. When you are ready to end this activity, give a five-minute warning and pass out a sheet of colored paper to each team. Tell the students to write down what they think caused the nerve damage problems in each mystery on two separate pieces of paper, one white and one colored.

Note: The following wrap-up discussions are best conducted immediately after this activity, but if you run out of time, this is a good break point.

Reveal the Suspects

1. Ask a member of each team to stand and announce what they think caused the problem in Mystery #1, then in Mystery #2. Record these on the chalkboard.

One teacher had her student teams "publish" their results by writing a brief conclusion, to place more value on the results of their research efforts.

2. Tell the students that you will now divulge the findings of the medical research team that worked on solving these mysteries in real life.

3. Ask for three dramatically-inclined student volunteers to come forward and sit or stand facing the class. Give them each a chemical name tag and the corresponding chemical suspect statement. Instruct the three not to look at their name tags. Tell them to read their statements to themselves and prepare to read them aloud at the appropriate time.

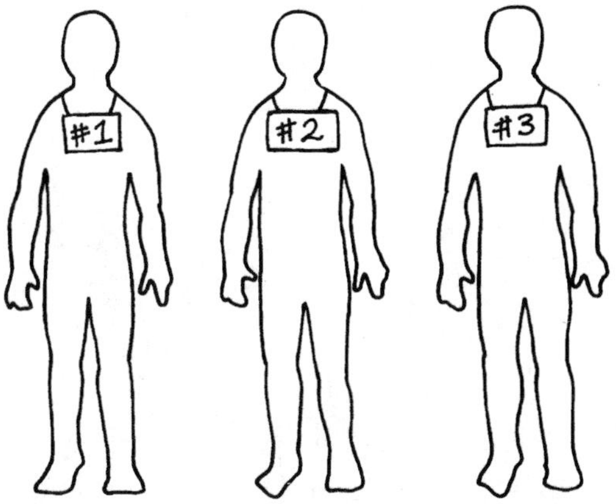

4. Explain that these three volunteers will play the part of three chemicals suspected of causing the neuropathies in the two mysteries. Continue by reading the following statements:

Teacher:
From their data, scientists learned that the workers with neuropathies in Mystery #1 had all been exposed to a particular chemical that the factory had just begun using as both an ink thinner and a cleaning agent. It had been brought in to replace a chemical that didn't meet new air pollution regulations. They first began using it in August 1972, but full use began in December 1972. Many workers had breathed in fumes from this solvent or had come into contact with this solvent on their skin. That chemical was... *(rip off post-it labeled #1 from Suspect #1's name tag)* ...**M*n*BK!**

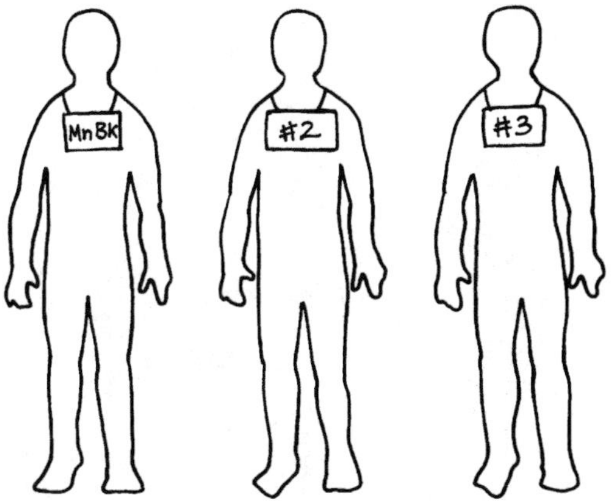

(Have Suspect #1 read her statement.)

Suspect #1—M*n*BK:
Ha! You're way off buddy! I was tested. Scientists found me to be safe!

Teacher:
Yes, you're right! Until that time, M*n*BK had been considered to be relatively harmless. Scientists had conducted research with animals, but... M*n*BK had been tested only for short term exposure in large doses, and was considered to be safe. It had never been tested in *small* amounts over a *long* period of time, which is how it caused nerve damage in this case.

From the studies of the chemicals in the lacquer thinner in Mystery #2, scientists found that the following chemical was the cause of neuropathy in glue sniffers... *(rip off post-it labeled #2 from Suspect #2's name tag)*...***n*-hexane!**

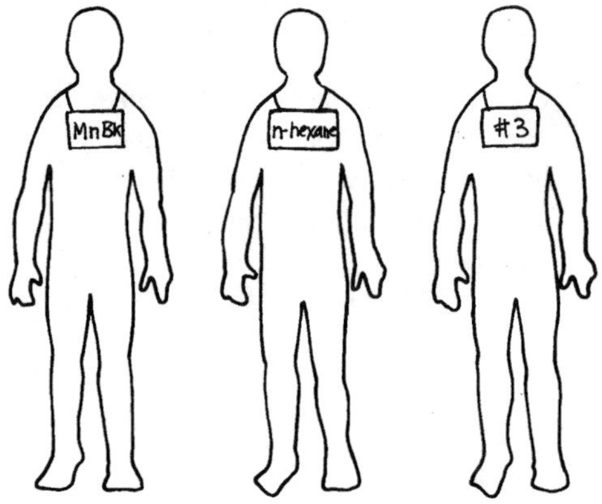

(Have Suspect #2 read his statement.)

Suspect #2—*n*-hexane:
No way! Uh-uh! I was tested too! I was found to be pretty safe! This is crazy!

Teacher:
Yes, the idea was resisted by many people at first. Some studies had been done in which animals were exposed to *n*-hexane, and they did not suffer neuropathies—*n*-hexane was used widely, and was regarded as being pretty safe—what scientists call having a *low toxicity potential.* But *n*-hexane fell into bad company—a chemical that brought out the worst in it.

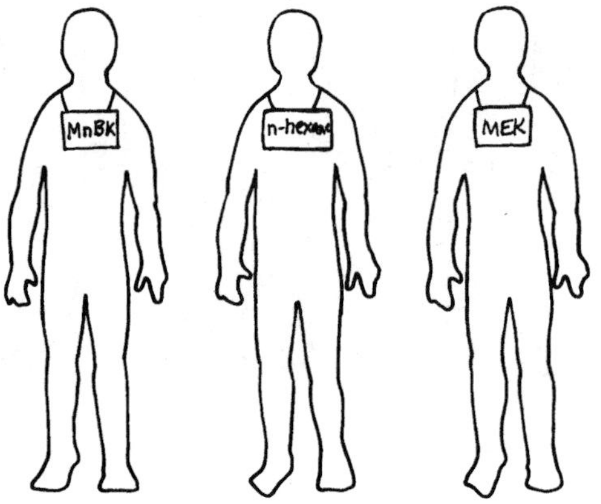

That leads us to a third chemical implicated in these mysteries. Let's expose the accomplice, responsible for aiding and abetting... *(rip off post-it labeled #3 from Suspect #3's name tag)*...**MEK!**

(Have Suspect #3 read her statement.)

Suspect #3—MEK:
I'm innocent! I'm innocent! To this date every study has proven that I am unable to produce nerve damage in any kind of animal! There it is. That's the truth. Deal with it!

Teacher:
You're right. On its own, MEK has been found to be unable to produce neuropathy in animals **but**—MEK **potentiates** *n*-hexane. In other words, it makes the nerve-damaging effects of *n*-hexane much worse. MEK also potentiates M*n*BK. While *n*-hexane on its own is not very toxic, researchers found that when combined with MEK, the damage to humans and animals was much worse. M*n*BK is toxic on its own, but mixed with MEK, it, too, causes greater nerve damage.

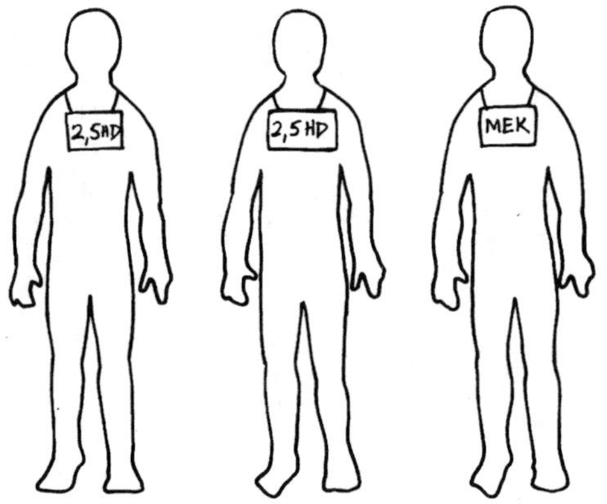

"In one class the two chemicals looked at each other and said, "Hey! Are we the same?!"

The mystery still isn't over. It's time to unmask and expose the real culprit. Both *n*-hexane and M*n*BK are broken down by the body (metabolized) to...*(rip off both MnBK and* n-*hexane post-its from Suspect #1's and #2's name tag)*...**2,5 HD** (2,5-hexanedione) which is responsible for much, if not all, of the neurological effects from repetitive exposure to these two solvents.

5. Thank your student volunteers and have them return to their seats.

6. Point out that all of these chemical suspects, M*n*BK, *n*-hexane, and MEK, are in **the same family of solvents—they are all *hexacarbon solvents.*** Some types of solvents, such as *certain* ones in the hexacarbon family, can cause nerve damage in people. This hazard was first discovered through these historic cases, of the workers in the fabric printing factory and the young men who sniffed lacquer thinner.

7. You may want to point out that unlike in the drama that they just enacted, chemicals are not guilty or bad. There are good and bad *uses* of chemicals, not good and bad chemicals. Hexacarbon solvents can be used safely with proper ventilation, protection against harm to the skin, and other safety precautions. However, these precautions were not known at the time, because the product testing done on these solvents was limited.

8. Conclude by saying that the medical research teams did a great job! Each group provided some piece of the puzzle. Like professional scientists, **working together,** they **learned** more about what was causing the health problems. They analyzed evidence from real-life mysteries and came to conclusions similar to those reached by the original medical research teams that tackled these problems. As a class, read aloud the following account so students can find out more about what really happened. Ask them to pay attention to how well their conclusions fit in with these real-life medical mysteries.

Be sure to validate the process all the groups and students went through in putting together each part of the mystery, even if they had only partial success, as is most likely. Providing this positive feedback to all students and groups helps counter negatively competitive feelings and helps students understand how groups of scientists learn from the work of others. It focuses students on the cooperative process of science.

What Really Happened

At a fabric printing factory in Columbus, Ohio, a small group of workers started showing signs of nerve damage (neuropathy), with pain and weakness in their arms and legs. This made doctors wonder if there was a problem. They did physical exams and tests on all 1,100 workers at the factory. They found that 79 workers already had neuropathies, and 182 more people had signs that they might be developing this serious problem. Where should the team of medical research specialists begin to look?

One teacher had several students act out What Really Happened.

Be sure to set aside time to discuss with your students what glue-sniffing is and some of its adverse effects. See the "Behind the Scenes" section if you need information about this. In some communities, this is a severe problem. Raising this issue also provides an opportunity to discuss other forms of drug abuse.

The medical research team suspected that workers were being exposed to a toxic chemical. They checked how many chemicals were used in the factory. There were over 275.

They carefully checked the results of the doctors' reports for more clues. All of the people with neuropathies had started having symptoms only in the past few months. The problem was probably something that had *recently changed* in the factory environment.

The team investigated whether any *new* chemicals had been brought into the factory. They also checked to make sure that the chemicals that had been in use for a long time had not been recently changed in some way.

They found only one big change had been made during the past seven years. Just the year before, the factory started using a new ink-thinner *solvent, MnBK (methyl-*n-*butyl ketone). Solvents* are liquids that help dissolve other materials. The team investigated more about this new solvent and why the factory had changed to it.

Solvents used in printing processes can often produce smelly vapors or fumes. The researchers discovered that the factory had changed to the new, less smelly solvent in order to better meet new air pollution regulations. The team checked into what was known about the safety of this new solvent. Until then, this new ink thinner was thought to be a relatively harmless chemical within a large family of solvents called *hexacarbons.* Because the solvent was thought to be safe, workers took no special precautions when handling it.

The team checked to see where in the factory this new solvent was used. It was used in several parts of the factory, but the greatest amount was used in the print room, where colors were printed on the fabric.

The research team quickly checked to see where all workers with nerve damage worked, and if they came into contact with this new solvent. The results of the investigation: All the workers with neuropathies had been exposed to this solvent by working with or being close to it—even those who did not work in the print room.

How were workers exposed to the solvent? The team discovered that the liquid solvent produced fumes or vapor that got into the air. Some workers were exposed to the solvent by breathing the vapors. Workers also became exposed if the liquid touched their skin or got into their mouths. The team discovered that the workers in the print department had not worn gloves to protect their skin. They washed their hands in the solvent to help remove ink stains. They also soaked rags with the chemical to clean their machinery. Some workers ate their lunches in the work area without first washing the solvent off their hands. It was discovered that the greater exposure to M*n*BK a worker had, the more severe their nerve damage.

The factory stopped using the new ink-thinning solvent immediately because it looked like exposure to the new solvent was related to the worker's health problems.

In other parts of the country and the world, there were already medical reports of serious health problems in young men who sniffed glue to get high. In Tampa, Florida, seven young men, who all had inhaled fumes of a certain lacquer thinner to get high, started to feel weakness and numbness in their arms and legs. Four men needed wheelchairs, two others became completely paralyzed and required artificial respiration. One died from breathing problems.

Researchers noticed the similarities between this situation and the one in the fabric printing factory. Chemical analysis of the lacquer thinner used for glue sniffing showed that it was *n*-hexane, a type of hexacarbon solvent, very similar to the ink thinner used in the fabric printing factory. While *n*-hexane did not usually cause neuropathy by itself, when mixed with another solvent that was present in the lacquer thinner (MEK), these two chemicals caused nerve damage. This might seem like the end of the story, but actually the mystery-solving work for scientists was just beginning. Several big questions still remained. Scientists needed to:

a.) *prove* that it was indeed the hexacarbon solvents causing the problem in each of the situations;

b.) learn *how much* of the chemicals produced the harmful effects, in order to know if they could ever be used in a safe way;

c.) do more research on the *long term* health effects of the solvents; and

d.) learn whether and how other *similar types of hexacarbon solvents* might also cause nerve damage.

Researchers conducted tests with laboratory animals. Both the ink-thinning and the glue-sniffing solvents produced the same kind of nerve damage in animals as seen in humans. Scientists looked at the effect of many different solvents on nerve cells they had grown in laboratory dishes. They also used chemical tests to find out what was similar and different about each solvent. These specific ink-thinning and glue-sniffing solvents harmed nerve cells, while some similar solvents did not. In this case, it was also important to see if effects changed or worsened when substances were combined. Scientists have continued their research on these and other solvents to ensure that the products we use in our work places and homes are safe.

Going Further

1. Tell students to imagine that it is 1974. The chemicals suspected of causing the neuropathies were just identified, and the students are the research team responsible for finding out more about the hazards of these solvents. Invite them to design experiments to prove that the ink-thinning and glue-sniffing solvents are the problem, to better determine the long-term effect of these chemicals on humans, and to find out if there is a safe level of exposure to these solvents. If students are familiar with the concept of controlled experimentation, this is an excellent opportunity to remind them of the requirements for a "fair test," and to have them evaluate their own and/or each other's experimental ideas from this standpoint, and to consider whether or not to test people, animals, in lab dishes, or in other ways.

2. Consider having kids dramatize the story of the Hexacarbon Solvent Mystery for another class. Challenge them to adapt it as a presentation before a congressional subcommittee.

3. See if you can obtain a copy of *Eleven Blue Men* by Berton Roueché. This out-of-print book contains a series of compelling epidemiological mysteries. See "Literature Connections" for more information.

4. Invite a product safety scientist (toxicologist) to visit your class. Call local companies that produce products or chemicals that must be tested, universities with medical research departments, occupational health scientists, or biomedical research organizations for suggestions.

EURON
n-hexane
MnBK
#3

Victim Name Tag Sheet

Mystery #1

Luis Marquez

Mystery #2

Steve Billings

Chemical Name Tag Sheet

M*n*BK
(methyl *n*-butyl ketone)

n-hexane
(normal hexane)

MEK
(methyl-ethyl-ketone)

2,5 HD
(2,5-hexanedione)

2,5 HD
(2,5-hexanedione)

Chemical Suspect Statements

Suspect #1:

Ha! You're way off buddy! I was tested. Scientists found me to be safe!

Suspect #2:

No way! Uh-uh! I was tested too! I was found to be pretty safe! This is crazy!

Suspect #3:

I'm innocent! I'm innocent! To this date every study has proven that I am unable to produce nerve damage in any kind of animal! There it is. That's the truth. Deal with it!

Victim Information Sheet for Luis Marquez—Mystery #1

(Conduct the interview standing, to distinguish this character from the second one, who is wheelchair-bound.)

Introduce yourself as a 22-year-old, male worker in a fabric printing factory in Columbus, Ohio. It is June, 1973.

Symptoms: I've been feeling weak. My hands aren't as strong as they used to be and my fingers get numb sometimes. I get severe headaches and have difficulty walking. My symptoms began in May, about 1 month ago. I'm in very good health otherwise. According to the doctors, there have been no outbreaks of neuropathy in the nearby town where I live.

Job: I work in a fabric printing factory, in the print room. I'm a printing machine operator. I know five other workers in my department who are suffering from similar symptoms. I started working here two and half years ago. I have never had any problems before. Most of the five of us who are experiencing problems have worked here for quite a few years without having any problems in the past.

The Factory: Our fabric printing factory employs 1,100 people. We get large rolls of cloth which are infused with vinyl. We laminate and coat them. The rolls are then taken to the print department (where I work), where we print them with one or more colors. They're dried in ovens, then rewound in rolls. They are then transported to inspecting rooms and the shipping area. The printed cloth is used in cars and offices and in many products.

Chemicals: There are about 275 different chemicals used in the factory. I'll give you a list of some of the chemicals the other researchers have narrowed it down to later, but in my department, we use various inks, and a couple of solvents in a trough around the machines. One of the solvents is called MEK, and the other is called M*n*BK. There are others as well.

Sometimes we use the solvents to clean things. Occasionally, I wash my shoes in a solvent when they get ink on them. Sometimes workers from other departments borrow a solvent to clean things. I know that it couldn't be the solvent that's the problem though, because I've heard it's safe. They brought in M*n*BK to replace another solvent that didn't meet the new environmental air pollution laws. We started using it in August last year, but full use really began in December.

Contact with the chemicals:

Do I ever eat in the print room? Yes, a bunch of us do.
Do I always wash my hands? Nope. Sometimes I wash 'em in the solvent to get off ink stains. It works really well.

Victim Information Sheet for Steve Billings—Mystery #2

(Conduct the interview while sitting, to represent that you are confined to a wheel-chair.)

Introduce yourself as one of seven white male patients, ages 17–22, who are experiencing similar symptoms between mid-February and late March, 1974. All live in the same area. Four are confined to wheelchairs and three are completely paralyzed—unable to breathe without an artificial respirator. It is late April, 1974.

Symptoms: It began with weakness in my arms and legs, and numbness that moved up my arms and legs. Now I'm so weak I can't walk, and I have to use a wheelchair. I'm not getting worse now, but I'm not getting any better either. I had to quit my job, because I couldn't lift things. I stumbled because I couldn't pick up my feet when walking, and I couldn't climb stairs.

Diagnosis: At first they thought I had infectious mononucleosis, but now they're calling it a neuropathy.

Treatment: I'm receiving high dosages of multiple vitamins, physical therapy and therapy for pneumonia, but it doesn't seem to be having any effect.

Job: Works as a clerk in a department store in Tampa, Florida. Do I work with dangerous chemicals? Just ethanol, but only small amounts.

Avoid divulging the following glue-sniffing information until after the students have begun their research, and have discovered for themselves that all seven of the patients had sniffed glue.

Questions about glue-sniffing: I don't actually sniff glue, I sniff, or "huff," lacquer thinner. I started huffing, then I couldn't stop. It became a habit. I've stopped now. Why did I do it? It's cheap. My friends and I would do it all evening. I usually huffed with a group of people. The "high" lasts about 5–15 minutes. I started huffing a few months ago. I quit huffing, but I kept getting worse for about eight weeks after I quit. **Now I wish I'd never started!**

Chemical List from the Fabric Printing Factory

There are about 275 different chemicals used in the fabric printing factory. We've narrowed the list of possible problem chemicals down to the following 17:

Date Factory Began Using Chemical	Chemical Name	What the Chemical is Used For
August '64	MEK (methyl-ethyl-ketone)	solvent
December '63	ethanol	solvent
January '65	methyl violet	textile dye
December '72	M*n*BK (methyl *n*-butyl ketone)	solvent
August '62	trisodium phosphate	industrial cleaner
December '63	carbon disulfide	solvent
January '59	methanol (methyl alcohol)	solvent
August '57	trichloroethylene	solvent
August '62	phthalate	polymer
August '62	aluminum sulfate	mordant
August '62	bismuth	pigment
January '59	copper sulfate	pigment
January '65	copper chloride	mordant
January '59	EDTA	detergent/cleaner
August '62	ferrous chloride	mordant
June '56	*n*-hexane	solvent
June '61	formaldehyde (formalin)	mordant

solvent—a chemical that dissolves other chemicals. Sometimes solvents are used for cleaning.

pigment—a chemical that makes something look a certain color. Dyes are made of pigments.

mordant—a chemical that helps pigments (or dyes) stick to cloth.

polymer—a material that is sometimes used to make synthetic fabrics or to treat fabrics so that they are more stain resistant.

List of Workers with Neuropathy

Fabric Printing Factory—Columbus, Ohio, USA.
Doctors have found that 79 workers have toxic peripheral neuropathy, and 182 have shown signs they might develop it. Here is a list of the workers with toxic peripheral neuropathy:

Name	Work Location
Daniel Adair	print room
Larry Amos	art layout room
Steven Baratz	print room
Brian Binderman	print room
Laksmi Chand	inspecting room
Carmine Colletti	print room
Miguel Cristales	dye-mixing room
Connor Deeny	print room
Jason Dobbs	print room
Thad Donnelly	oven-drying room
David Elva	janitorial services —all rooms
Steven Fiske	print room
John Fitzgerald	janitorial services —all rooms
Gerald Flynn	print room
Joshua Forrest	dye-mixing room
Jacob Genetti	print room
Sam Ginsburg	print room
Jane Guzman	embossing room
Kim Harlington	print room
James Hobard	plastic coating room
Peter Ingle	print room
Jim James	print room
Stanley Keller	print room
Andy Kennard	janitorial services —all rooms
Otto Kent	print room
Mathew Keppner	materials storage room
Pat Kraft	print room
Lashanna Kudumu	print room
Jacquey Kuric	plastic coating room
Barbara Lima	inspecting room
Arturo Limonv	print room
Ephram Lipanovich	janitorial services —all rooms
Tony Lippincott	plastic coating room
Paul Littlebear	print room
Luis Marquez	print room
Connie Martin	stripping room
Mike McGrew	print room
Lynn Musik	stripping room
Michiko Nagashima	print room
Van Thuong Ng	print room
Binh Ngo	inspecting room
Binh Van Nguyen	print room

Name	Work Location
Jennifer Ogutu	materials storage room
Tomas Olivera	janitorial services —all rooms
Angelo Pardini	print room
Jonathan Pelletier	oven-drying room
Scott Peppers	print room
Louise Perez	oven-drying room
Darlene Posada	shipping room
Bernard Rice	cutting room
Valerie Rice	print room
Scott Rich	stripping room
Gilbert Rieben	inspecting room
Ray Riegert	print room
Carole Rigo	janitorial services —all rooms
Denny Riley	print room
Lincoln Ritter	inspecting room
Rebecca Roper	plastic coating room
Kevin Rower	print room
David Rynders	print room
Janet Sachs	janitorial services —all rooms
Gabriel Salazar	print room
Simon Salcido	plastic coating room
Laura Sanshun	janitorial services —all rooms
Joseph Schwin	print room
Steve Seabrooks	inspecting room
Melba Sievers	print room
Gary Suto	janitorial services —all rooms
Mario Tambini	plastic coating room
Gus Tanaka	embossing room
Brenda Taylor	print room
Brad Thomas	pre-pressing room
Irene Thomas	print room
Jennifer Tinker	plastic coating room
Tim Tsu	plastic coating room
Miguel Velasco	janitorial services —all rooms
Arnold Wells	print room
Anne Wu	print room
Kwok-Ying Hui	oven-drying room

Map of the Fabric Printing Factory

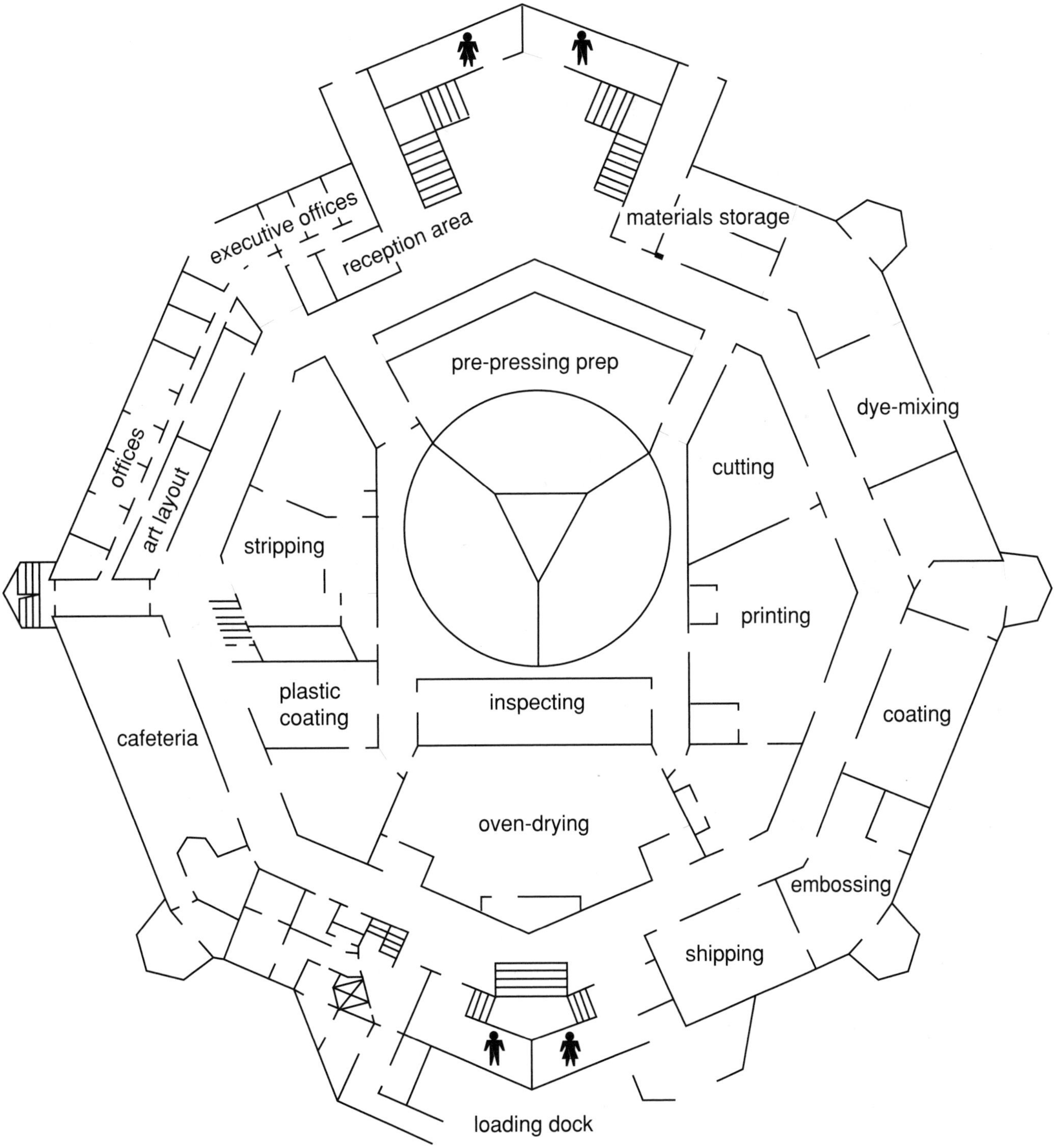

Job Descriptions of Workers in Print Room

The print room workers are exposed to various inks and MEK and M*n*BK—in troughs attached to the printing machines.

Job titles of print workers with neuropathies

Name	Job Title	Name	Job Title
Daniel Adair*	printing machine operator	Luis Marquez	printing machine operator
Steven Baratz*	printing machine operator	Mike McGrew	helper
Brian Binderman	helper	Michiko Nagashima*	printing machine operator
Carmine Colletti	helper	Van Thuong Ng	printing machine operator
Connor Deeny*	printing machine operator	Binh Van Nguyen*	printing machine operator
Jason Dobbs*	printing machine operator	Angelo Pardini*	ink pan washer
Steven Fiske	helper	Scott Peppers*	printing machine operator
Gerald Flynn*	printing machine operator	Valerie Rice*	printing machine operator
Jacob Genetti*	printing machine operator	Ray Riegert*	printing machine operator
Sam Ginsburg*	printing machine operator	Denny Riley*	printing machine operator
Kim Harlington*	printing machine operator	Kevin Rower	helper
Peter Ingle	printing machine operator	David Rynders	helper
Jim James	helper	Gabriel Salazar*	printing machine operator
Stanley Keller	helper	Joseph Schwin	printing machine operator
Otto Kent	printing machine operator	Melba Sievers*	printing machine operator
Pat Kraft	helper	Brenda Taylor	printing machine operator
Lashanna Kudumu	printing machine operator	Irene Thomas	helper
Arturo Limonv*	printing machine operator	Arnold Wells*	printing machine operator
Paul Littlebear*	printing machine operator	Anne Wu	printing machine operator

* These workers have the most severe nerve damage.

Job descriptions

Printing Machine Operators: Spend nearly 100% of their time at printing machines, 5%–15% at the back of the machine where solvents are most concentrated.

Helpers: Spend about 50% of their time in proximity of the print machines.

Ink Pan Washers: Clean ink pans with solvent.

#1—Sam Washington, age 19, carpenter's apprentice. Paralyzed, on artificial respirator.

Monday	Tuesday	Wednesday	Thursday	Friday	Saturday	Sunday
Food eaten: eggs bacon orange juice peanut butter and jelly sandwich milk candy bar gum spaghetti salad milk	*Food eaten:* eggs toast orange juice pizza cola crackers gum candy bar hamburger milk	*Food eaten:* wheat cereal orange juice peanut butter and jelly sandwich milk apple tuna casserole	*Food eaten:* eggs bacon toast orange juice spaghetti salad soda chocolate candy bar gum pasta primavera milk	*Food eaten:* wheat cereal milk peanut butter and jelly sandwich apple cola steak salad ice cream	*Food eaten:* pancakes syrup milk hot dog apple cola hamburger fries gum ice cream	*Food eaten:* eggs bacon orange juice cheese sandwich grapes cola beef burrito chips and salsa gum pudding
Activities: work touch football watched T.V. smoked 3 cigarettes	*Activities:* work watched T.V.	*Activities:* work touch football	*Activities:* work sniffed glue smoked 2 cigarettes went to movie	*Activities:* work watched T.V.	*Activities:* went to mall watched T.V. went to movie	*Activities:* rode bike watched T.V.

#2—Michael Barrientos, age 20, waiter. Confined to wheelchair.

Monday	Tuesday	Wednesday	Thursday	Friday	Saturday	Sunday
Food eaten:	*Food eaten:*	*Food eaten:*	*Food eaten:*	*Food eaten:*	*Food eaten:*	*Food eaten:*
coffee	coffee	toast	muffin	muffin	muffin	muffin
candy bar	cereal	orange juice	orange juice	coffee	coffee	coffee
apple	cola	coffee	salad	salad	salad	tuna sandwich
milk	crackers	pizza	soda	bread	apple	banana
burrito	candy bar	milk	chocolate candy bar	cola	cola	cola
gum	spaghetti	apple	gum	enchilada	hamburger	burrito
	salad	beef burrito	steak	ice cream	fries	chips and salsa
	gum		salad	beer	milkshake	gum
	milk				gum	
Activities:	*Activities:*	*Activities:*	*Activities:*	*Activities:*	*Activities:*	*Activities:*
work	work	work	work	work	went to mall	went to mall
played tennis	watched T.V.	smoked 5 cigarettes	watched T.V.	went to movie	watched T.V.	
watched T.V.			sniffed glue		sniffed glue	
smoked 4 cigarettes			smoked 2 cigarettes		went to movie	

#3—Michael Kowalsky, age 22, dishwasher. Confined to wheelchair.

Monday

Food eaten:
bagels
orange juice
taco
milk
gum
fish sticks
gum
apple
milk

Activities:
work
baseball
watched T.V.

Tuesday

Food eaten:
eggs
toast
orange juice
pizza
cola
crackers
candy bar
chicken
fries
green beans
milk

Activities:
work
skateboarded

Wednesday

Food eaten:
bagels
orange juice
gum
roast beef sandwich
milk
apple
chicken
baked potato
cake

Activities:
work
skateboarded

Thursday

Food eaten:
bagels
orange juice
pizza
apple
soda
gum
rice
corn
milk

Activities:
work

Friday

Food eaten:
bagels
eggs
milk
gum
sandwich
chocolate candy bar
cola
corn
salad
chicken
ice cream

Activities:
work
went to movie

Saturday

Food eaten:
bagels
milk
hot dog
plums
soda
chicken sandwich
gum
ice cream

Activities:
went to mall
watched T.V.
skateboarded

Sunday

Food eaten:
eggs
bagels
orange juice
cheese sandwich
grapes
cola
beef burrito
chips and salsa
gum
pudding

Activities:
skateboarded
sniffed glue
watched T.V.

#4—Tim Watkins, age 17, Jackson High School. Paralyzed, on artificial respirator.

Monday	**Tuesday**	**Wednesday**	**Thursday**	**Friday**	**Saturday**	**Sunday**
Food eaten:	***Food eaten:***	***Food eaten:***	***Food eaten:***	***Food eaten:***	***Food eaten:***	***Food eaten:***
wheat cereal	wheat cereal	wheat cereal	wheat cereal	wheat cereal	wheat cereal	wheat cereal
breakfast drink	breakfast drink	orange juice	breakfast drink	breakfast drink	breakfast drink	sausage
salad	ham sandwich	gum	pizza	gum	pizza	orange juice
cola	apple	fish sticks	banana	ham sandwich	raisins	Thai food:
carrot	cola	cola	cola	cherries	watermelon	rice and
gum	crackers	apple	gum	chocolate candy bar	cola	vegetables
beans	candy bar	chips and salsa	beans	cola	rice	cherries
cornbread	beans	cookies	corn	corn	macaroni and	cola
	biscuit		cake	salad	cheese	beef burrito
	cookies		milk	chicken	gum	gum
				baked potato	ice cream	cookies
				cookies		
Activities:	***Activities:***	***Activities:***	***Activities:***	***Activities:***	***Activities:***	***Activities:***
school	school	school	school	school	swimming at pool	read book
read book	read book	sniffed glue	drama rehearsal	drama rehearsal	watched T.V.	
		drama rehearsal	watched T.V.		read book	
					dancing at party	

#5—Jeff Smith, age 18, Franklin High School drop-out, fast food burger restaurant worker. Paralyzed, on artificial respirator.

Monday	Tuesday	Wednesday	Thursday	Friday	Saturday	Sunday
Food eaten:	*Food eaten:*	*Food eaten:*	*Food eaten:*	*Food eaten:*	*Food eaten:*	*Food eaten:*
chips	wheat cereal	chips	crackers	wheat cereal	chips	pizza
cola	apple	gum	cheese	gum	cheese	grapes
banana	soda	cola	hamburgers	chocolate candy bar	pizza	milkshake
pastrami	candy bar	hamburgers	candy bar	soda	raisins	hamburgers
gum	hamburgers	fries	fries	corn	watermelon	fries
polish dog	fries	milkshake	milkshake	fish steak	cola	gum
beer	candy	cookies	salad	fries	gum	cookies
		beer	gum	cookies	ice cream	beer
			milk		beer	
Activities:	*Activities:*	*Activities:*	*Activities:*	*Activities:*	*Activities:*	*Activities:*
worked on motor-cycle	work	work	work	work	swimming at beach	work
smoked 10–15 cigarettes	smoked 10–15 cigarettes	watched T.V.	smoked 10–15 cigarettes	sniffed glue	watched T.V.	smoked 10–15 cigarettes
	worked on motor-cycle	sniffed glue		smoked 10–15 cigarettes	party	
		smoked 10–15 cigarettes		worked on motor-cycle	smoked 10–15 cigarettes	

#6—Joe Lambly, age 19, food store cashier. Confined to wheelchair.

Monday	Tuesday	Wednesday	Thursday	Friday	Saturday	Sunday
Food eaten:	*Food eaten:*	*Food eaten:*	*Food eaten:*	*Food eaten:*	*Food eaten:*	*Food eaten:*
wheat cereal	eggs	eggs	eggs	wheat cereal	eggs	pancakes
orange juice	bacon	bacon	toast	milk	bacon	syrup
peanut butter and jelly sandwich	toast	orange juice	orange juice	spaghetti	orange juice	milk
milk	orange juice	peanut butter and jelly sandwich	milk	salad	hot dog	cheese sandwich
apple	pizza	milk	peanut butter and jelly sandwich	soda	apple	grapes
tuna casserole	cola	candy bar	apple	chocolate candy bar	cola	cola
	crackers	gum	cola	gum	hamburger	beef burrito
	gum	spaghetti	steak	pasta	fries	chips and salsa
	candy bar	salad	salad		gum	gum
	hamburger	milk	ice cream		ice cream	pudding
	milk					
Activities:	*Activities:*	*Activities:*	*Activities:*	*Activities:*	*Activities:*	*Activities:*
work	work	work	work	work	went to bar	went to bar
watched T.V.	watched T.V.	went to bar	went to movie	sniffed glue	watched T.V.	watched T.V.
smoked 2 cigarettes		smoked 3 cigarettes		went to bar	went to movie	smoked 7 cigarettes
				smoked 8 cigarettes	smoked 5 cigarettes	

#7—Steve Billings, age 21, department store clerk. Confined to wheelchair.

Monday	Tuesday	Wednesday	Thursday	Friday	Saturday	Sunday
Food eaten:	*Food eaten:*	*Food eaten:*	*Food eaten:*	*Food eaten:*	*Food eaten:*	*Food eaten:*
eggs	pizza	bagels	eggs	bagels	bagels	bagels
bagels	grapes	orange juice	toast	eggs	orange juice	milk
orange juice	milkshake	gum	orange juice	milk	pizza	hot dog
cheese sandwich	hamburgers	roast beef sandwich	pizza	gum	apple	plums
grapes	fries	milk	cola	sandwich	soda	soda
cola	gum	popcorn	crackers	chocolate candy bar	gum	chicken sandwich
beef burrito	cookies	apple	popcorn	cola	rice	gum
chips and salsa	beer	chicken	candy bar	corn	corn	ice cream
gum		baked potato	chicken	salad	milk	popcorn
pudding		cake	fries	chicken	popcorn	
			green beans	popcorn		
			milk	ice cream		
Activities:	*Activities:*	*Activities:*	*Activities:*	*Activities:*	*Activities:*	*Activities:*
work	work	work	work	sniffed glue	swam in pool	played soccer
watched T.V.	watched T.V.	went to bar		work	watched T.V.	watched T.V.
				went to movie	played soccer	

Lacquer Thinner Ingredients

(Note: the "glue" sniffers actually sniffed lacquer thinner)

Chemical Name
MEK (methyl-ethyl-ketone)
MiK (methyl-isobutyl-ketone)
n-hexane
methanol (methyl alcohol)
toluene
isobutyl acetate
acetone
ethylene glycol

Lacquer Thinner Ingredients

(Note: the "glue" sniffers actually sniffed lacquer thinner)

Chemical Name
MEK (methyl-ethyl-ketone)
MiK (methyl-isobutyl-ketone)
n-hexane
methanol (methyl alcohol)
toluene
isobutyl acetate
acetone
ethylene glycol

Lacquer Thinner Ingredients

(Note: the "glue" sniffers actually sniffed lacquer thinner)

Chemical Name
MEK (methyl-ethyl-ketone)
MiK (methyl-isobutyl-ketone)
n-hexane
methanol (methyl alcohol)
toluene
isobutyl acetate
acetone
ethylene glycol

What Really Happened

At a fabric printing factory in Columbus, Ohio, a small group of workers started showing signs of nerve damage (neuropathy), with pain and weakness in their arms and legs. This made doctors wonder if there was a problem. They did physical exams and tests on all 1,100 workers at the factory. They found that 79 workers already had neuropathies, and 182 more people had signs that they might be developing this serious problem. Where should the team of medical research specialists begin to look?

The medical research team suspected that workers were being exposed to a toxic chemical. They checked how many chemicals were used in the factory. There were over 275.

They carefully checked the results of the doctors' reports for more clues. All of the people with neuropathies had started having symptoms only in the past few months. The problem was probably something that had *recently changed* in the factory environment.

The team investigated whether any *new* chemicals had been brought into the factory. They also checked to make sure that the chemicals that had been in use for a long time had not been recently changed in some way.

They found only one big change had been made during the past seven years. Just the year before, the factory started using a new ink-thinner *solvent*, *MnBK (methyl-n-butyl ketone)*. *Solvents* are liquids that help dissolve other materials. The team investigated more about this new solvent and why the factory had changed to it.

Solvents used in printing processes can often produce smelly vapors or fumes. The researchers discovered that the factory had changed to the new, less smelly solvent in order to better meet new air pollution regulations. The team checked into what was known about the safety of this new solvent. Until then, this new ink thinner was thought to be a relatively harmless chemical within a large family of solvents called *hexacarbons.* Because the solvent was thought to be safe, workers took no special precautions when handling it.

The team checked to see where in the factory this new solvent was used. It was used in several parts of the factory, but the greatest amount was used in the print room, where colors were printed on the fabric.

The research team quickly checked to see where all workers with nerve damage worked, and if they came into contact with this new solvent. The results of the investigation: All the workers with neuropathies had been exposed to this solvent by working with or being close to it—even those who did not work in the print room.

How were workers exposed to the solvent? The team discovered that the liquid solvent produced fumes or vapor that got into the air. Some workers were exposed to the solvent by breathing the vapors. Workers also became exposed if the liquid touched their skin or got into their mouths. The team discovered that the workers in the print department had not worn gloves to protect their skin. They washed their hands in the solvent to help remove ink stains. They also soaked rags with the chemical to clean their machinery. Some workers ate their lunches in the work area without first washing the solvent off their hands. It was discovered that the greater exposure to M*n*BK a worker had, the more severe their nerve damage.

The factory stopped using the new ink-thinning solvent immediately because it looked like exposure to the new solvent was related to the worker's health problems.

In other parts of the country and the world, there were already medical reports of serious health problems in young men who sniffed glue to get high. In Tampa, Florida, seven young men, who all had inhaled fumes of a certain lacquer thinner to get high, started to feel weakness and numbness in their arms and legs. Four men needed wheelchairs, two others became completely paralyzed and required artificial respiration. One died from breathing problems.

Researchers noticed the similarities between this situation and the one in the fabric printing factory. Chemical analysis of the lacquer thinner used for glue sniffing showed that it was *n*-hexane, a type of hexacarbon solvent, very similar to the ink thinner used in the fabric printing factory. While *n*-hexane did not usually cause neuropathy by itself, when mixed with another solvent that was present in the lacquer thinner (MEK), these two chemicals caused nerve damage. This might seem like the end of the story, but actually the mystery-solving work for scientists was just beginning. Several big questions still remained. Scientists needed to:

a.) *prove* that it was indeed the hexacarbon solvents causing the problem in each of the situations;

b.) learn *how much* of the chemicals produced the harmful effects, in order to know if they could ever be used in a safe way;

c.) do more research on the *long term* health effects of the solvents; and

d.) learn whether and how other *similar types of hexacarbon solvents* might also cause nerve damage.

Researchers conducted tests with laboratory animals. Both the ink-thinning and the glue-sniffing solvents produced the same kind of nerve damage in animals as seen in humans. Scientists looked at the effect of many different solvents on nerve cells they had grown in laboratory dishes. They also used chemical tests to find out what was similar and different about each solvent. These specific ink-thinning and glue-sniffing solvents harmed nerve cells, while some similar solvents did not. In this case, it was also important to see if effects changed or worsened when substances were combined. Scientists have continued their research on these and other solvents to ensure that the products we use in our work places and homes are safe.

NEURON

NEURON

Activity 5: Learning What is Safe

In this activity, your students investigate how animals and humans learn what is safe to eat and how there is a need for research and regulation applying to foods, drugs, cosmetics and their safety. The class enacts a simulation of hungry wolves encountering some "strange" foods and how the wolves attempt to learn what is safe to eat. A discussion follows, which leads students to understand the limits of using our senses to determine the safety of substances and how we as a society of humans attempt to learn what is safe.

For homework (or during one or two additional class sessions), students read an article and write a letter to the editor about a true story that occurred in the 1930s, about an eyelash and eyebrow dye called Lash-Lure. This tragic story led to the development of the Federal Food, Drug, and Cosmetic Act of 1938, enabling the Food and Drug Administration (FDA) finally to begin to protect people by regulating these substances.

What You Need

For the class:

- ❏ 1 package (8 oz.) of elbow macaroni (or other pasta that comes in small individual pieces) *
- ❏ 1 spoon for stirring the macaroni as it cooks
- ❏ 1 pot for cooking macaroni
- ❏ access to a stove, a sink, and a refrigerator
- ❏ 1 colander
- ❏ 5 large ziplock plastic bags
- ❏ 4 colors of food coloring
- ❏ 5 flavorings (such as salt, garlic powder, lemon juice, various food extracts, sugar, cinnamon, curry powder, etc.)
- ❏ 1 cafeteria tray
- ❏ several paper towels or a piece of paper large enough to cover the tray

For each student:

- ❏ 1 copy of the homework article, The Case of Lash-Lure (master on pages 83–85)

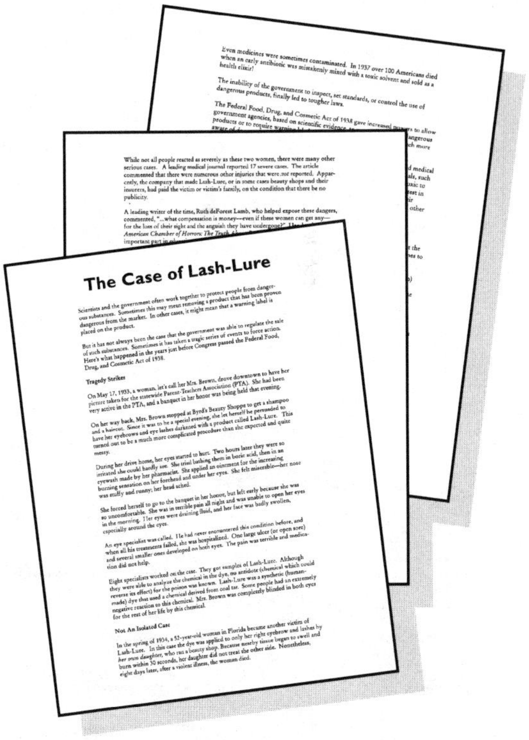
The Case of Lash-Lure

* ***Please note***: All of your students will want to taste the macaroni. Be sure to make enough so that everyone can have a taste. If you are presenting this activity to multiple classes, you might want to make a double batch. This requires very little extra effort on your part.

Getting Ready

Before the Day of the Activity

1. The "strange" foods used in the hungry wolves simulation are piles of cooked macaroni, each colored and flavored in a different way. Plan how you will color and flavor five different portions of macaroni. Here is one possible plan:

- green macaroni (with garlic powder)
- red macaroni (with cinnamon)
- blue macaroni (with vanilla extract and sugar)
- yellow macaroni (with curry powder)
- white macaroni (with salt)

Note: Don't feel constrained to follow this plan, rather choose a plan which uses things you have on hand. As you make your choices, try and get at least one flavor and smell that will be objectionable to some students and at least one flavor and smell that will be pleasant to some students. Also, consider choosing colors that will somewhat mask the appearance (if any) of the flavoring. For instance, use curry powder on yellow, not white, macaroni.

2. Prepare the "strange" food.

Cook the macaroni. Slightly undercook an eight ounce package of elbow macaroni, stirring occasionally. *Do not add salt to the cooking water.*

Drain the macaroni. Pour the macaroni into a colander and rinse very well with cold water (for several minutes!) to remove the sticky starch coating that makes macaroni stick together.

Color the macaroni. Divide the macaroni equally into five large ziplock bags, using your fingers to separate any clumps. Add several drops of food coloring to one bag of macaroni, seal the bag, and use your hands (on the outside of the bag) to gently mix the coloring so it covers all of the macaroni. If you have trouble getting the food coloring distributed on all of the macaroni, add a few drops of water to the bag. If you want a more vibrant color, add several more drops of coloring. Repeat this procedure with a different color for three other bags of macaroni. The fifth bag of macaroni can remain white.

Flavor the macaroni. Add flavorings to all five bags according to your plan. There is no exact formula for how much flavoring to add—just add enough so there is a distinct flavor and odor. The simulation works best if the flavors are not subtle, so be heavy handed!

Store the macaroni. Refrigerate the macaroni until you are ready to use it. Use within several days.

3. Duplicate one copy of the homework article, The Case of Lash-Lure, for each student (master on pages 83–85).

The Day of the Activity

1. Place the colored, flavored macaroni in five piles on a tray. If you are presenting this activity to multiple classes, just put enough macaroni on the tray for one class and then replenish the piles before the next classes. Cover the tray with several paper towels or a large piece of paper so students cannot see the macaroni.

2. For homework, students read a short article entitled The Case of Lash-Lure and then write a "letter to the editor." Some teachers prefer to have students do this during class. Decide if you want to assign it as homework after Activity 5 or schedule an additional session or two so they can do it in class.

Please note: Even if you do decide to assign the article and letter as homework, you may still want to schedule a specific time for your students to discuss the article or share their letters to the editor. Many teachers have found that students need time to process this information in the group. If you would like to provide time to specifically debrief the Lash-Lure story or for students to share the letters they have written, then schedule this discussion time soon. Later, in Activity 9, when students talk generally about the issues of experimenting with animals and humans, they can bring issues or examples from this Lash-Lure discussion into that session.

Hungry Wolves Simulation

1. Tell your students that they are going to again pretend to be wolves. This time they are going to investigate how wolves learn what is safe to eat.

2. Ask them to imagine that they are all members of a pack of wolves. They have been without food for a while and are very hungry. Several wolves run across what appears to be food and are checking it out. We need several volunteers to be those pack members. (Warn the volunteers that they must be willing to eat some foods with unknown tastes.)

3. Choose four or five volunteers and have them come to the front of the classroom. Explain that you will show them the food items in just a moment, after you explain the procedure.

4. Describe the procedure. Each "wolf" needs to eat one food item. They will take turns choosing and eating an item. Remind them that this will be a silent activity. Wolves **can** communicate non-vocally by using a variety of facial gestures and body postures. Tell the wolf volunteers that as they investigate and then taste the food, they should show their reactions and be expressive. (This is key to the success of the activity.) Tell the others to carefully watch the actions and reactions of the volunteers. Point out that as wolves the volunteers should not be self-conscious nor should they keep secrets. Because wolves do not use a spoken language, they are very expressive with their bodies, facial gestures, and sounds (or vocalizations). The wolf volunteers should be expressive too!

If you think your volunteers might be inhibited, you may want to help students practice being expressive non-verbally by asking them to practice looking: curious, fearful, like they have just eaten something delicious, something awful, something so-so, etc.

5. After the wolf volunteers understand what to do, remind the rest of the wolf pack (the class) that they should not speak either. Their job is to learn what they can about whether these food items are safe to eat by watching their fellow wolves. You might want to tell them that you will be asking them to report what they learned at the end of the simulation. Some teachers ask their students to record their observations.

Note: There will be many students in your class who want to participate in the most active roles—the hungry wolves. Reassure them now that everyone who wants to will get to taste the macaroni at the end of class. Some teachers have let the entire "wolf pack" make food choices after observing the wolf volunteers. Others have chosen to do the simulation more than once so more students are wolves. You may want to play this "by ear," depending on classroom dynamics at the time of the activity.

6. Uncover the tray of food items and have the wolf volunteers begin. You may need to remind them of their task, encourage them to be expressive, and keep the action moving. It is not necessary that the wolves go in any order as they taste the foods, as long as they go one at a time. In fact, it is interesting to see which wolves take risks, which wolves copy others, and which wolves hold back. These are all common wolf and human behaviors! Some teachers like to record the food choices on the board as they are made.

7. After each wolf volunteer has tasted one food item, you can either end the simulation, or have them go around one more time and taste a second food item.

Note: The goal of the simulation is for the wolves to exhibit a variety of learning behaviors (sniffing, acting curious, choosing a food item after observing another wolf's positive response to it, avoiding a food item after observing another wolf's negative response to it, etc.). You will want to continue for a second round if these behaviors could not be observed the first time. You might also want to continue if your students are engaged and having fun.

What Did You Learn?

1. Thank the wolf volunteers. Tell the rest of the wolf pack that at the end of today's class, you will allow them to taste the food items if they wish. For now, you'd like them to become students again.

Alternatively, you could invite each student in the class to file by the tray of macaroni, choosing one to taste based on what they learned from watching the wolf volunteers.

2. Lead a discussion of the simulation.

  a. Ask the wolf pack:

  - What did you learn about these foods by watching these wolves interact?
  - What behaviors did you observe that indicated that a food was disliked? liked?
  - In what ways did you see that these wolves learned from each other?

b. Ask wolf volunteers:

- What are some things that you learned?
- Did color play a role in your choices? If so, how? (You might want to point out that while humans and many animals use color to direct food choices, wolves are color blind.)
- What strategy did you use to choose a food?
- Did anyone use a different strategy?
- What color would you choose next? Why?

3. Send the wolf volunteers back to their seats.

4. Summarize by saying that people, like wolves and other animals, learn to avoid bad smelling and tasting things through their senses, memories of bad experiences, and their observations of how others respond to certain foods.

5. You might want to point out that this kind of learning, related to survival, happens all the time for many different kinds of animals, including humans. For instance, birds eat red cherries off trees but not other varieties of red poisonous berries.

Birds that successfully avoid dangerous berries pass their genes on to their offspring. "Poison-berry-avoiding" birds may then come to dominate the population with their inherited or instinctual behaviors.

6. Ask the students for their ideas about how birds might learn this. If your students don't come up with all of these ideas, you might want to add some. [Maybe the taste/smell provides enough warning by itself and birds will either not taste or spit it out. Maybe birds learn if they get sick after eating a berry and then associate that sickness with the berry. Parent birds may teach their young to avoid poison berries. Birds may learn by watching other birds get sick or die.]

When There Are No Sensory Clues...

You may want to point out that wolves and other animals do *eat things which are bad for them. An example of this is the case of automobile anti-freeze (ethylene glycol). Dogs and cats are attracted to this liquid because it smells and tastes good to them. They often seek out containers of it in garages and yards. Animals can get very sick or die from drinking it.*

1. Point out that, unfortunately, not all things that are hazardous have a bad taste or odor. In these cases, learning has to occur by observing what happens when someone comes into contact with that substance. Do they get sick? It may take observing a bad reaction many times to make the connection (like in the Hexacarbon Solvent Mystery). Sometimes being able to **prove** that a substance is hazardous has taken generations (as in the case of cigarette smoking).

2. As humans, we have more options than wolves. Ask students, "What are some of the things that we, as a society of humans, do to avoid potentially dangerous substances?" [We can test substances in a laboratory. They can be analyzed (using chemical tests and special equipment) to see if they are like other known hazardous substances (like the connection that was made between the two hexacarbon solvents). They can be tested on animals to see their reaction to the substance. They can be tested on cell cultures to see what happens to those cells.] If your students don't come up with many ideas, you might want to add a couple. Don't feel compelled to tell them everything, as they will encounter all of this information in the Lash-Lure article.

3. Summarize the session by saying that in this country we have something called the Food and Drug Administration—the FDA. This is a federal agency whose role is to help protect humans from hazardous foods, drugs, and cosmetics. We don't have to taste everything ourselves, like the wolves, to see if there is a hazard. There are regulations that help ensure that those things we eat, ingest, and use on our bodies are safe. Scientists and researchers work to help ensure that products of companies are safe, and in recent years the public in general has been very concerned with safety and health issues. This doesn't eliminate all danger (spoiled or contaminated food, long-term effects of substances formerly thought to be safe, new findings about substances once thought to be safe, etc.) but it provides a certain degree of protection.

Safety is not always easy to determine—or to agree on! Sometimes there is controversy about the safety of substances or processes, where some people think something presents a reasonable risk (given the potential benefit) and others feel the risk is too great. You might want to have your students investigate the cases of x-rays and/or cigarette smoking to see historically how we learned what we know about their health risks. The case of using fluoride in water is interesting, as the controversy still continues!

Introducing the Homework: The Case of Lash-Lure

1. Explain that there was a time, within the lifetime of students' grandparents, when there weren't federal regulations to protect us. For homework, you'd like them to read an article about a true story that prompted the establishment of the Federal Food, Drug, and Cosmetic Act of 1938. This congressional act empowered the then weak Food and Drug Administration (FDA) to begin to regulate food, drugs, and cosmetics. Be sure to warn the students that the article is gruesome!

One teacher chose to strengthen students' personal connection to the Lash-Lure situation by asking if they or someone in their family uses cosmetics, dyes their hair, has a tattoo, etc. Lash-Lure is a product that was used to dye eyebrows and eyelashes.

2. Ask students to write a letter to the editor about the article after they have read it. If your students are not familiar with what a letter to the editor is, you might want to explain that these letters are often written in response to newspaper articles. Letters that raise interesting points or

present other points of view are sometimes published in the newspaper.

Their letter can focus on any of the issues raised in the article, such as:

- the importance of protecting people by testing products,
- the controversy of using animals to test food, drugs, and cosmetics.

Note: The Case of Lash-Lure is a true story that includes some upsetting occurrences (a woman dies, another is blinded, etc.). This tragedy is precisely what led to the establishment of important health and safety regulations in our country. In turn, the need to test products led to the prevalent use of laboratory animals in testing food, drugs, and cosmetics. Reading this article is likely to make a deep impression on your students regarding: a) the need for product testing and consumer protection, b) the profit motivation of some large businesses (like the creators of Lash-Lure), and c) the use of animals in product testing. You will find that this reading and writing assignment, and any subsequent discussion of it, are likely to produce strong reactions in your students. As such, it has great potential as a powerful learning experience.

Some teachers have brought in letters to the editor from a local newspaper to read to students so they can better understand what their own letters might be like.

Writing a letter to the editor will provide your students with a way to express some of their feelings and thoughts about the content of the article. This makes it appropriate for the letter to be from them. Some teachers have offered their students the option of writing the letter as if they were a product safety scientist, the president of a cosmetic company, an animal rights activist, or some other person.

During the Lash-Lure controversy, the chemical (derived from coal tar) that caused the harmful effects was termed by a rival manufacturer as the "criminal ingredient." It's worth noting, however, that an ingredient or a chemical in and of itself cannot be "criminal." Everything is made of ingredients, of chemicals—they are not intrinsically "bad" or "good," they just are! It all depends on how chemicals are used, how different chemicals interact, the ways in which people fail to protect against harmful effects they may have, etc.

The Case of Lash-Lure

Scientists and the government often work together to protect people from dangerous substances. Sometimes this may mean removing a product that has been proven dangerous from the market. In other cases, it might mean that a warning label is placed on the product.

But it has not always been the case that the government was able to regulate the sale of such substances. Sometimes it has taken a tragic series of events to force action. Here's what happened in the years just before Congress passed the Federal Food, Drug, and Cosmetic Act of 1938.

Tragedy Strikes

On May 17, 1933, a woman, let's call her Mrs. Brown, drove downtown to have her picture taken for the statewide Parent-Teachers Association (PTA). She had been very active in the PTA, and a banquet in her honor was being held that evening.

On her way back, Mrs. Brown stopped at Byrd's Beauty Shoppe to get a shampoo and a haircut. Since it was to be a special evening, she let herself be persuaded to have her eyebrows and eye lashes darkened with a product called Lash-Lure. This turned out to be a much more complicated procedure than she expected and quite messy.

During her drive home, her eyes started to hurt. Two hours later they were so irritated she could hardly see. She tried bathing them in boric acid, then in an eyewash made by her pharmacist. She applied an ointment for the increasing burning sensation on her forehead and under her eyes. She felt miserable—her nose was stuffy and runny; her head ached.

She forced herself to go to the banquet in her honor, but left early because she was so uncomfortable. She was in terrible pain all night and was unable to open her eyes in the morning. Her eyes were draining fluid, and her face was badly swollen, especially around the eyes.

An eye specialist was called. He had never encountered this condition before, and when all his treatments failed, she was hospitalized. One large ulcer (or open sore) and several smaller ones developed on both eyes. The pain was terrible and medication did not help.

Eight specialists worked on the case. They got samples of Lash-Lure. Although they were able to analyze the chemical in the dye, no antidote (chemical which could reverse its effect) for the poison was known. Lash-Lure was a synthetic (human-made) dye that used a chemical derived from coal tar. Some people had an extremely negative reaction to this chemical. Mrs. Brown was completely blinded in both eyes for the rest of her life by this chemical.

Not An Isolated Case

In the spring of 1934, a 52-year-old woman in Florida became another victim of Lash-Lure. In this case the dye was applied to only her right eyebrow and lashes by *her own daughter,* who ran a beauty shop. Because nearby tissue began to swell and burn within 30 seconds, her daughter did not treat the other side. Nonetheless, eight days later, after a violent illness, the woman died.

While not all people reacted as severely as these two women, there were many other serious cases. A leading medical journal reported 17 severe cases. The article commented that there were numerous other injuries that were *not* reported. Apparently, the company that made Lash-Lure, or in some cases beauty shops and their insurers, had paid the victim or victim's family, on the condition that there be no publicity.

A leading writer of the time, Ruth deForest Lamb, who helped expose these dangers, commented, "...what compensation is money—even if these women can get any—for the loss of their sight and the anguish they have undergone?" Her book, *American Chamber of Horrors: The Truth About Food and Drugs*, played an important part in educating people about the need for more government regulation.

The Question of Risk

In those days, the Food and Drug Administration did not have the power to seize these products and remove them from the market. Lash-Lure, for example, continued to be used widely. The government did try to warn the public against this "caustic 'beautifier' capable of burning the very eyeballs out of your head," in the words of Ruth deForest Lamb. Many newspapers carried the government warning.

But the manufacturer of Lash-Lure did not stop making the product or change it. Instead, they just made people sign the form below before using Lash-Lure. Customers signed statements before the treatment saying they would not blame the Lash-Lure company if they were injured by the product. Here is what that form said:

> The ....
> (Name of beauty shop)
>
> Guarantees to Dye the Eyelashes and Eyebrows of
>
> Name..
> Street ....
> City ....
>
> Being fully aware that some people are sensitive to dyes because of their physical condition which causes a dermatitis or other injury, I am willing and do assume the risk involved in this treatment and I agree to make no claim against the beauty shop or Lash-Lure Research Laboratories, Inc., and to hold them harmless in the event of the occurrence of such possible consequences.
>
> I have read the foregoing and understand the contents thereof.
>
> Signed ....
> (Customer)
>
> Dated ....
>
> (This Waiver when signed to be retained by beauty shop)

Knowing what you know about Lash-Lure, would you sign the above?

Regulation and Research

Hair dye was just one of many cosmetics of that time that could be dangerous. Toxins such as arsenic, quinine, resorcin, and mercury were commonly used then in various cosmetics and other personal care products.

Even medicines were sometimes contaminated. In 1937 over 100 Americans died when an early antibiotic was mistakenly mixed with a toxic solvent and sold as a health elixir!

The inability of the government to inspect, set standards, or control the use of dangerous products, finally led to tougher laws.

The Federal Food, Drug, and Cosmetic Act of 1938 gave increased powers to allow government agencies, based on scientific evidence, to prevent the use of dangerous products or to require warning labels. Since then, we have all become much more aware of dangers in products and contamination of the environment.

Scientists worked on these problems in other ways as well. They developed medical tests, such as the Draize test for eye and skin irritation. This test uses animals, such as rabbits, to determine whether or not a substance might be damaging or toxic to human eyes. Some researchers have pointed out that had there been such a test in the 1930s, and laws that required companies to demonstrate the safety of their products, the death, blindness, and other severe injuries from Lash-Lure and other dyes would probably not have occurred.

More Recent Issues

There is an important need for regulation of dangerous or toxic substances, but the amount of government regulation has always been hotly debated. When it comes to scientific testing, there has also been controversy.

In order for a substance to be proven safe (or for its dangers to be clearly known) scientific testing is needed. Many of these tests have involved animals of many different kinds. In recent years, animal activists have led strong campaigns, as one example, against animal testing in the cosmetics industry. One full page ad in the New York Times accused a large cosmetics firm of blinding rabbits for "beauty's sake."

There are many different kinds of tests, not all of which involve animals. Scientists continue to search for new, different, and better ways to scientifically test for toxicity. Many large companies employ scientists and other researchers to better ensure product safety.

Some of today's tests rely much less on what is called "whole animal testing." One new approach, *in vitro* toxicology, allows scientists, rather than working with live animals, to work with organs, tissues, or cells. *In vitro* means: in glass or observable in an artificial environment, such as a Petri dish or test tube. Sometimes tests are developed that can tell whether a substance is toxic or not using, for example, a blood sample from an animal or a human.

Controversy continues, both about animal testing and about how much government regulation is needed to protect the public. Learning about the tragic experiences of people like Mrs. Brown that led to government regulation and testing can help all of us be more informed when such issues arise in our own lives.

BABY
Genie
I miss

Activity 6: The Story of Genie

This activity begins with a discussion of how "enriched" environments facilitate learning and "impoverished" environments impair learning. The teacher briefly shares two classic cases, of "Victor" and "Genie," two children raised in severely isolated environments, who were unable even to speak when they were each discovered. Scientists investigated the question of whether these children were permanently damaged by their impoverished upbringing or whether, when put in an enriched environment, these adolescents would learn language and other things normally learned in childhood. Students go on to read a short article telling about the Genie story and discuss the ethics of learning by conducting research on humans.

At the end of the activity, students hear about research conducted on rats by Dr. Marian Cleeves Diamond and her lifetime quest to find out if spending time in "enriched" environments causes the brain to grow in different ways than in "impoverished" environments. This sets the stage for the next activity when your students actually conduct a "classroom brain research" simulation, based on the real research done by Dr. Diamond.

If you or your students are especially intrigued by the case studies of Victor and Genie, consider getting one of the two highly recommended videos featuring these two case studies. Seeing these will make this research come alive for your students. See "Getting Ready" #2 for more information about these videos. Also, see the "Resources" section for information on these videos as well as information about some commonly available books on the subject.

What You Need

For the class:

- ❏ *(optional)* videos of the case studies of Victor and/or Genie, see #2 in "Getting Ready," below, for more details.

For each student:

- ❏ 1 copy of the article The Story of Genie (master on pages 92–95)

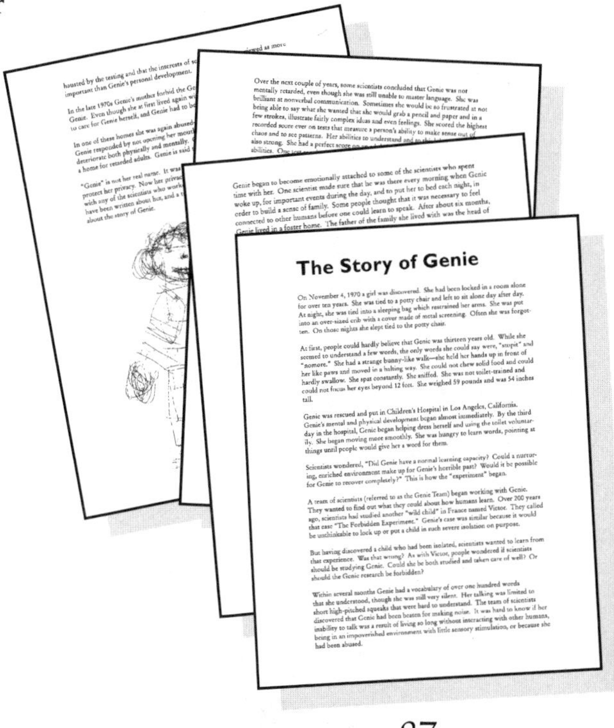

The Story of Genie

On November 4, 1970 a girl was discovered. She had been locked in a room alone for over ten years. She was tied to a potty chair and left to sit alone day after day. At night, she was tied into a sleeping bag which restrained her arms. She was put into an over-sized crib with a cover made of metal screening. Often she was forgotten. On those nights she slept tied to the potty chair.

At first, people could hardly believe that Genie was thirteen years old. While she seemed to understand a few words, the only words she could say were, "stopit" and "nomore." She had a strange bunny-like walk—she held her hands up in front of her like paws and moved in a halting way. She could not chew solid food and could hardly swallow. She spat constantly. She sniffed. She was not toilet-trained and could not focus her eyes beyond 12 feet. She weighed 59 pounds and was 54 inches tall.

Genie was rescued and put in Children's Hospital in Los Angeles, California. Genie's mental and physical development began almost immediately. By the third day in the hospital, Genie began helping dress herself and using the toilet voluntarily. She began moving more smoothly. She was hungry to learn words, pointing at things until people would give her a word for them.

Scientists wondered, "Did Genie have a normal learning capacity? Could a nurturing, enriched environment make up for Genie's horrible past? Would it be possible for Genie to recover completely?" This is how the "experiment" began.

A team of scientists (referred to as the Genie Team) began working with Genie. They wanted to find out what they could about how humans learn. Over 200 years ago, scientists had studied another "wild child" in France named Victor. They called that case "The Forbidden Experiment." Genie's case was similar because it would be unthinkable to lock up or put a child in such severe isolation on purpose.

But having discovered a child who had been isolated, scientists wanted to learn from that experience. Was that wrong? As with Victor, people wondered if scientists should be studying Genie. Could she be both studied and taken care of well? Or should the Genie research be forbidden?

Within several months Genie had a vocabulary of over one hundred words that she understood, though she was still very silent. Her talking was limited to short high-pitched squeaks that were hard to understand. The team of scientists discovered that Genie had been beaten for making noise. It was hard to know if her inability to talk was a result of living so long without interacting with other humans, being in an impoverished environment with little sensory stimulation, or because she had been abused.

Getting Ready

Before the Day of the Activity

1. Duplicate one copy of the article The Story of Genie, for each student (master on pages 92–95).

2. (*Optional)* Obtain the film by Francois Truffaut entitled *The Wild Child* and/or the NOVA video called *The Secret of the Wild Child.* Both of these offer scientifically accurate, moving accounts of two children, each raised in impoverished circumstances. The Truffaut film documents the true story of Victor, a child who lived by himself in the woods of southern France. He was found in 1800 at the age of 12, "animal in behavior, human in form." The film is based on the notebooks of the scientist who studied Victor.

The NOVA video spends some time on the story of Victor but features the tragic story of a girl named Genie who spent her entire childhood strapped to a chair and isolated in a barren room. She was discovered in 1970, at the age of 13. The video shows Genie's struggles to learn and what scientists learned about learning as they worked with her. **If you do obtain these highly recommended features, schedule a time prior to Activity 7 in which your students can watch excerpts from them or even view them in their entirety.**

Enriched and Impoverished Environments

1. Begin the session by pointing out that as humans we are driven to learn. Curiosity is a trait of humans and other animals. Whether it be to learn how to protect ourselves or just to find out something we didn't know before—we go to great lengths to learn. Conclude by saying that learning results not just in our survival—**learning causes us to thrive.**

2. Point out that our environment makes a huge difference in how well we learn. **Imagine trying to learn how to count in two different situations:**

- **An "enriched" environment** with lots of materials you can hold and count, people to interact with who can count with you, counting books to look at with numbers in them, being able play counting games;

or

• **An "impoverished" environment** where you are all by yourself in an empty or boring room, without any other people, and no things you could touch or hold, no books or games.

3. Ask, "In which environment would you learn to count best, an enriched or an impoverished one?" (You may want to clarify that in this case "enriched" does not mean "rich," but stimulating and socially interactive.)

4. Tell your students that over the centuries people have learned a lot about learning through the many cases of children raised in strange circumstances:

• There are cases of "wild children" who are raised by animals or who survive on their own in nature. The stories of these wild children are told in popularized books, movies, legends, and scientific accounts. Many of us are familiar with the tale of Mowgli that was popularized through the stories of Rudyard Kipling and the Walt Disney *Jungle Book* movies. Fewer have heard of Victor, a child who walked out of the forest in the year 1800 at age 12. He often walked on all fours and was unable to speak. At first, people weren't even sure he was human!

• There are also cases of "closet children." These are horrible situations in which children have been kept in closets or rooms by themselves for long periods of time. One of the most extreme cases is of a girl referred to as "Genie" who was kept locked in a room for over ten years. She was discovered in 1970 at the age of 13. She could barely walk or even swallow. She could not talk.

5. Explain that both "wild children" and "closet children" have been exposed to extremely impoverished environments. "Wild children" do have lots of stimulation from living in nature, but they are deprived of interacting with other humans, human language, and culture. "Closet children" receive very little stimulation.

6. Say that when these children have been discovered, many different kinds of scientists have been very interested, particularly those who study how humans learn language. Both Victor and Genie were studied very carefully. Scientists wanted to know what would happen if

In addition to Victor in France, there are over fifty documented wild children discovered in the last seven centuries. These include: the Hesse wolf-child; the Irish sheep-child; Kaspar Hauser (the first Lithuanian bear-child); Peter of Hanover, (the second Lithuanian bear-child); Tomko of Zips (the third Lithuanian case, also called the Karpfen bear-girl); the Salzburg sow-girl, Clemens the Overdyke pig-child; Dina Sanichar of Sekandra, the Indian panther-child; the Justedal snow-hen; the Mauretanian gazelle-child; the Teheran ape-child; Lucas the South African baboon-child; and Edith of Ohio.

While the experiment of isolating a child would never be done on purpose, when this happens through some unfortunate circumstance, people are curious to learn from it. The study of Victor in 1800 was referred to as "The Forbidden Experiment" at the time, precisely for this reason. Many people thought it cruel to subject the child to ongoing tests and experiments. Later, the same issues arose in the study of Genie. The ethics of experimenting in these ways on humans is a large issue and one that eventually contributed to the end of the study of Genie's progress. Ironically, in the case of Genie, many people believe that the tests and caring attention that Genie received from the team of scientists that worked with her were an important source of stimulation and enrichment for her. When the testing ended, Genie quickly began to regress. There are of course many other factors involved. Some of this is discussed in the story. Some of the books and videos listed in the "Resources" section present a detailed study of this fascinating case and the ethics of experimenting with human lives.

Your students may want to know more about Genie's early conditions and her parents. While not everything is known, it is thought that it was her severely disturbed father who was the instigator of the terrible abuse. Her mother, abused to some extent herself, was also blind at the time, although she later recovered some sight surgically. Very shortly after authorities found Genie, her father committed suicide. (Several books on Genie are listed in the "Resources" section.)

these children were put in an enriched environment—would they now be able to learn language and other things that they had been unable to learn in their impoverished environments? Or had their brains been permanently affected by having been in impoverished environments?

Reading and Discussing The Story of Genie

1. Tell the students that today they are going to read a story about Genie—one of the most studied closet children. Decide whether you want students to read the article silently or whether you want to read it aloud as a class. Distribute copies of the story and have them begin.

2. After reading the story, your students will want to share their reactions. Allow time for open-ended discussion about the story.

3. Steer the discussion back to the concept of impoverished and enriched environments and the question of whether the environment in which humans are raised can affect how a person's brain develops. Ask students what they think about this.

4. Ask the class whether they think it was wrong for scientists to study Genie. After some discussion, ask, "Is it possible for scientists to learn about learning without studying humans?"

5. End by saying that there is a scientist, named Dr. Marian Cleeves Diamond, who wondered about some of the same questions that the Genie team wondered, especially: Does learning change the structure of our brains? Dr. Diamond has spent a large part of her life studying whether being in impoverished environments (where little learning occurs) will cause your brain to grow differently than spending time in enriched environments (where lots of learning occurs). She conducted her studies with rats, not humans.

6. Tell students that in the next two activities, they will get a chance to learn more about Dr. Marian Diamond's research, as they conduct some simulated experiments based on her research.

Going Further

1. If you were not able to have the entire class watch the recommended videos, individuals or groups of students could look for them and report to the class.

2. Students could do research projects to learn more about Victor or about other "wild children."

The Story of Genie

On November 4, 1970 a girl was discovered. She had been locked in a room alone for over ten years. She was tied to a potty chair and left to sit alone day after day. At night, she was tied into a sleeping bag which restrained her arms. She was put into an over-sized crib with a cover made of metal screening. Often she was forgotten. On those nights she slept tied to the potty chair.

At first, people could hardly believe that Genie was thirteen years old. While she seemed to understand a few words, the only words she could say were, "stopit" and "nomore." She had a strange bunny-like walk—she held her hands up in front of her like paws and moved in a halting way. She could not chew solid food and could hardly swallow. She spat constantly. She sniffed. She was not toilet-trained and could not focus her eyes beyond 12 feet. She weighed 59 pounds and was 54 inches tall.

Genie was rescued and put in Children's Hospital in Los Angeles, California. Genie's mental and physical development began almost immediately. By the third day in the hospital, Genie began helping dress herself and using the toilet voluntarily. She began moving more smoothly. She was hungry to learn words, pointing at things until people would give her a word for them.

Scientists wondered, "Did Genie have a normal learning capacity? Could a nurturing, enriched environment make up for Genie's horrible past? Would it be possible for Genie to recover completely?" This is how the "experiment" began.

A team of scientists (referred to as the Genie Team) began working with Genie. They wanted to find out what they could about how humans learn. Over 200 years ago, scientists had studied another "wild child" in France named Victor. They called that case "The Forbidden Experiment." Genie's case was similar because it would be unthinkable to lock up or put a child in such severe isolation on purpose.

But having discovered a child who had been isolated, scientists wanted to learn from that experience. Was that wrong? As with Victor, people wondered if scientists should be studying Genie. Could she be both studied and taken care of well? Or should the Genie research be forbidden?

Within several months Genie had a vocabulary of over one hundred words that she understood, though she was still very silent. Her talking was limited to short high-pitched squeaks that were hard to understand. The team of scientists discovered that Genie had been beaten for making noise. It was hard to know if her inability to talk was a result of living so long without interacting with other humans, being in an impoverished environment with little sensory stimulation, or because she had been abused.

Genie began to become emotionally attached to some of the scientists who spent time with her. One scientist made sure that he was there every morning when Genie woke up, for important events during the day, and to put her to bed each night, in order to build a sense of family. Some people thought that it was necessary to feel connected to other humans before one could learn to speak. After about six months, Genie lived in a foster home. The father of the family she lived with was the head of the Genie Team.

Genie continued to recover and develop. She ran, giggled, and smiled. People commented that in some ways she seemed like a normal 18–20-month-old child. If you were to give her a toy, she would feel it gently first with her fingertips. Then she would rub it against her mouth and face, using her lips to feel the object. Genie did not seem to know when to use her eyes and when to use her sense of touch.

Genie's scientist "friends" took her on daily outings—walks through the neighborhood, visits to stores. Genie was so curious and hungry for experiences. She would demand to know the names for all the things in stores, almost faster than she could be told. She would pick up items and intently explore them. Even strangers felt compelled to help her learn about the world. A butcher, who knew nothing about Genie, used to hand her an unwrapped bone, piece of meat or fish each time she passed by his shop. She would explore it by rubbing it on her lips and face. Other strangers would go out of their way to give Genie things. Somehow her thirst for learning about her world showed.

Many scientists came from all over to meet and observe Genie. They argued and debated about what research to do, as did the Genie Team itself. What could Genie best help scientists discover about learning? Could they conduct their research without interfering with her well-being?

Genie's vocabulary grew by leaps and bounds, but she was still not able to string words together into meaningful sentences. Normal children begin by learning to say simple sentences, like "No have toy." Soon they are able to say "I not have toy." Eventually they will learn to say, "I do not have the toy." Later they will refine the sentence to say, "I don't have the toy." Genie seemed to be stuck at the first stage. We do learn many words from experience, from seeing, hearing, reading, and asking. But some scientists think that learning how to speak in sentences and sensing how words get put together in logical order also depends on something that is built into our brains from birth. Was Genie's brain missing something which was necessary for learning language?

Scientists began to wonder if Genie was mentally retarded. If she was, had she been mentally retarded from birth? Had she been injured? Or was the retardation a result of her brain being deprived of good nutrition and/or stimulation? How had her poor diet and isolated upbringing affected her growing brain?

Over the next couple of years, some scientists concluded that Genie was not mentally retarded, even though she was still unable to master language. She was brilliant at nonverbal communication. Sometimes she would be so frustrated at not being able to say what she wanted that she would grab a pencil and paper and in a few strokes, illustrate fairly complex ideas and even feelings. She scored the highest recorded score ever on tests that measure a person's ability to make sense out of chaos and to see patterns. Her abilities to understand and to think logically were also strong. She had a perfect score on an adult-level test that measured spatial abilities. One test required that she use a set of colored sticks to recreate a complicated structure from memory. She was not only able to build the structure perfectly, she built it with sticks of the exact same color as the first structure! Despite all this, Genie remained unable to master the basics of language.

Scientists wondered—could she **ever** be taught to speak? If so, how would her brain have to grow and adapt to do so? Could a teenager still learn to talk or is the structure of language something that must be learned in the early years of life when the brain is growing and changing so much?

In most humans, both sides of the brain are involved in every task, but some tasks result in more electrical activity on the right side of the brain and some in more activity on the left side of the brain. Scientists noticed that Genie was particularly good, quick, and confident at those tasks that involved more of the right brain. She was hesitant at tasks that require equal coordination between the two sides of the brain. She failed at tasks that involved more of the left brain, such as language.

One of the last tests that was done on Genie measured what parts of her brain were active as she conducted different kinds of tasks. Scientists were shocked at how unbalanced the activity in her brain was. There was almost no left brain activity. Her tests looked similar to tests of children who had to have their left brains removed.

Some scientists thought this explained her inability to learn language. Whether this was correct or not, it raised the question: Why was her brain activity so lopsided? Does the left brain develop in those critical early years of life when Genie was so isolated? Does the left brain need to receive stimulation and hear language to develop?

After about five years of researching Genie's progress, the Genie Team lost their funding from the government agency that had awarded the research grant. The scientists at this agency felt that the Genie Team was not doing good scientific research because the tests Genie was being given were not producing enough new information. At the same time that these people felt that Genie wasn't being tested enough, others felt that Genie was being over-tested.

Genie's mother, encouraged by one of Genie's old teachers, tried to sue the Genie Team for "cruel" treatment of Genie. Their lawsuit claimed that Genie was exhausted by the testing and that the interests of science were being viewed as more important than Genie's personal development.

In the late 1970s Genie's mother forbid the Genie Team from having contact with Genie. Even though she at first lived again with her mother, her mother was unable to care for Genie herself, and Genie had to be sent to a series of foster homes.

In one of these homes she was again abused—this time punished for vomiting. Genie responded by not opening her mouth for several months. Genie began to deteriorate both physically and mentally. Genie's mother moved and placed Genie in a home for retarded adults. Genie is said to still live in a home for retarded adults.

"Genie" is not her real name. It was first given to her by the scientists in an effort to protect her privacy. Now her privacy is guarded by her mother. She has no contact with any of the scientists who worked with her and came to love her. Several books have been written about her, and a television documentary program was also made about the story of Genie.

Genie's drawing of her mother cradling a baby Genie.

Development of the Human Cerebral Cortex

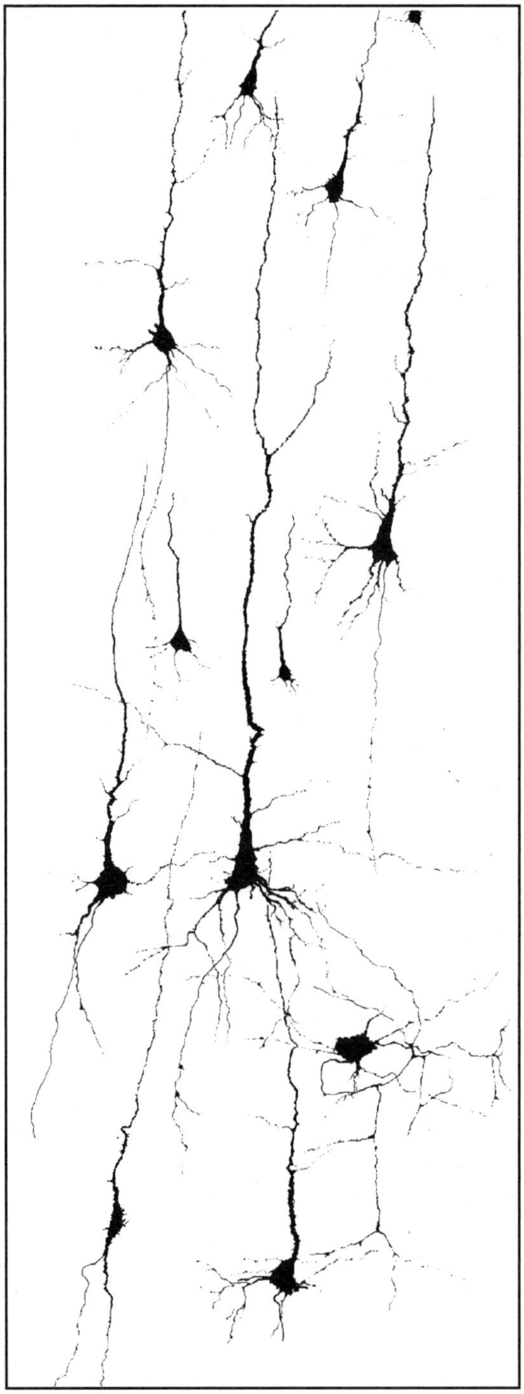

Cerebral cortex neurons in a newborn child. *(from Volume I)*

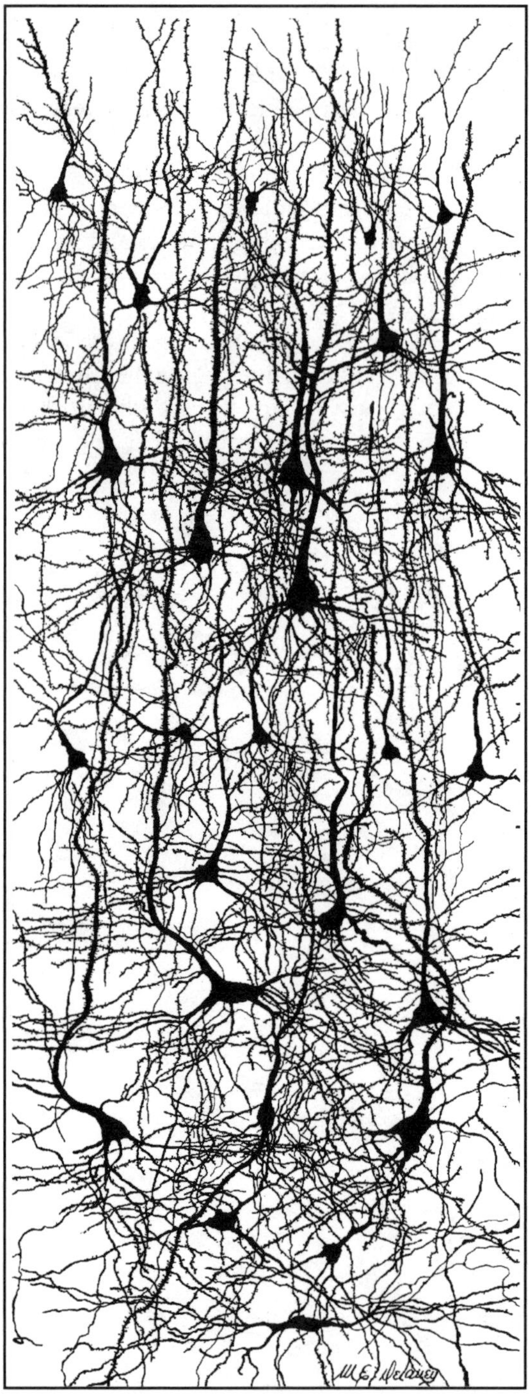

Cerebral cortex neurons in a two-year-old child. *(from Volume VI)*

Illustrations modified and adapted from *The Postnatal Development of the Human Cerebral Cortex* by J. Leroy Conel, Harvard University Press, Cambridge, Massachusetts, 1939-1967.

Activity 7: Learning and Environment (Part I)

In this activity, your students conduct "brain research" as they collect and graph data from diagrams of rat brain cells. Based on real research by Dr. Marian Cleeves Diamond, this "classroom brain research" enables students to investigate the hypothesis that learning changes the very *structure* of the brain.

Don't feel that you must pre-teach about brains and brain function. It is not necessary for you or your students to know anything specific about the brain before this activity—except that it is involved in learning! Students will learn about neurons early in the session—this will prepare them for their task of comparing and measuring the size of different neurons. Our experience is that students (and teachers!) want to learn more about brains after having participated in this activity—as such it is a great *introduction* to brain science. See the "Resources" section for names of good sources for learning more about brain anatomy and function.

What You Need

For the class:

- ❏ 5 Rats in Cages (Control Group plus Experimental Groups 1–4) diagrams (masters on pages 104–108)
- ❏ 5 Rat Brain Cell (Control Group plus Experimental Groups 1–4) diagrams (masters on pages 109–113)
- ❏ overhead transparencies of:
  - Rat Brain Cell—Control Group diagram (master on page 109)
  - Circle Grid (master on page 114)
  - Dendrite Graphing Sheet (master on page 115)
  - Instructions for Dendrite Graphing (master on page 116)
- ❏ overhead projector
- ❏ 1 transparency pen
- ❏ several rolls of masking tape
- ❏ 5 different colors of crayons, markers, or colored pencils

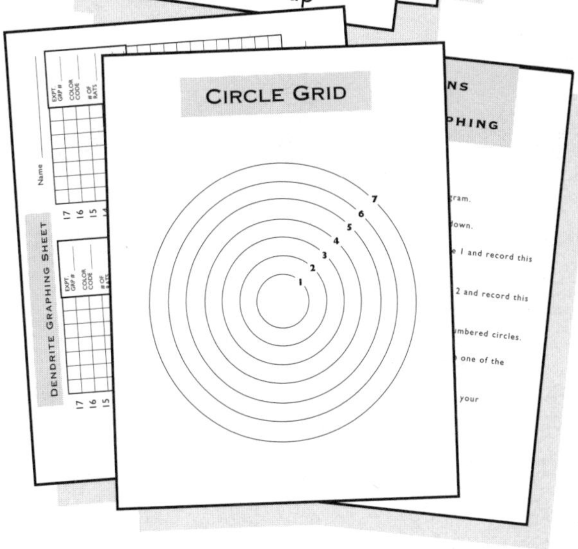

For each team of four students:

- ❏ 4 Rat Brain Cell—Control Group diagrams (master on page 109)
- ❏ 1 set of four diagrams paper-clipped together. The set consists of one each of the following diagrams:
  - Rat Brain Cell—Experimental Group 1 (master on page 110)

- Rat Brain Cell—Experimental Group 2 (master on page 111)
- Rat Brain Cell—Experimental Group 3 (master on page 112)
- Rat Brain Cell—Experimental Group 4 (master on page 113)

❑ 4 blank overhead transparencies (to make circle grids)
❑ 4 Dendrite Graphing Sheets (master on page 115)
❑ 1 or 2 manila file folders
❑ pencils

Note: If you are presenting this activity to multiple groups, you can reuse all student sheets except the Dendrite Graphing Sheets. To make your job easier, have on hand file folders for the next class of students. See the note at the end of this activity on page 103 instructing you to have students place sheets to be reused in these new folders, so that you will be practically set up for the next class. All you'll need to add are new Dendrite Graphing Sheets.

Getting Ready

Note: We're aware that preparation for this activity involves a lot of copying and collating. We've tried to control the flurry of papers by suggesting a method of color-coding and other ways to organize the papers. The copied sets can also be reused by other classes, representing simulated data sets. As you weather the storm of papers, it's worth remembering that this activity allows your students to simulate an experimental experience in a much less expensive and more accessible (and possible!) way than having students do the real research of examining brain cells with microscopes.

Before the Day of the Activity

1. Duplicate one copy of each of the Rats in Cages (Control Group plus Experimental Groups 1–4) diagrams (masters on pages 104–108). Use a different colored marker, pencil, or crayon to color in the color-code square on each of these drawings.

2. Duplicate a Rat Brain Cell—Control Group diagram (master on page 109) for each student and one for yourself. Make an overhead transparency of it for use in your demonstration.

3. Duplicate a set of four Rat Brain Cell diagrams from Experimental Groups 1–4 (masters on pages 110–113) for

each team of four students. Make an extra set for yourself. Paper clip one set together for each team.

4. Make a Circle Grid for each student by duplicating the master (see page 114) onto a blank overhead transparency. Make one extra for your demonstration.

5. Duplicate a Dendrite Graphing Sheet (master on page 115) for each student and make an overhead transparency of it for use in your demonstration.

6. Make an overhead transparency of the Instructions for Dendrite Graphing (master on page 116).

7. Place the following materials in a manila folder for each team of four students:

- ❑ 4 Rat Brain Cell—Control Group diagrams
- ❑ 1 set of Rat Brain Cell—Experimental Groups 1–4 diagrams
- ❑ 4 Circle Grids
- ❑ 4 Dendrite Graphing Sheets

The Day of the Activity

1. Set up the overhead projector. Put the Rat Brain Cell—Control Group diagram on the overhead and have the other transparencies and masking tape nearby.

2. Tape up the five Rats in Cages diagrams in a place where everyone will be able to see them. Next to each diagram, tape up the five corresponding Rat Brain Cell diagrams.

3. Have the file folders and lengths of masking tape ready to distribute to each research team.

Marian Diamond's Experiment

1. Tell your students that today they are going to do "brain research" similar to the research done by Dr. Marian Diamond. Remind them that Diamond wondered whether learning changes the structure of our brains. She set out to discover if spending time in "enriched" environments causes the brain to grow in different ways than in "impoverished" environments.

2. To answer this question, Diamond compared rats in a standard cage environment with rats in impoverished and enriched environments.

Dr. Marian Cleeves Diamond is one of the authors of this unit. As a Professor at the University of California at Berkeley she continues to conduct research on the brain; she also served as the Director of the Lawrence Hall of Science for five years. Many students, particularly girls, are inspired by talking with Dr. Diamond, learning about her life and how she has been driven to learn about learning. We have included an optional article about her in this guide so you and your students can learn more about her and her research. It is best read after Activity 8.

3. Focus the students' attention on the five Rats in Cages diagrams you have posted on the wall. Tell the students that these represent the cage environments that Diamond used in her experiments. She and her research team tried to set up some cage environments that were enriched, and some that were impoverished.

4. Start with the Rats in Cages—Control Group diagram. Explain that this is the standard environment for rats used by research labs around the nation. The rats are fed a standard diet that contains everything an animal needs for healthy development. Tell them that this "normal" situation is called the "control group" because it is what the other groups are compared to.

A great variety of metal objects or "toys" were used to "enrich" the cage environments, including wheels, things to climb on, and kitchen utensils.

5. Then introduce the four Rats in Cages—Experimental Groups 1–4 diagrams, pointing out the features of each cage environment (size of cage, number of rats, presence of toys). Ask the students, "What might make these environments impoverished from a rat's point of view? What might make them enriched?"

6. Tell students they will be collecting and comparing data from some of the experiments that Marian Diamond and her research team did, and that they will be using methods very similar to those used by her team to investigate learning in rats.

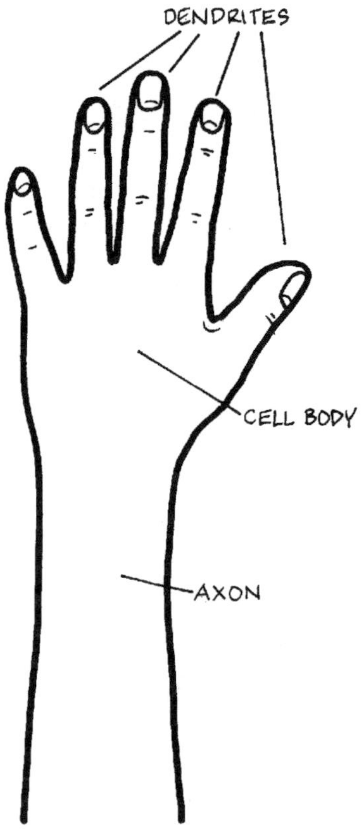

HAND AS MODEL OF NEURON

Introducing Neurons

1. Tell them that at first it was hard for Diamond to decide how to compare the rats' brains. She and her research team tried many different ways, including comparing individual brain cells from the brains of the rats.

2. Introduce brain cells (***neurons***) to your students in the following way:

a. Have students hold up their hands with their fingers extended. Ask them to imagine that their hand is a giant nerve cell or ***neuron.***

b. Explain that the palm of the hand represents the ***cell body.*** This is where the ***nucleus*** would be.

c. The arm represents the ***axon.***

d. The fingers represent ***dendrites.***

See "Behind the Scenes" and books in the "Resources" section for more information on neurons, dendrites, axons, and other aspects of brain anatomy and structure.

3. Mention that, of course, neurons are very tiny. One neuron would fit on the point of a pin! There are approximately 100 billion (100,000,000,000) neurons in your brain!

4. Turn on the overhead projector and show students the Rat Brain Cell—Control Group diagram. Tell them that this is a diagram of a typical brain cell found in the ***cerebral cortex*** of a rat's brain. Ask students to point out the cell body, the axon, and the dendrites.

The cerebral cortex, also called the cerebrum, is the outer surface of the brain, sometimes referred to as the "thinking" part of the brain.

5. Re-emphasize that one of the things Diamond's research team did was focus on comparing individual brain cells from the brains of rats that spent time in impoverished environments to those that spent time in enriched environments. That is just what students are going to do today.

You might want to mention that the axon extends much further in real life. Also, in this diagram, the cell body looks dark. This is just what the brain cells looked like after Diamond's research team prepared them with a special staining technique that uses a silver compound to darken the cell body and make the dendrites more conspicuous, so they are easier to see.

Comparing Neurons

1. Point out the five posted Rat Brain Cell diagrams from the brains of rats who spent time in the different cage environments shown in the Rats in Cages diagrams. Tell them that their challenge will be to measure the differences between these brain cells.

2. Ask, "What are some of the ways we could measure the differences in these brain cells?" Accept all answers. Tell your students that their ideas are similar to some that Diamond's research team first had. After trying out different ways of measuring, the research team ended up using the same measurement technique that the students will use, after you demonstrate it to them.

The brain cell drawings they will use in this activity are based on a synthesis of Diamond's research findings over the years. They are not actual images, but drawings that are similar to what the researchers observe when they are making measurements of cells.

Demonstrate How to Count Dendrite Crossings

1. Focus the class on the overhead transparency of the Rat Brain Cell—Control Group diagram. Explain that the Diamond research team decided to use a circle grid to measure and compare cells. Put the circle grid on the overhead for them to see. Say that they developed very precise rules for using the grid, so that even new graduate students who joined the team could quickly learn to measure cells reliably.

2. Use the overhead to model the procedure the students will follow:

- Tell the students they will tape the diagram of the brain cell being measured to their desk so it won't move around. (Show this to students by taping the transparency to the overhead.)

- Then they will place their transparency of the circle grid so its center is on the center of the cell body, and tape it down too. (Again, do this with your transparencies, being sure to tape the circle grid securely to the brain cell diagram and then tape both to the overhead.)

Deciding where the center of the cell body is and lining it up with the center of the circle grid may be challenging for your students. It was for Diamond and her research team, too! It's okay if it isn't exact. The goal is not for the students to come up with identical results, but rather for them to go through similar processes to those that real scientists do, making judgments and estimations. Contrary to what many people may think, science is not always exact!

- Begin with circle #1 and demonstrate how to count the number of times the circle grid line crosses a dendrite. Have the students do this with you. Beware: the cell body can't be counted, only the points at which the dendrites extend from the cell body. Also, don't count the axon!

One teacher color-coded the axon (by drawing a colored line over it) so it would be easier to remember that you don't count it.

*There are **0** dendrite crossings at circle #1.*

- Show students how to record the number of crossings for circle #1 on the Dendrite Graphing Sheet, by placing an "X" on the line labeled "circle grid line 1" at the correct number of crossings. (To do this, you will need to remove the taped overheads carefully so they don't slip apart from one another, show students how to record on the transparency of the graphing sheet, and then replace the two taped overheads. You will need to do this a couple more times. While this is a bit awkward, we have found that showing students how to use the Dendrite Graphing Sheet is a very effective way to clarify something that is otherwise confusing to some students.)

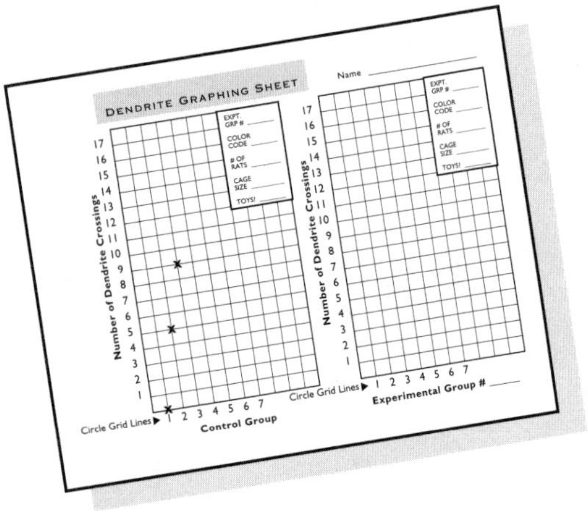

*There are **5** dendrite crossings at circle #2.*

- Count the number of crossings for circle #2 and record the number on the Dendrite Graphing Sheet by making another "X" at the intersection of the graph lines for circle grid line 2 and the number of dendrite crossings. (Don't count the axon!)

*There are **9** dendrite crossings at circle #3.*

- Continue until your students understand the process. There is no need to complete the graph.

3. Explain that each team of four students will be its own research team. Each person in the team will individually count and graph the dendrite crossings for a rat brain cell from the Control Group. Then each student in the team

will individually count and graph one of the four Experimental Groups. When they are through, each team will have a complete set of graphs to compare the brain cells of rats from all of the different cage environments.

Depending on how the grid is centered, the number of dendrite crossings may vary. This is okay and should not change the overall results significantly.

4. Say that they will each need to record information about the Control Group and the Experimental Group on their graphing sheet. Point out the "tag" in the upper corner of each graphing sheet where this information is to be written. Point out the color-code square on each posted Rats in Cages diagram. This is the color code for that experimental group. If you think your students need more clarification, you might want to model filling out the tags by doing so on the transparency of the graphing sheet.

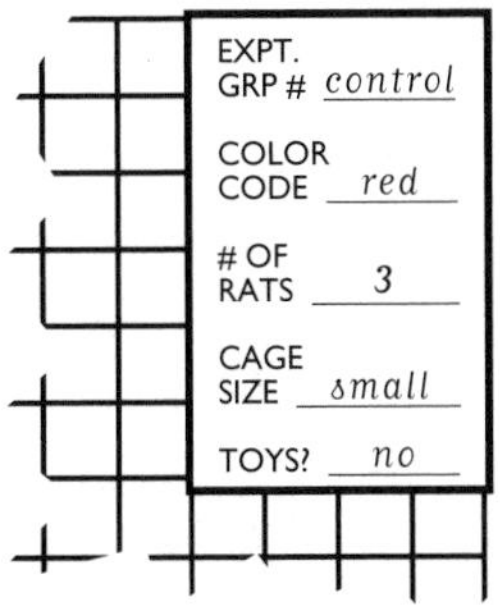

"Research Teams" Measure Brain Cells

1. After students understand what they are to do, put a transparency of the Instructions for Dendrite Graphing on the overhead. Distribute file folders with student materials and lengths of masking tape. Divide students into groups of four and have them begin.

With younger students, you may want to separate the steps by having them do the control graph, then stopping to make sure they've understood, before they go ahead to graph the experimental groups. You would then also explain writing information on the "tag" in the upper corner of each graph.

2. As they work, circulate around the room to check on their progress. Invite students to ask questions and to share observations of interesting things the graphs reveal.

3. As they complete the task, have them replace their materials in the folder, label the folder with their team members' names, and return them to you for safe-keeping.

Note: If you are doing this with multiple classes, have the students put their completed graphing sheets in their team's folder, and give them a second folder into which they can put the circle grids and all of the Rat Brain Cell diagrams. These new folders will then be nearly ready to be given to the next group—just add new Dendrite Graphing Sheets.

4. Tell them that in the next activity, they will have an opportunity to work in their teams to interpret the graphs.

Color code

CONTROL GROUP: 3 RATS, SMALL CAGE, NO TOYS

Color code

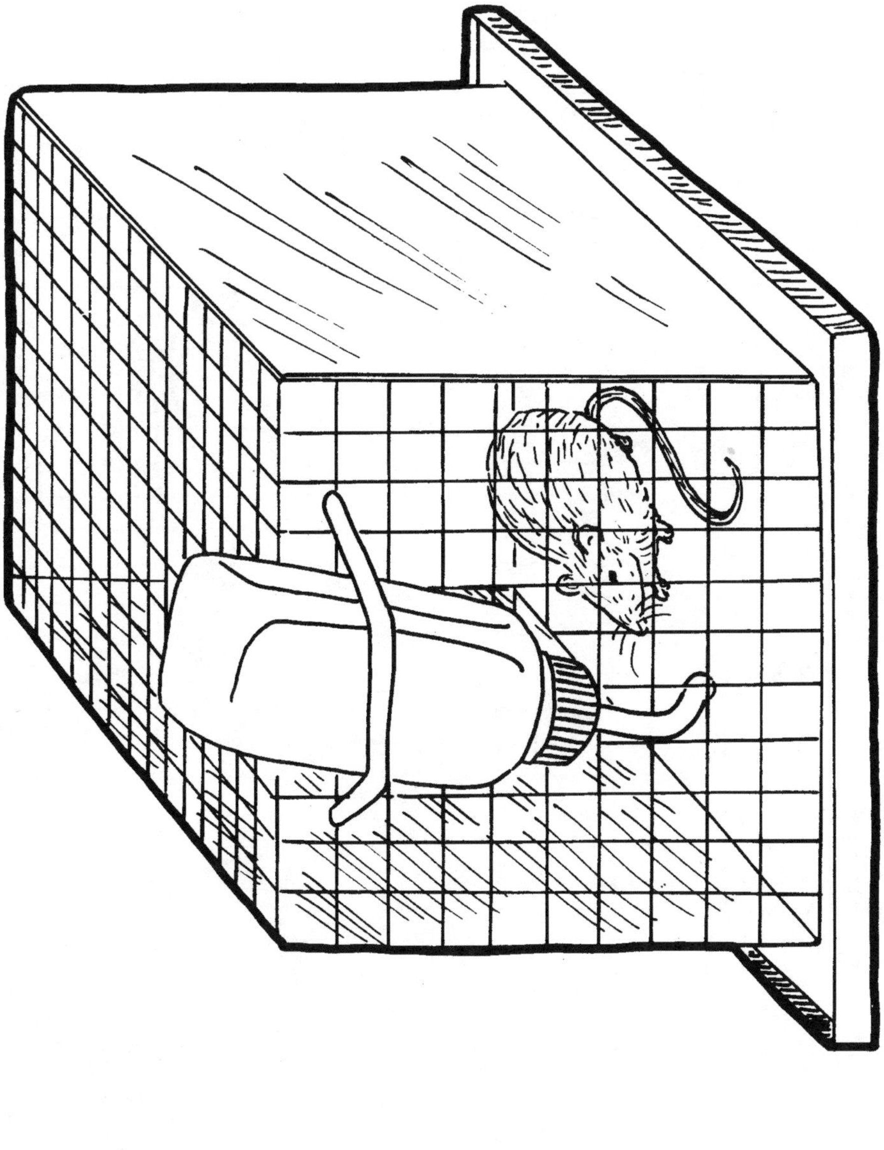

EXPERIMENTAL GROUP 1: 1 RAT, SMALL CAGE, NO TOYS

EXPERIMENTAL GROUP 2: 1 RAT, LARGE CAGE, TOYS

Color code

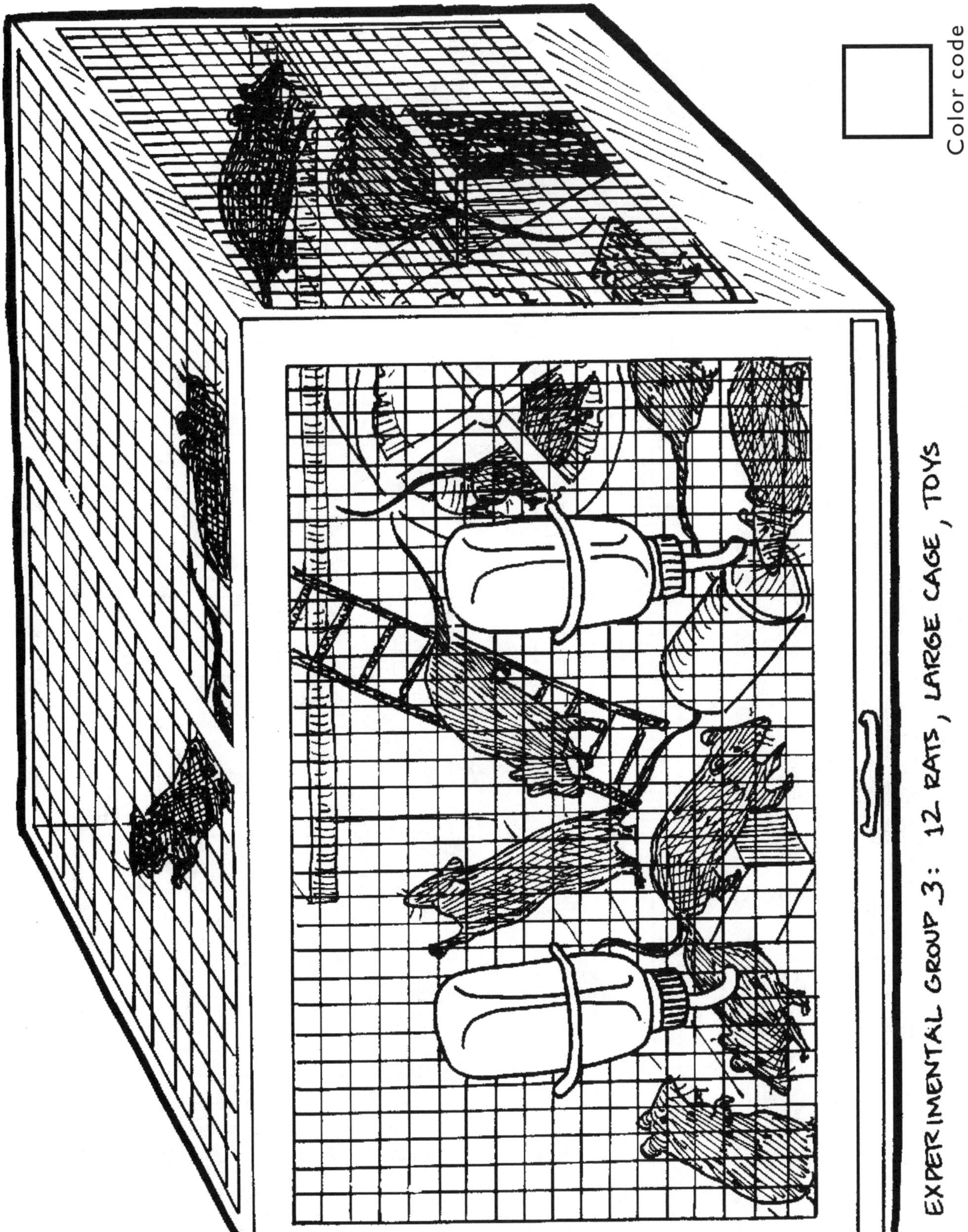
Color code
EXPERIMENTAL GROUP 3: 12 RATS, LARGE CAGE, TOYS

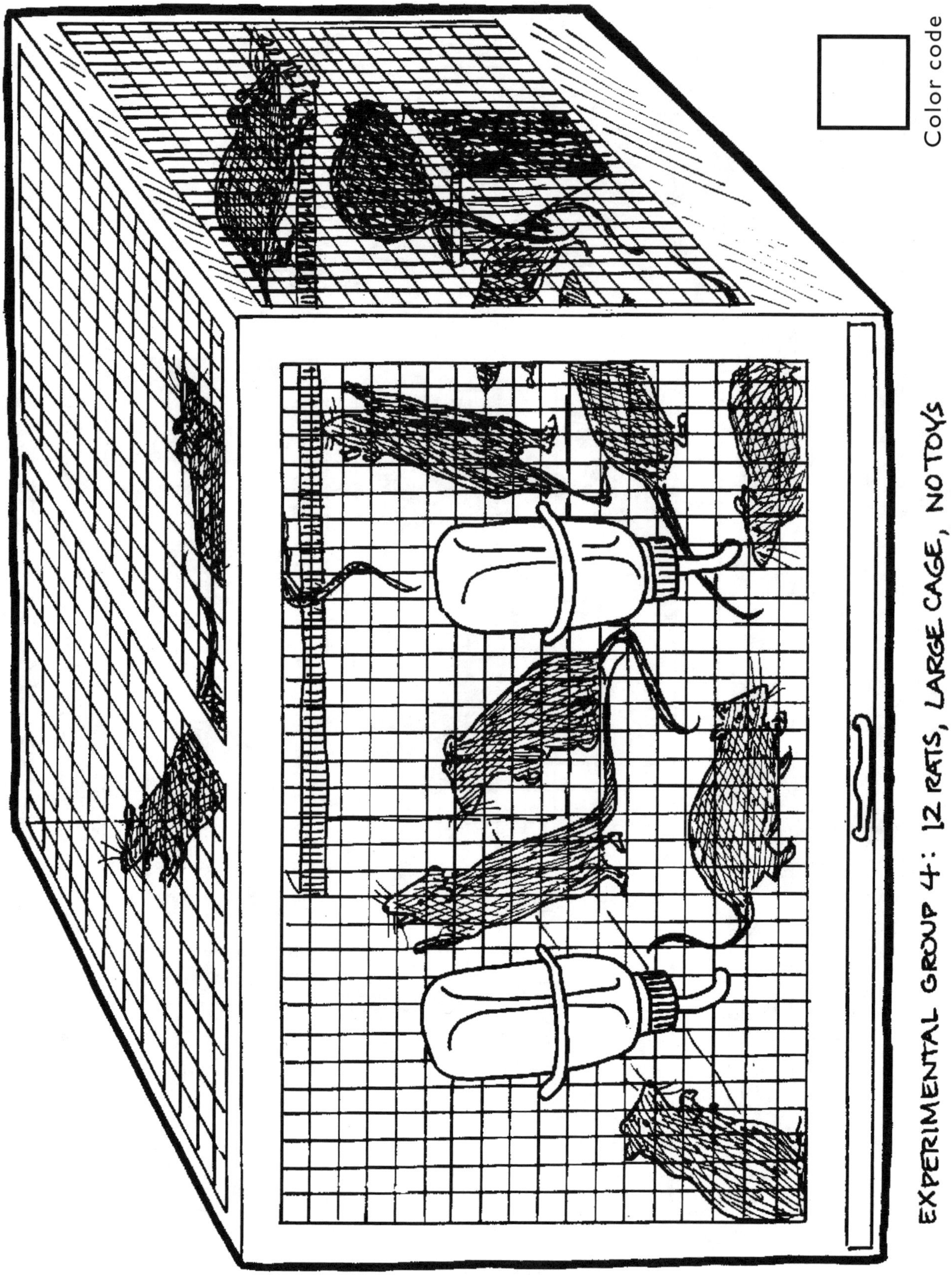
Color code
EXPERIMENTAL GROUP 4: 12 RATS, LARGE CAGE, NO TOYS

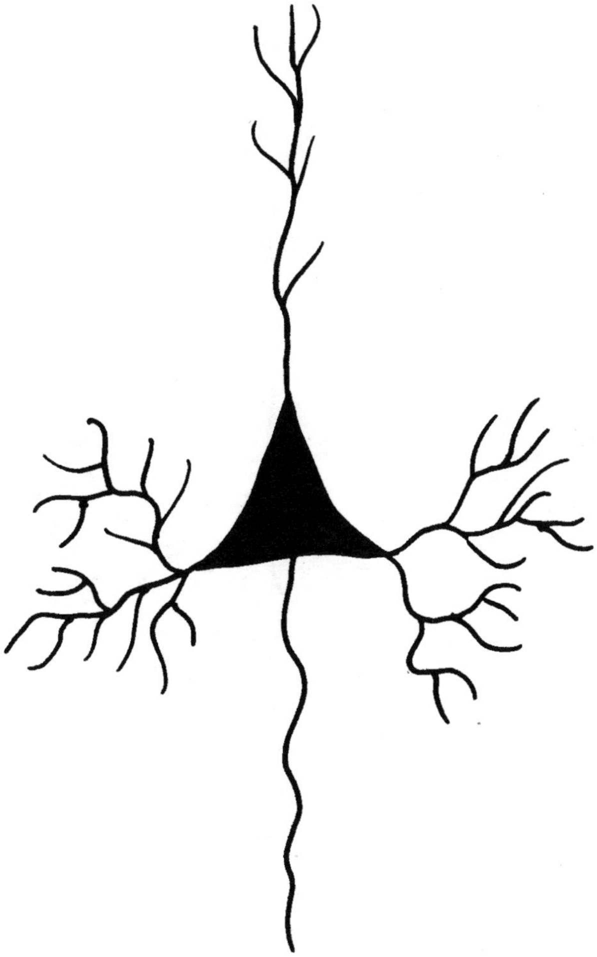

Control Group

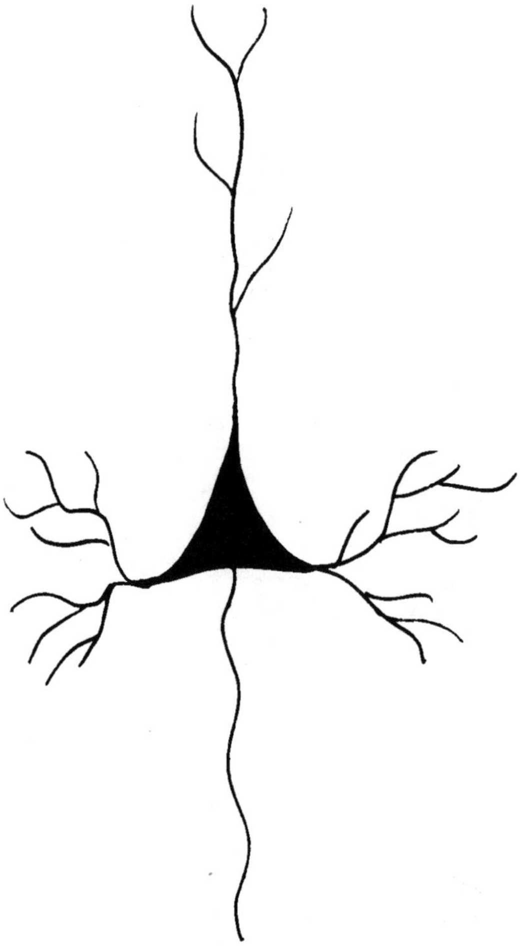

Experimental Group I

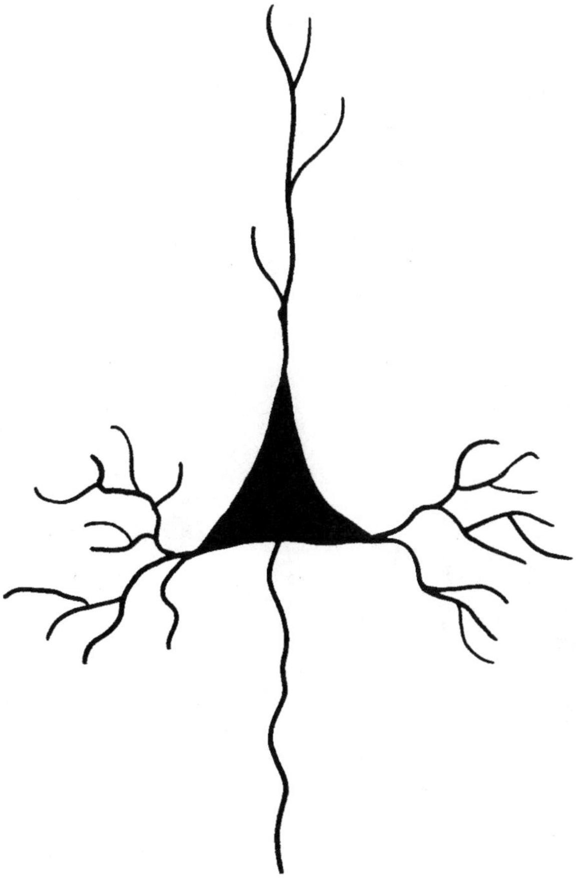

Experimental Group 2

Experimental Group 3

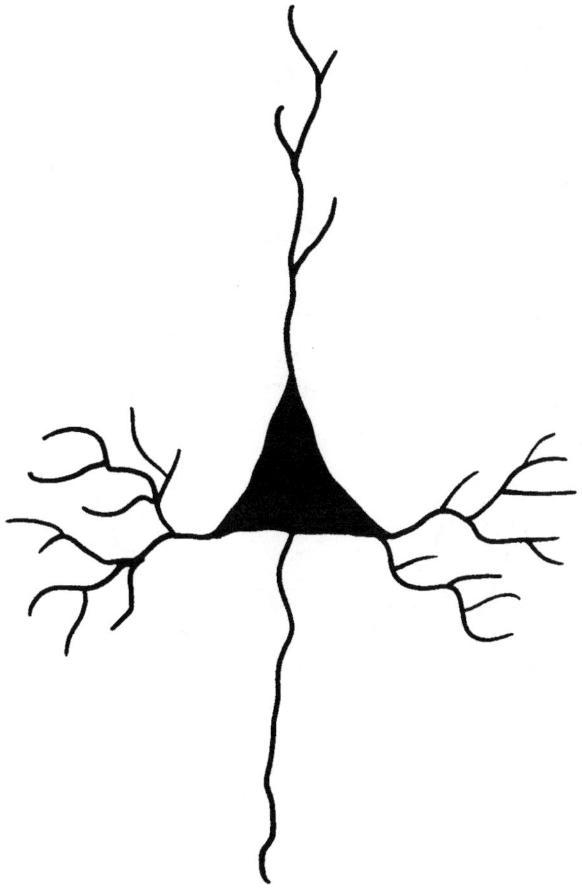

Experimental Group 4

CIRCLE GRID

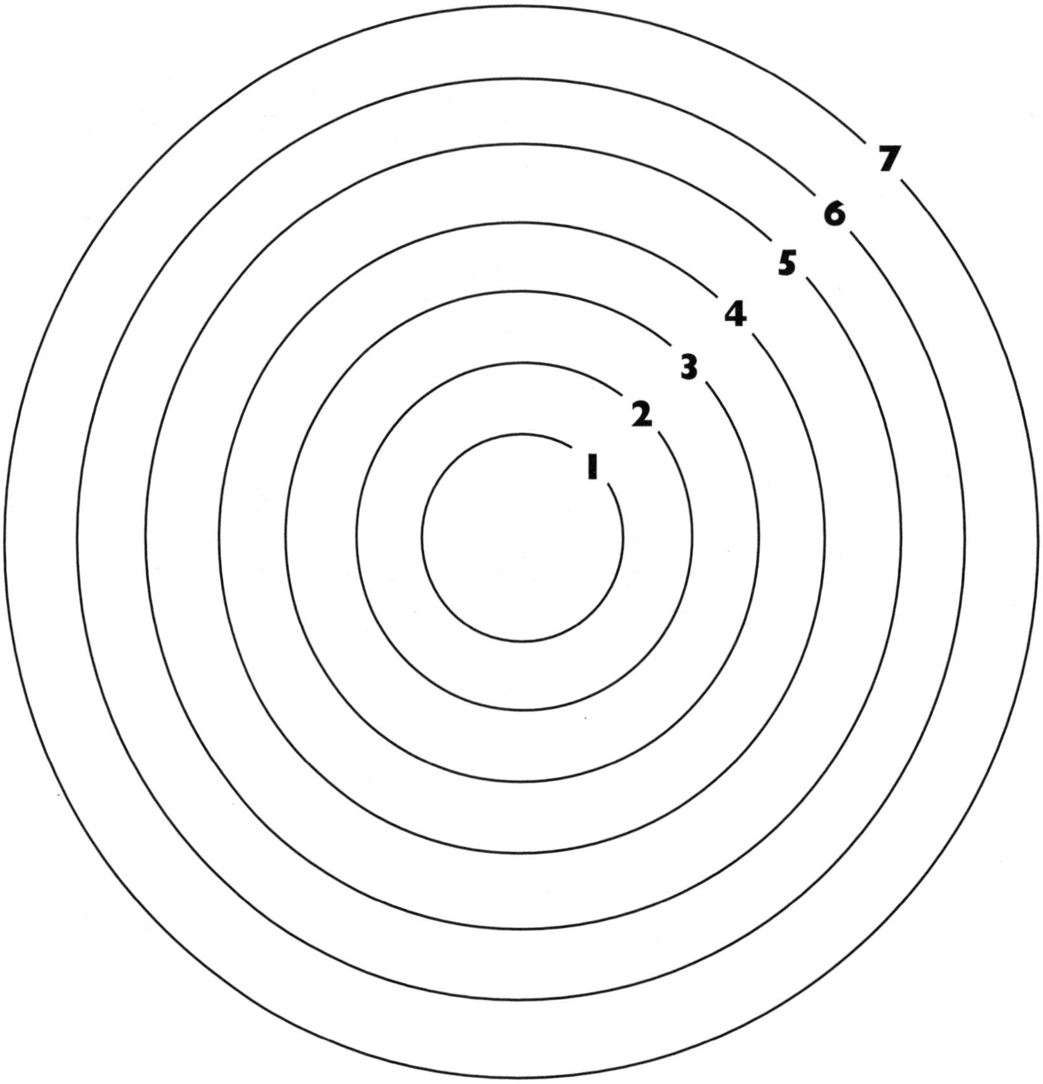

DENDRITE GRAPHING SHEET

Name ______________

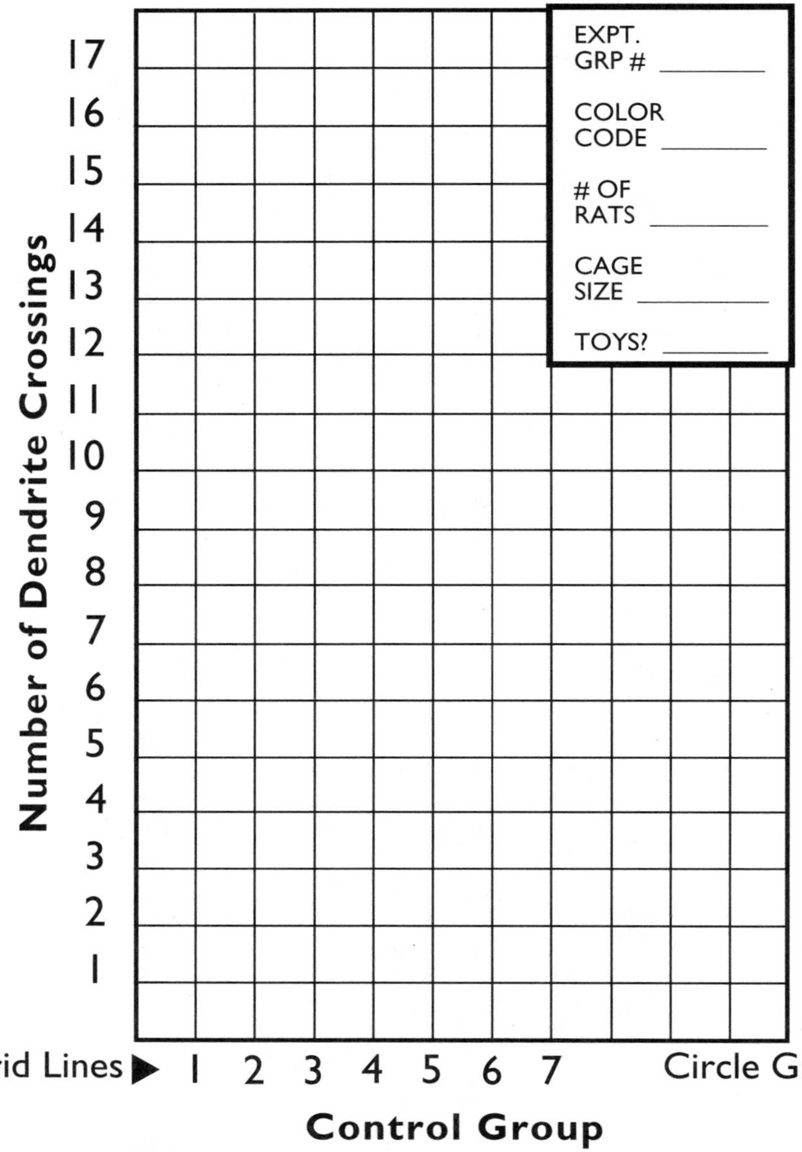

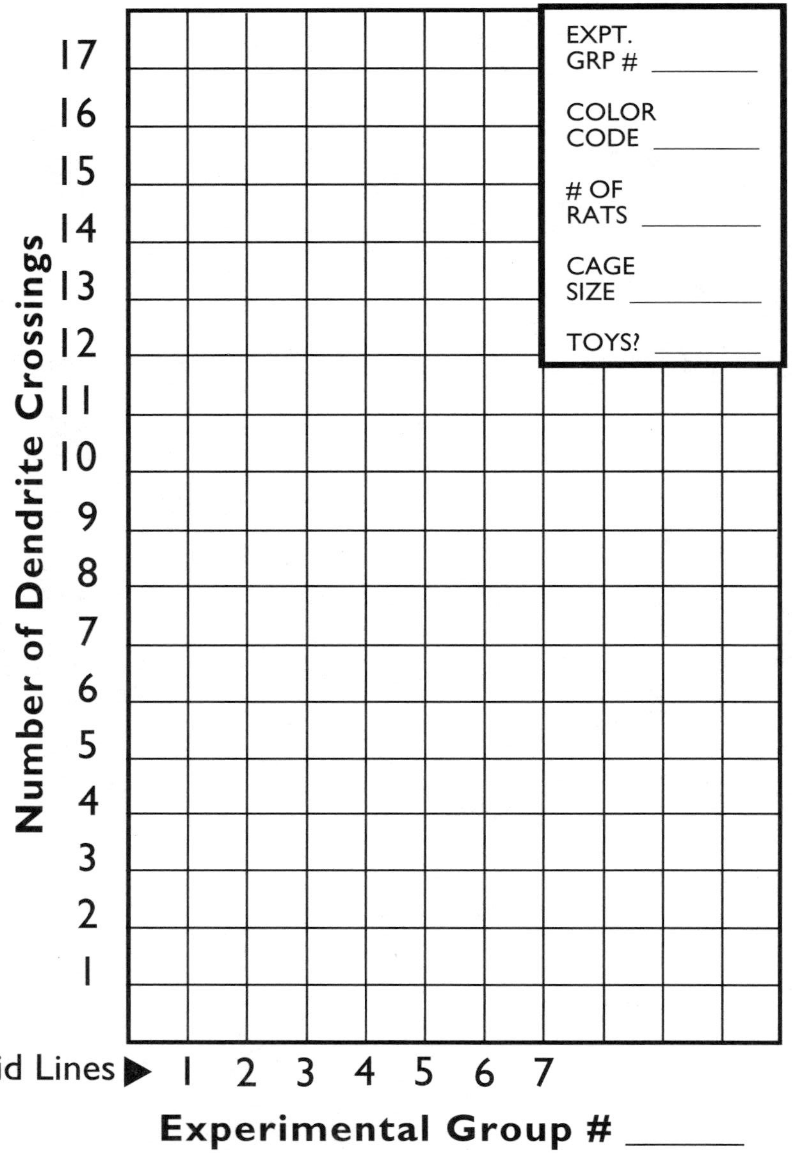

INSTRUCTIONS *for* DENDRITE GRAPHING

1. Tape down Rat Brain Cell—Control Group diagram.

2. Center circle grid on the cell body and tape it down.

3. Count the number of dendrite crossings on circle 1 and record this number on the graphing sheet.

4. Count the number of dendrite crossings on circle 2 and record this number on the graphing sheet.

5. Continue counting and recording for each of the numbered circles.

6. Repeat this process to measure a rat brain cell from one of the **Experimental Groups.**

7. Record information about the **Control Group** and your **Experimental Group** on the graphing sheet (group #, color code, number of rats, etc.).

Activity 8: Learning and Environment (Part II)

In this activity, students again work in their "research teams" to compare data they collected from brain cells of rats raised in "impoverished" environments and those raised in "enriched" environments. The fun begins as students use their critical thinking skills to tease out the effect of different variables and draw conclusions.

Students are excited to share some of their findings—among other things, they discover that not only do "enriched" environments result in *increased growth* of rat brain cells (as compared to the control group), "impoverished" environments result in *decreased growth* of rat brain cells. The activity ends with a discussion about the possible implications for humans of these studies on the rat brain.

What You Need

For the class:

- ❑ 5 Rats in Cages (Control Group plus Experimental Groups 1–4) diagrams (color-coded, from Activity 7)
- ❑ 5 Rat Brain Cell (Control Group plus Experimental Groups 1–4) diagrams (from Activity 7)
- ❑ masking tape
- ❑ overhead transparencies of:
    - Completed Dendrite Graphing Sheet—Control Group and Experimental Group 1 (master on page 126)
    - Questions to Consider (master on page 127)
- ❑ overhead projector

For each team of four students:

- ❑ file folder from Activity 7 containing their completed Dendrite Graphing Sheets
- ❑ pencils
- ❑ 1 or more sheets of blank paper
- ❑ (*optional*) 1 copy of What's Really Going On In There? (master on pages 128–131)

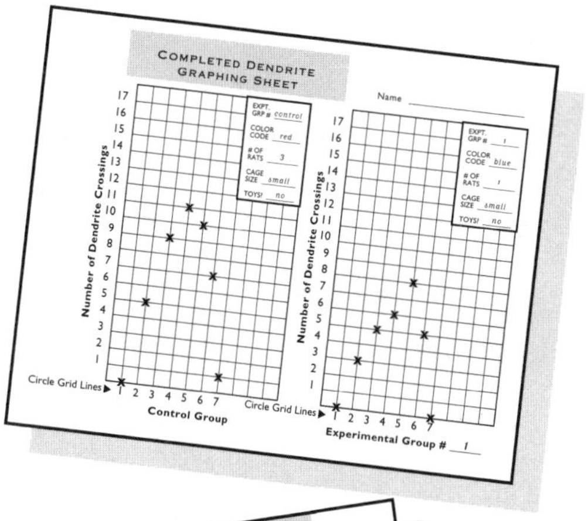

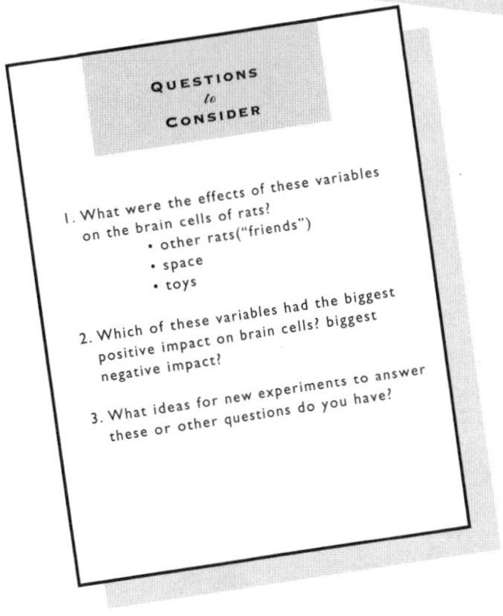
Questions to Consider

1. What were the effects of these variables on the brain cells of rats?
    - other rats("friends")
    - space
    - toys
2. Which of these variables had the biggest positive impact on brain cells? biggest negative impact?
3. What ideas for new experiments to answer these or other questions do you have?

Getting Ready

Before the Day of the Activity

1. Make an overhead transparency of the Completed Dendrite Graphing Sheet—Control Group and Experimental Group 1 (master on page 126).

2. Make an overhead transparency of Questions to Consider (master on page 127).

The Day of the Activity

1. As in Activity 7, post the five Rats in Cages diagrams and the corresponding five Rat Brain Cell diagrams.

2. Set up the overhead projector. Place the transparency of the Completed Dendrite Graphing Sheet on the overhead.

3. Have file folders and blank paper on hand ready to distribute to research teams.

4. *(Optional)* If you want your students to read What's Really Going On In There? for homework, then duplicate copies of the story for each student (master on pages 128–131).

Delving Into Data

1. Tell the students that today they will work in their research teams to draw conclusions about their data. Explain that this is one of the most enjoyable parts of research! After what has been usually weeks or months (or sometimes even years!) of conducting an experiment and collecting data, finally scientists can sit down, look at the results, and make discoveries. This is the time when scientists see if their initial questions were answered, make new discoveries, and generate new questions.

2. Remind the students of the questions asked by the Diamond research team: Are the brains of rats raised in impoverished environments different from the brains of rats raised in enriched environments? Specifically, they wanted to know if there was an effect on the brain from these variables: living with other rats ("friends"), in different-sized cages, and/or with toys.

3. Model the process of drawing conclusions based on data as follows:

- Have the class focus first on Experimental Group 1 compared to the Control Group. Ask, "What is the difference between these two experimental groups?" [One group had one rat, another had three rats. Everything else was the same in these two groups.]

Depending on your students' prior experience with identifying and controlling variables, you may want to take this opportunity to talk about experiments. A ***variable*** is any condition in an experiment that can vary or change. A ***controlled experiment*** is one in which all variables except the one being investigated are held constant. In the case of Experimental Group 1 and the Control Group, the uncontrolled variable is the number of rats.

- Show them the transparency of the Completed Dendrite Graphing Sheet—Control Group and Experimental Group 1. Ask them what they can say about the brain cells in these two groups based on the data in these graphs? [there are more crossings in the Control Group; there are more dendrites in the first two grid lines for the Control Group; etc.]

- Encourage the students to draw conclusions about what the data might mean. Ask, "What conclusions could you draw from the data?" [being with "friends" causes more dendrites to grow; being with "friends" is stimulating to the brain; etc.] Point out that sometimes there is more than one inference that can be made. Record these statements on the board, modeling what students will soon do in their teams.

4. Tell the class that you would like them to work in their research teams to draw further conclusions based on their results. As they do, ask them to consider the following questions (show Questions to Consider on the overhead):

a. What were the effects of these variables on the brain cells of rats?

- other rats ("friends")
- space
- toys

b. Which of these variables had the biggest positive impact on brain cells? biggest negative impact?

c. What ideas for new experiments to answer these or other questions do you have?

5. Have students generate conclusion statements (just as you did together earlier) and record those statements on a sheet of paper. Ask them to be prepared to share these statements with the rest of the class.

Drawing Conclusions—the Fun Part!

1. When students understand what they are to do, have them begin.

If students were surprised to see how small the changes were between the rat brains exposed to different environments, point out that by using statistical methods with large numbers of rats, these small differences have been shown to be significant, meaning that they could not have occurred by chance. That's why they are called experimental ***groups.***

2. Circulate as they work, asking questions to encourage logical thinking and stimulate inquisitive minds.

3. After about 15–20 minutes, focus the class' attention on you. Invite research teams to share one conclusion they made about the data.

4. After students have presented some of their findings, share some of Diamond's findings. (See information in box on page 123.) Summarize or excerpt as appropriate for your class.

What has Marian Diamond's research shown?

Diamond's first discovery showed that rats in enriched environments developed a significantly thicker cerebral cortex as compared with rats in impoverished environments. For the first time in history, she and her group demonstrated that experience and environment can affect the structure of the brain.

The thickness of the cerebral cortex was one important sign of change, but over the years, Diamond and her team were able to become more exact. They learned that the neurons in the brains of rats who lived in enriched environments were also larger, and so were the nuclei of those cells. Using a staining technique, they counted and measured the neuron and glial cells, and the number and length of the branches or dendrites that grew out from the cells.

By setting up an experiment with rats in a standard environment, or a control group, they learned that enriched environments led to increased brain growth (compared to standard environments). They also learned that impoverished environments led to decreased brain growth. This demonstrated that not only did enrichment improve a brain, but you could also have environments that caused a loss of brain power.

They learned that impoverished environments had the biggest negative effect when a rat was young. They discovered that not only did rats who had toys and friends develop a thicker cerebral cortex and more and longer dendritic branches—both friends and toys were needed for this to happen. Rats with only friends and no toys—or with only toys but no friends—did not show such increased growth.

Diamond also experimented with different variables, such as the age of rats and the length of time they were exposed to the enriched or impoverished environments. It was discovered that it was never too late for the enriched environment to have a positive impact on the brain. Even extremely old rats developed a significantly thicker cerebral cortex and longer dendritic branches when placed in an enriched environment. Given a healthy diet, and healthy blood and oxygen supply, parts of the brain keep changing and growing when they are being stimulated.

Although scientists had previously thought the brain did not change during a lifetime, parts of it can grow (or decrease) and its structure can be influenced by stimulation, social situation, and environment—throughout an entire lifetime.

Learning from this Research

1. Stimulate students to make inferences from the Diamond research by asking provocative questions such as:

- "Do you think this research would hold true for humans—that neurons will lose some of their dendrites if a person goes from an enriched environment to an impoverished one?"
- "What would an enriched environment for humans be like, or an impoverished environment?"
- "What advice would you give to the parents of a new baby?"
- "What advice would you give to a friend?"
- "What advice would you give to your grandparents?"
- "What does this research say about the old proverb 'It's never too late to change?'"

2. Explain that while such research could never be performed on humans, there has been other research conducted on human brains, with results that indicate some of the same effects of stimulation and enrichment on brain health. At a convent in Minnesota, for example, a group of aging nuns have agreed to take part in a long term study. This order of nuns is college-educated and they engage in regular "mental exercise," including doing crossword puzzles, solving brain teasers, playing Jeopardy, attending lectures, playing musical instruments, etc. Of the 150 retired nuns living at this convent, over 25 are older than 90 years old. When they die, many of these nuns donate their brains to the research study. Early reports show these nuns experience much less memory loss, dementia, and Alzheimer's disease than others their same age. Preliminary results suggest there are more dendrites and other growth in the cortex of their brains than in brains of less mentally-active people of the same age.

Going Further

1. Ask students to write a letter to someone (a grandparent, a friend who watches too much TV, the parents of a new baby, or someone else) telling about these research findings and how they relate to choice of lifestyle.

2. Some of your students may want to research the original articles in which Marian Diamond and her colleagues reported their findings, so they can get a sense of the level of detail involved. References for some of these articles appear in the "Resources" section on page 177.

3. Have students investigate research done on human brains. They can start by reading the article on "Brain Calisthenics" in *Life* magazine (July 1994). They may want to write to the scientists involved in the study to find out the latest results.

4. Have students read about people whose unique talents and abilities have helped scientists and others learn more about the brain, including autistic children and adults, sometimes known as "savants." The film *Rain Man* focused on one such individual. Oliver Sacks, the neurologist whose work led to the book and film *Awakenings* has written on autistic individuals as part of a *New Yorker* series ("A Neurologist's Notebook"). One article focused on an autistic woman veterinarian and the adaptations she devised to help herself function in the work-a-day world. The January 1995 issue focuses on Stephen Wiltshire, an autistic boy from England who has become famous due to his amazing artistic abilities. This subject also fits in with the ideas about "multiple intelligences" raised earlier in this guide. Oliver Sacks has also written *An Anthropologist on Mars: Seven Paradoxical Tales*, a book of case studies on autism.

5. Consider having a friendly rat visit the classroom so that students may hold it and observe its behavior.

Since this teacher's guide was first published, Dr. Diamond, in collaboration with Janet L. Hopson, has published a book on resources to help stimulate growing minds. Entitled Magic Trees of the Mind: How to Nurture Your Child's Intelligence, Creativity, and Healthy Emotions from Birth through Adolescence, *it is published by Penguin USA, 1999 (paper) and Dutton, 1998 (hardcover).*

We highly recommend the "Neuroscience for Kids" website which provides a regular e-newsletter free to those who sign up and has lots of excellent and accessible information.

http://faculty.washington.edu/chudler/neurok.html

Completed Dendrite Graphing Sheet

Name ______________________

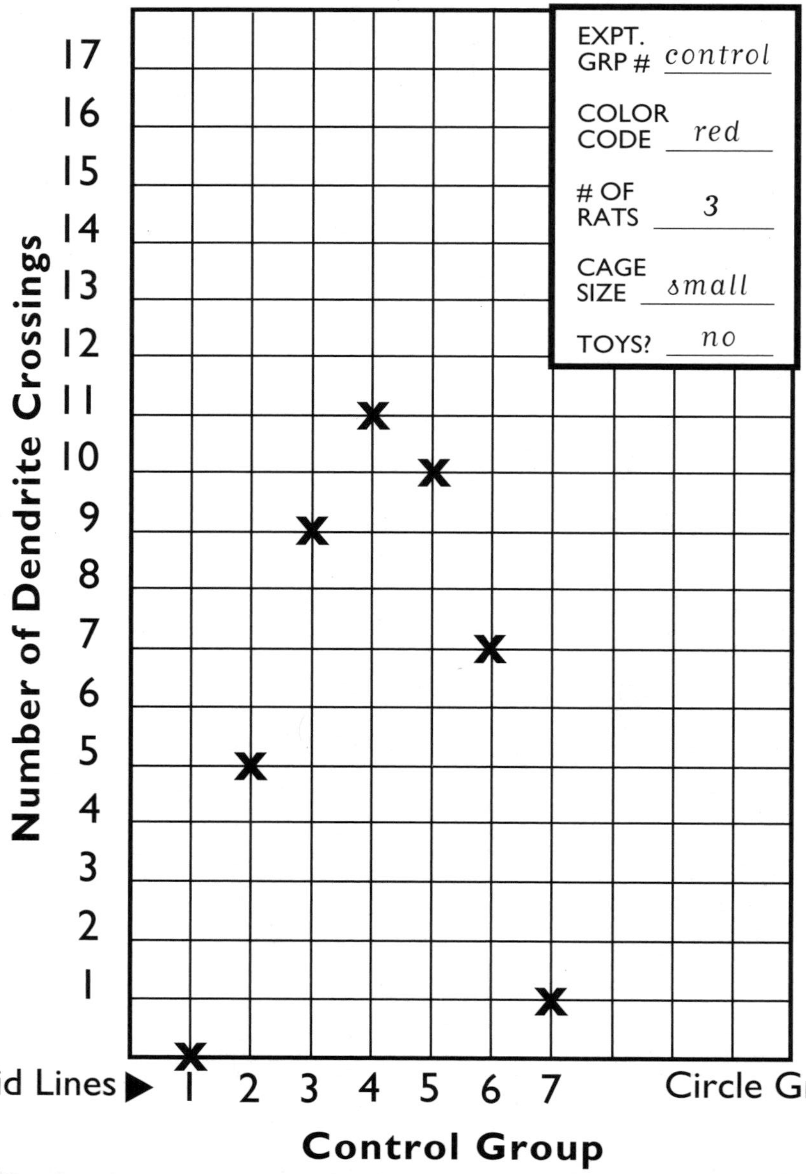

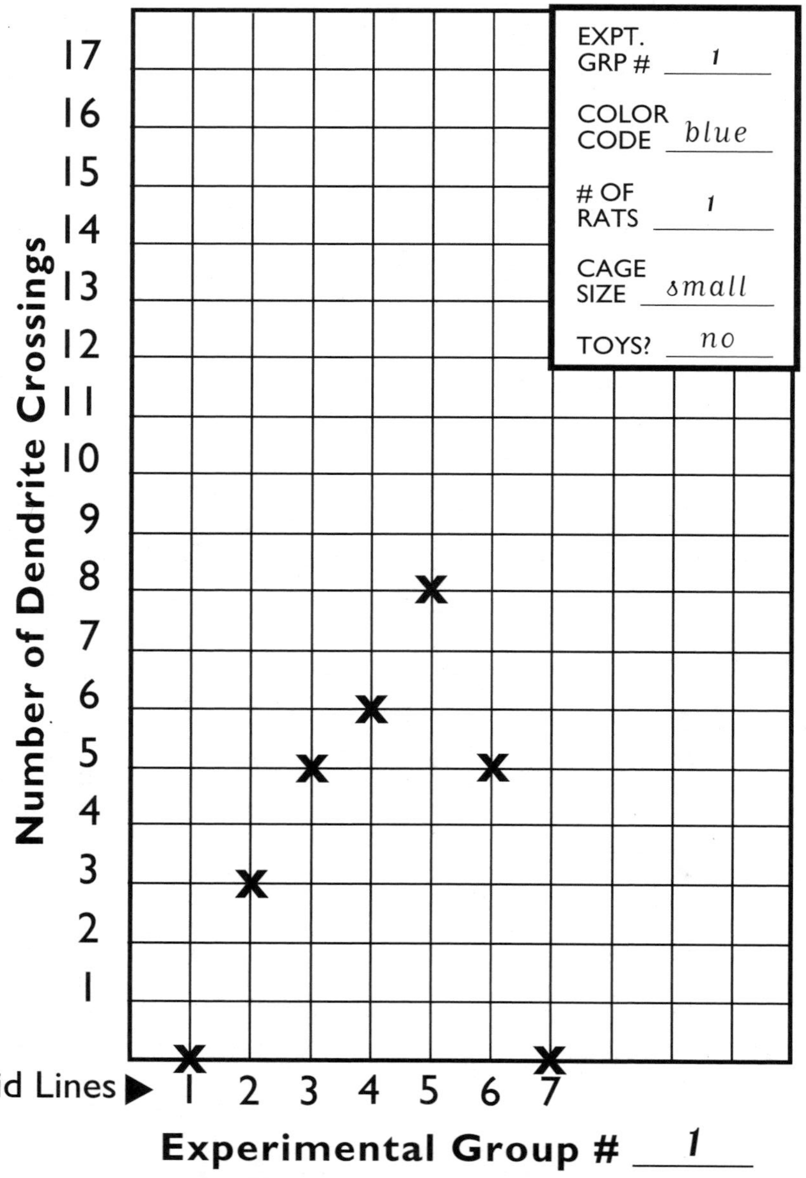

Questions *to* Consider

1. What were the effects of these variables on the brain cells of rats?
    - other rats("friends")
    - space
    - toys

2. Which of these variables had the biggest positive impact on brain cells? biggest negative impact?

3. What ideas for new experiments to answer these or other questions do you have?

What's Really Going On In There?

The Story of Dr. Marian Cleeves Diamond's Research on the Brain

From her earliest days, Marian Cleeves Diamond remembers being fascinated with how our brains work. Falling in a pool when she was about four years old, before being quickly rescued, what flashed through her mind was: "I wonder what's happening inside my brain right now..."

She grew up in the mountains just north of Los Angeles, California, the youngest of six children. Her father was a doctor, and he often asked his children interesting questions like: "How is it you can eat ice cream and a hot dog and the temperature in your body remains the same?"

Mr. Engstrom, her junior high biology teacher, was a strong influence. She also liked a physiology course in high school. Marian Diamond remembers looking at people's eyes and wondering what was going on behind them—what's really going on in there?

As a teenager, she visited the hospital where her father worked and was fascinated when she saw a human brain for the first time. After she graduated from the University of California at Berkeley, she continued working toward her Ph.D., and had made up her mind to specialize in the brain.

Marian Diamond's unique contributions in the human search for knowledge about the brain, that most complex and powerful part of our bodies, were also inspired by a magazine article. Dr. Diamond says, "I still remember that moment in 1958, sitting in the green leather chair in the living room while my children were playing. I was reading a *Science* magazine article. Three researchers at U.C. Berkeley demonstrated there was a difference in the amounts of certain chemicals in the brains of rats—depending on different experiences the rats had. I said—aha! **From that moment on, I knew what I wanted to do."**

The scientists who wrote the article were using two ***strains*** of rats developed at Berkeley in the 1920s by a psychology professor who observed that some rats ran mazes differently than others. He raised a "maze-bright" strain and a "maze-dull" strain by mating the fastest maze runners together and the slowest ones together, generation after generation. But it was not until the 1950s that psychologists and chemists got together to find out if there was a **chemical** difference in the brains of these two strains. They found out that there was. The "maze-bright" strain had more ***acetylcholinesterase*** (pronounced: ah-see'-tull-ko-lin-est'-ur-aze), an enzyme that plays an important role in completing the sending of signals in the brain.

Did the chemical differences also mean there were differences in the **structure** or actual physical make-up of the brain? That was what Marian Diamond wanted to know. If the answer turned out to be "yes" it would be a very important finding, because **until that time most scientists believed that the brain did not change its structure after a person or animal was very young.**

One of Dr. Diamond's favorite quotations is from the great French scientist, Louis Pasteur, who said, "Chance favors the prepared mind." When her chance came she was ready and determined. Her research team included two psychologists and a biochemist, with herself as the anatomist. She remembers this time of teamwork as among the happiest days of exciting research she ever experienced.

They all sat down to plan experiments, brainstorming together, then went off to test hypotheses in different ways. It took a while to figure out the best methods to measure changes in brain structure. They learned that the thickness of the ***cerebral cortex*** could be more easily measured in **rats** than in many other animals—no one before had done it in the way their team worked out. (The cerebral cortex in humans is the part of the brain that has to do with thinking and analyzing, judging, solving problems, and planning.) Planning their procedures very carefully, Marian Diamond's team began their experiments.

After several years of intense research, the group published their first scientific paper. It compared the thickness of the cerebral cortex in rats that lived in **"enriched environments"** to that of rats in **"impoverished environments."** In an enriched environment, rats lived with other rats ("friends") in a large cage, about one-meter square, with lots of toys, ladders, and other objects to investigate. A rat in an impoverished environment lived by itself in a smaller cage, with no toys. **The findings showed that the rats in enriched environments developed a significantly thicker cerebral cortex.** The team published their findings in *Science* magazine and were thrilled with the attention their experiments received. **For the first time in history, it was demonstrated that experience and environment can affect the actual structure of the brain.**

The thickness of the cerebral cortex was one important sign of change, but over the years Marian and her team were able to become more exact. They learned that the ***neurons*** (or nerve cells) in the brains of rats who lived in enriched environments were also larger, and so were the ***nuclei*** of those cells. Using a staining technique, they counted and measured the neuron and ***glial cells***, and the number and length of the branches or ***dendrites*** that grew out from the cells.

Experiment followed experiment to confirm findings and learn more. The more they learned, the more questions they had. For instance, though they knew that enriched environments produced rats with more brain growth than those in impoverished environments, they wondered how these brains compared to those of rats who lived in environments that were "standard"— neither enriched nor impoverished.

By setting up an experiment with rats in a standard environment, or a ***control group,*** they learned that enriched environments led to *increased* brain growth (compared to standard environments). They also learned that impoverished environments led to *decreased* brain growth. What an important finding this was! Not only did enrichment improve a brain, but you could also have environments that caused a loss of brain power.

They learned that impoverished environments had the biggest negative effect when a rat was young. They discovered that not only did rats who had toys and friends develop a thicker cerebral cortex and more and longer dendritic branches—***both* friends and toys were needed for this to happen**. Rats with *only* friends and no toys—or with *only* toys but no friends—did not show such increased growth. **In class, when you and your team compared the different images of the brain cells, you were doing the same kinds of things scientists do to find out more about the brain.**

The research team also experimented with different *variables,* such as the age of rats and the length of time they were exposed to the enriched or impoverished enviroments. **It was also discovered that it was never too late for the enriched environment to have a positive impact on the brain.** Even extremely old rats developed a significantly thicker cerebral cortex and longer dendritic branches when placed in an enriched environment. Given a healthy diet, and healthy blood and oxygen supply, parts of the brain keep changing and growing when they are being stimulated, regardless of age.

The original finding was reconfirmed again and again—although scientists had previously thought the brain did not change during a lifetime, parts of it can grow (or decrease) and its structure can be influenced by stimulation, social situation, and environment—throughout an entire lifetime.

Many scientists believe that findings in rats tell us a great deal about human brains. Marian Diamond compares rats learning mazes to the human learning process. In her lab, rats encounter mazes of increasing difficulty. A new barrier is added every day for 19 days, after which time brain changes can be detected. She believes that, in the same way, human brains also change their structure and chemistry when we are challenged and try to solve problems—**when we learn.**

Education has always been very important to Dr. Diamond and she is one of the most popular professors at the University of California at Berkeley. Using the slogan "each one, teach one," she assigns her college anatomy students to spend time in elementary school classrooms, helping younger students learn about the human body. In 1990, she became Director of the Lawrence Hall of Science, a well-known science education center. She is also one of the authors of *The Human Brain Coloring Book,* a widely-used text and workbook on the anatomy of the brain.

Marian Diamond sparkles with energy when she discusses what scientists may find out in the future. If you were in her office right now, she might take you over to an enlarged photograph on the wall and show you how to carefully count brain cells. She would tell you how special each individual person is, saying, "No two brains are alike. No one believed it when I said I wanted to study brains. But you have to follow *your* heart, do what *you* are most interested in doing, even if no one else out there is doing it yet—your brain has to play its own tune. That's what I tell young people today!"

YOUR BRAIN HAS TO PLAY ITS OWN TUNE...

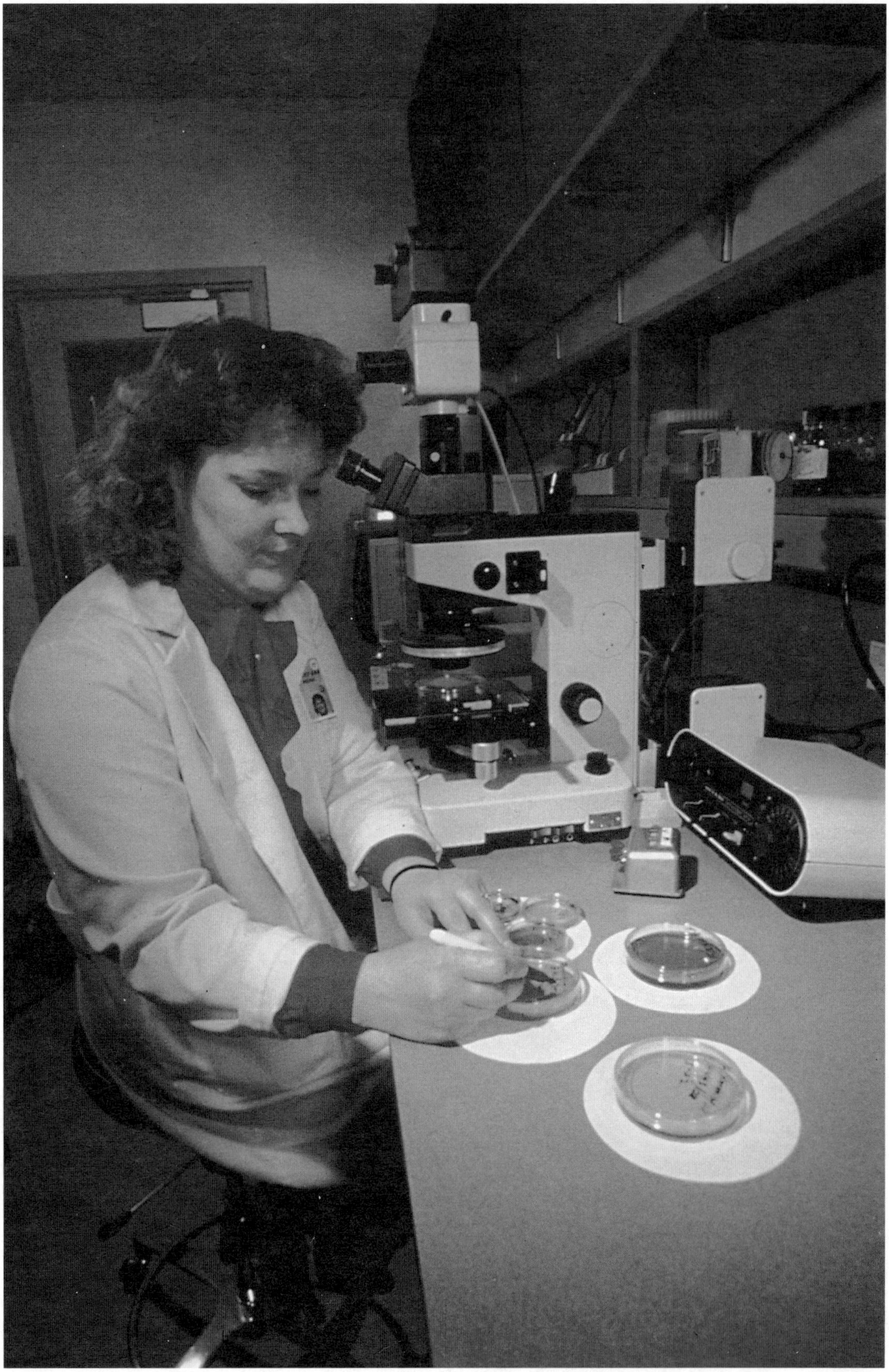

Activity 9: Ethics of Learning

In this activity, your students discuss the problems and benefits of learning by conducting research in three of the standard ways: using humans; using animals; and *in vitro* studies (cell and tissue cultures).

The teacher helps strike some balance in the discussion so students can begin to grasp the complexity of the situation. Many students bring their previous experience as well as what they've learned in this unit into the discussion. Many portions of this unit provide grist for this complex and controversial discussion. The purpose of the discussion is not to teach any one point of view, but to air some of the issues, encourage students to further explore them, and make up their own minds.

Note: Some classes are finished with the ethics discussion after about twenty minutes; others get very involved and want to keep going. Follow your students' interest level.

Benefits and Problems of Research

1. Tell the class that in this unit, they have learned about some of the research done by scientists: The Hexacarbon Solvent Mystery, the story of Lash-Lure, the research done with Genie, and Marian Diamond's brain research.

2. Ask them to think of the *benefits of this research.* What was discovered? How did this help humans? Point out that this research involved different types of testing such as *in vitro* tests, chemical analysis, animal research, and human testing.

You may want to point out that the appropriate test method depends on what is being investigated, what the questions being asked are, and what information is already known. You may also want to point out that, typically, in the modern research world, in vitro *testing, if appropriate, would be done first, followed by animal testing, with human testing last. You may want to consider structuring the discussion in this order.*

Make a list of their ideas on the board under the heading, "Benefits of Conducting Research." If ideas are slow in coming, you might want to give groups of four students an opportunity to discuss it among themselves and then share their ideas.

3. Ask them to now think about the *problems of conducting research using humans.* If they need prompting, ask: "What problems arose in the study of Genie?" Remind them that one of the ways scientists test new products, new drugs, new methods of surgery, other medical techniques, etc., is by conducting what are called "human clinical trials." This means that they try them out on some human volunteers

after animal studies or *in vitro* research predict that humans won't be harmed under the test conditions.

Make a list of their ideas on the board under the heading, "Problems of Conducting Research on Humans."

4. Ask them to think about the *problems of conducting research using live animals.*

Make a list of their ideas on the board under the heading, "Problems of Conducting Research on Animals."

5. Finally, ask them to think about the *problems of conducting* in vitro *research.* Remind them that *in vitro* involves the use of living cells (such as blood samples or tissue cultures) in a Petri dish or test tube. If they need prompting, ask, "Would you be able to measure how the entire body would react to a test substance?" For example, how could you measure blood pressure in a test tube?

Make a list of their ideas on the board under the heading, "Problems of Conducting *In Vitro* Research."

6. Summarize by saying that we saw what happened in situations (such as the Lash-Lure and Hexacarbon Solvent stories) where people died and/or were damaged by products that weren't tested adequately. Protecting ourselves in these cases requires learning as much as we can about these products through testing.

One teacher found that her students were embarrassed to share their opinions on ethics in front of their peers. She first had them discuss in smaller groups and then gave the assignment of writing their personal views to the teacher. Later this teacher read excerpts from their writing aloud, to depict the range of views.

"My students demonstrated wonderful higher order thinking. They knew that if they felt strongly about one research method over another, they needed justification. Their statements of justification were powerful and a true verification of how much they learned. It was gratifying to see some students alter their views over the course of the discussion." —Seventh grade teacher

However, each of the types of testing listed above, (human clinical trials, live animal testing, and *in vitro* testing) has its problems or issues. Weighing the problems and the benefits is difficult because there is rarely a perfect solution. If the complexity of the choices is not clear to your students, you might want to pose some of the following questions:

- Would you be upset if you found out that the material used in the walls of our school building was dangerous and might result in some students becoming permanently damaged? Would you expect the safety of these materials to have been tested?

- How would you feel if there wasn't a drug or a cure for a friend of yours with a fatal disease? Would you want scientists to research possible drugs that could help?

The purpose of this discussion is not to teach any one particular viewpoint, but to clarify some of the issues, enabling students to arrive at their own viewpoints.

7. Explain that scientists are working to develop alternatives to testing living animal or human subjects, but even those alternatives generally rely on data from previous research using animals or humans. For instance, computers are being used more often to model the possible effects of harmful new substances. However, to make these predictions, computers must first be programmed with information learned from past animal studies on closely-related substances. Computers cannot, of course, re-create the unexpected variables and complexities of living forms. While some of these alternatives can reduce the need to experiment on humans and animals, they can't eliminate it in all cases.

Some manufacturers advertise that their products are "not tested on animals" or are "cruelty-free." While these goals (along with product safety) would be shared by most people, in fact the labels are deceiving and misleading. Most such products use ingredients that have already been proven safe based on past animal testing information. Since there are no U.S. government standards to define this advertising claim, "not tested on animals" may really mean:

- The exact final product formula was not tested on animals, but single ingredients or ingredient combinations were;
- The manufacturer did not conduct animal testing, but the ingredient supplier did;
- The manufacturer did the animal testing in another country;
- The ingredients or the finished products have not been tested within the past five years.

In reality, almost all ingredients in use today have been safely tested on animals at some time, by someone.

Carl Cortex
Nose
Sara Bellum

Activity 10: The Learning About Learning Play

To close the unit, students do a dramatic reading of a light-hearted play that summarizes some of the highlights of what they have learned in the unit in a memorable way. Teachers have found this activity to be fun for their students, and also to help bring the many conceptual threads of this unit together.

The play can also help introduce the idea that, just as there are many different ways that people learn, there are also many ways to organize learning that have educational value. During this unit, for example, they designed and experienced the learning and teaching of mazes; pondered what helps and hinders learning; pretended to be wolves with a need to learn on two different occasions; served on research teams investigating two real-life health-related mysteries; read and discussed true, compelling stories; simulated the research approaches of brain scientists; had opportunities to reflect on what they've learned in small groups and as a class; and, now—for a grand finale—they take part in Common Sense: The GEMS Learning About Learning Play!

One teacher divided his class into groups of six and had each group of students do their own play reading. While this approach loses the effect of having an attentive, laughing audience, it has the advantage of involving every single student. If you decide to do this, you will need to modify the "Getting Ready" instructions below.

What You Need

For the class:

- ❑ 7 copies of Common Sense: The GEMS Learning About Learning Play (master on pages 140–146)
- ❑ a highlighter pen
- ❑ 6 half-sheets of 8 ½" x 11" card stock
- ❑ 6 lengths of string (3' each)
- ❑ 1 single-hole paper punch
- ❑ a large, dark-colored felt marker

Getting Ready

Before the Day of the Activity

1. Duplicate seven copies of Common Sense: The GEMS Learning About Learning Play (master on pages 140–146). *(Optional)* If you want students in the audience to read along, then duplicate enough copies for the "audience" as well as for the six actors and yourself.

2. Write the name of one character on one copy of the play. Go through that copy with a highlighter pen, highlighting

the lines that character says. Do this for the other five characters on the five other copies. You may also want to highlight, perhaps in a different color, the stage directions on all copies, so the actors' attention will be drawn to them. The last copy is for you.

3. Make a necklace-style name tag for each character in the play.

- Use the half-sheets of card stock.
- Punch holes in the upper two corners of each half sheet.
- Thread a piece of string through the holes and tie the two ends together.
- Use the dark-colored marker to write the character's names on the card stock.

4. (*Optional*) Some teachers have had the class make costumes and props for the play. This, of course, takes more time and planning but results in a rich experience for all.

The Day of the Activity

1. Put the name tag necklace and the script for each character together, so you can hand them out easily.

2. Think about who you will choose to read the parts of the six characters. Make sure you choose students who are good readers.

3. Decide if you want to gather the actors together for a few minutes, to alert them to the stage directions, point out some lines or difficult words that may need some advance coaching, and consider any other staging or dramatic issues. This is not necessary, but can be helpful. Plan a time to do this if you want to.

GO!

What Have We Learned About Learning?

1. Change gears by telling the class that now they will reflect on the entire *Learning About Learning* unit in a fun way. Tell them that you need some volunteers to be characters in the Learning About Learning Play. (You will

already have done this if you decided to gather actors together beforehand for a brief partial rehearsal.)

2. Choose six volunteers and have them come up to the front of the classroom. Give them each a name tag to wear (so others know who they are) and a script. Organize them in the order in which they appear.

- Sara Bellum and Carl Cortex
- Rat
- Nose, Eye, Hand

3. Tell the class that the characters in the play are two students who have just completed the *Learning About Learning* activities, just like they have, along with a Rat who took part in Marian Diamond's experiments, and a giant Nose, Eye, and Hand. Begin the play by reading the narrator's paragraph.

One teacher had his students write their own plays to summarize what they learned in the unit.

4. Have the characters read their parts. (You may want to narrate at certain points in the stage directions. If you've gathered with the actors earlier, it's preferable not to narrate, but to let them go ahead and act out the stage directions.)

5. When the play is over, lead a discussion to summarize and wrap up the unit.

Common Sense:
The GEMS Learning About Learning Play

Characters:
Sara Bellum
Carl Cortex
(students who have just taken part in the GEMS *Learning About Learning* activities)
Rat (who has taken part in Marian Diamond's research)
Nose
Eye
Hand

Narrator: The scene is a giant underground maze, a cave. Two students, Sara Bellum and Carl Cortex, are lost, and are running through the tunnels. They stop to catch their breath.

Carl: Dang, how we gonna get out of here?

Sara: I don't know, but the sooner the better.

Carl: Why did we leave the tour group?

Sara: It wasn't my idea, Einstein. Hey, where's that sandwich? We could use it to do the Hansel and Gretel thing.

Carl: I don't think so...

Sara: Why not, what happened?

Carl: *(looking guilty)* I was hungry.

Sara: Ah man, now we're really stuck!

Carl: This is a little harder than those finger mazes we did.

Sara: I know, huh? In a real maze those dead-ends can be painful. *(rubs nose or head)*

Carl: Ah, but can't you just feel those dendrites branching in your brain right now? I guess this is what they call an enriched environment for a rat. I could sure use a non-enriched environment right now. Sitting on my couch watching re-runs of the *Home Shopping Network* would suit me just fine. So, yeh, maybe my dendrites would shrivel up, but I'd be comfortable.

Sara: I wish we could talk to one of Marian Diamond's rats, maybe one of those maze-veterans could help us out.

Carl: I feel like one of Marian Diamond's rats right now.

Sara: Come on. We'll never get out of this rathole if we just sit here. Let's try that way...*(points)*

Carl: O.K. let's roll. *(both jog in place in one direction)*

Sara: Hey, have you noticed that the ceiling seems to be getting lower?

Carl: I know, we better watch out, we might hit our heads.

Sara: Yeah, good thing we noticed...

(BONK! Both slowly collapse to the ground, then slowly start to get up holding their heads)

Sara: What happened?

Carl: I don't know, but I could sure use an unnamed major brand of pain reliever right now.

Sara: I know, huh? Hey, who's that? *(Rat enters)*

Carl: What the...

Rat: *(in rap style)*
I'm a Diamond rat
You're in my habitat
Let's talk about this place
So you don't fall on your face.

Sara: You know Carl, I don't think we're in Kansas anymore...

Carl: A rappin' rat! O.K.—Now I've seen everything!

Sara: *(to rat)* Are you here to help us find our way out?

Rat: Yeah, I got your back.

Carl: O.K. then, which way should we go?

Rat: Come on, man! If I give you too many directions, you won't learn how to get out. 'Member the finger maze activity. It works best if someone gives you hints, and allows you to discover stuff for yourself. Too much direction, and you'll never learn.

Sara: So what's our first hint then?

Rat: Use your senses.

Carl: Like which sense, I've got five!

Rat: Well, you could use my favorite sense. *(gestures towards Nose, who comes jogging in)*

Carl: *(pointing at Nose)* Woh! Check it out—look what's running this way!

Sara: It's a giant running nose.

Carl: Gross! Looks like it needs a trim and a wipe.

(Nose runs up, stops and sniffs)

Nose: I prefer to be called a proboscis!

Sara: Picky picky picky...

Carl: What? Are we supposed to **smell** our way out of here?

Nose: Hey, learning starts with me. C'mon, remember how you were able to find your fellow wolves in that smelling activity. Let's give it a try. Let's see if we can smell fresh air and follow the smell. This way, let's go.

(Carl and Sara sniff around following the nose, moving around through tables and desks, sniffing all the while)

Nose: Woh! That smells nasty. *(they all back off like they just smelled something horribe)* Let's not go that way.

Sara: Hey Nose, you are useful.

Nose: That's right, your sense of smell is important to warn you when something might be harmful.

Carl: So Nose, you'll let us know if there are any bad chemicals ahead, right?

Nose: Well, chemicals aren't really good or bad. There are good and bad **uses** of chemicals. And not all bad-smelling chemicals are bad for you! Like broccoli! Smells nasty, but it's good for you.

Rat: I'm tired of always hearin' people dissin' chemicals. Our nerves, taste, and nose are made up of chemicals, and they can't work without chemicals.

Sara: I know. I keep forgetting. Everything is made of chemicals, not just things with long names.

Carl: Even water is a chemical!

Sara: Yeah, but back to our little chemical-detecting sense of smell—I don't think we can live on nose alone. Remember that some things hardly smell at all and still can be very dangerous, like that Lash-Lure dye! Sometimes you need more than just smell, or you're history.

Carl: Yeah, I don't think we're gonna get out of here on smell alone.

Nose: Oh ye of little faith...

(they run up against a wall)

Nose: Ouch!

Sara: What's up?

Nose: *(embarrassed)* Heh, heh. Wrong way, I think I just discovered a wall!

Carl: You were a big help.

Rat: Well, I guess smelling is my favorite sense because us rats have a better developed sense of smell.

Carl: So how about another hint, Rat?

Sara: Yeah, c'mon. Give us a hand.

Rat: Since your smell is not sufficiently intense
In fact it's dense
Let's move towards the groove
Of a different sense.

Sara: How about sometime in this century, Rat?

Rat: In the blink of an eye—BAM!

(Eye enters)

Carl: Cool. It's a giant Eye.

Sara: Oh Wondrous Eye. All-seeing one. What wisdom do you have for us?

Eye: *(looks around squinting for a bit)* Dang, it's dark in here!

Carl: *(disappointed)* Uh, eye-guy, we knew that!

Sara: Well Rat, looks like we're gonna need some more help.

(Hand enters)

Hand: Hey Sara, Carl, Rat, Nose, Eye—What's up? Gimme five!
(slaps each of their hands)

Sara: So Hand, can you help us learn how to get out of here?

Eye: No way. Without the sense of sight, you're lost!

Hand: Well, they do say that the best learning is hands-on.

Carl: I'm a tactile learner.

Eye: That's very touching!

Sara: You know we did learn the mazes in class starting with our fingers. Let's try it.

(Hand feels way around obstacles around room. Sara and Carl and the rest follow. Suddenly they all run into a wall.)

Hand: There's a wall here.

Eye: *(holds eye like it's bruised)* We noticed.

Hand: *(trying to explain)* O.K., so that was the wrong way, but don't you think that in trying to find out which way to go we need to discover which ways **not** to go?

Sara: Yeah, but that won't do us any good if we don't remember it. I think we've already been this way before.

Carl: It's kind of like that macaroni activity. After trying a few, we knew that certain colors tasted good, and others tasted lousy. I guess if a person didn't learn, they'd keep eating them at random, eating both good and bad. We were able to avoid the weird ones after we learned which ones they were.

Eye: So you used your sense of sight to tell which was bad and which was good.

Nose: You could've smelled them. I'm great at detecting chemicals!

Sara: You know Carl, we're getting all this sensory information, but somehow we need to figure out how to get it to our brains so we can remember it.

Rat: You've got a lot of nerve!

Sara: Say what?

Rat: That's what your **nerves** are for. They carry these messages to the brain and together the brain, the nerves, and the body react to whatever is being sensed!

Carl: That's interesting, Rat. Hey you know, since you know so much about this stuff, maybe it would help us get out of here if you tell us about your experiences in the mazes of Marian Diamond.

Sara: Yeah, tell us.

Rat: Well, at first we started out with just one barrier, then the scientists added one more barrier each day until there were 19, and by that time my cell nuclei were bigger and my little rat brain dendrites were branching all over the place!

Carl: So, I guess when I tried the finger mazes or counted dendrites on brain cells, my own brain cells grew, and my own dendrites got longer and more complicated.

Sara: And here in this "amazing" situation, we must be adding forests of dendrites.

Rat: Yeah, some of the rats in the lab lived in a boring environment, a real bunk hood with no toys and no friends. The one I lived in was stimulating, with toys and friends. We learned that, for us, having challenges made for healthier, more developed brains, like my lovely specimen. *(proudly points at own head)*

Carl: So we can say that learning seems to help brains to grow; it's healthy for our brains, and also important for our survival. But how do we learn?

Eye: Well, like Carl said earlier, you learn through experience. You also learn through what we, your senses, tell you. The senses, nerves, and the brain all work together when you learn.

Carl: You mean, learning means using what we *already know* to make sense out of new experiences or information? It's not just storing new information in our heads! I think I get it!

Rat: Hey, check out the branching dendrites on Carl! The man is thinkin'!

Sara: So when we have experiences, we remember them. I guess that's part of learning...we use our memory. Our brains are able to store so many things, and to remind us of them and even put them together in new ways—like some incredible computer.

Carl: Word!

Sara: You know there are ways we learn as individual humans, but there are also ways we learn as a society.

Carl: I heard that! It was pretty cool to see how scientists figure things out. I was surprised to learn how learning like this can be such a team effort. There were hecka scientists tracking down the Hexacarbon Solvent Mystery! Same with Lash-Lure.

Sara: It's a trip to think that together—our whole society of humans—we're figuring out how the world works, how our bodies work, how our minds work, what's dangerous, what's not...I mean, don't you just feel like an ant in an ant colony?

Carl: Yeah, and there's a kid with a magnifying glass hovering up above us. Nah, really, I guess I feel more like an individual brain cell in a huge brain.

Sara: You know with all this talk about how we learn—I feel like we're looking in a mirror...we're learning about how *(louder and louder)* we learn about how we learn about how we learn about how we learn about how we learn about how we learn...

Carl: Watch out Sara, you're gonna blow a fuse!

(Nose, Eye, Hand, and Rat all silently move off stage.
Sara stops, shakes her head and wakes up. Carl is rubbing his eyes.)

Sara: Wh... wh... what happened?

Carl: I guess we banged our skulls and were knocked out.

Sara: I had the weirdest dream. It was all about learning, and a rat, and a giant running nose.

Carl: For real? I had the same dream! *(both look at each other with big frightened eyes)*

Both: Ahhhhhhhhhhhh!

Carl: I'm outa here, this place is giving me the creeps!

Sara: O.K., O.K., let's try to put this all together ourselves. Let's see if we've learned something. We've already checked out a lot with our senses. Now if we use our memory to remember our previous experiences we know that we can't go that way *(points)* or that way or that way. How about that-a-way?!

(they walk in place in that direction, and find their way out into the sunlight)

Carl: Alright, we're finally outa there. Hey, how come all of a sudden it was so easy to find our way out? That Rat and Nose didn't lead us out of there.

Sara: I know why!

Carl: Why?

Sara: Because we used something that knows more about everything else than it knows about itself.

Carl: Sorry Sara, I think my dendrites have branched enough for the day. I give up.

Sara: You'll figure it out someday.

—— THE END, OR IS IT THE BEGINNING? ——

Going Further (for the entire unit)

1. Ask students to apply what they've learned about learning. Have them learn about a skill or a topic that interests them, remembering the list of things that help learning that were generated in class. Have them share their new findings/abilities with the class including the methods they used for learning.

2. Illustrate the power of different modes of learning in the following way. Teach your students how to do something very visual, like folding an origami crane. First teach them using only auditory instructions (no visual clues). Pass out folding paper. Can anybody fold the crane correctly? Then teach them by folding a crane in front of them once. Then pass out the paper and see who is successful. Finally, give them a diagram with instructions, folding paper, and take them through the process, step-by-step, allowing them to fold along with you. Have a discussion about hands-on learning, and the value of multi-sensory information.

"We invited a Japanese teaching assistant to teach origami three ways: 1) in Japanese; 2) in English (with no visuals); and 3) in English with visuals and hands-on participation. Boy! Frustration to elation! It was a very dramatic illustration of the barriers and facilitators of learning."
—Sixth grade teacher

3. Have students do research projects stimulated by what they've learned in the unit, such as finding out more about: the anatomy and physiology of the brain; cases of children like Genie or other unusual individuals whose background or condition sheds light on the human learning process; language acquisition; issues of occupational health and product safety and how scientists, manufacturers, government at all levels, and society as a whole respond; or other issues this unit may have raised for your students.

4. Have your students write or call local chapters of The American Heart Association, The American Lung Association, The American Cancer Society, the American Diabetes Association, etc. to find out the nature of their research.

5. Have students interview scientists, laboratory technicians, and/or graduate students who do human and animal research. Have them publish their own newsletter sharing what they learned.

6. With modeling clay or playdough, have your students construct a model of a brain. This three-pound organ, containing 100 billion nerve cells, can store more information than the Library of Congress—and scientists have only uncovered a small amount of what there is to know about it! Have students use what they learned about learning to learn about the brain. Assign pairs or groups of students various brain structures to research. Have them teach the

class about that structure and its function. Their lesson should include: 1) the name of the brain structure they were assigned; 2) the location of the structure on the clay brain (they may have to bisect the brain to show where it is!); 3) the functions of that structure; 4) additional interesting information, such as diseases associated with that structure, current medical research, the person who discovered it, etc.; 5) a chance for their peers to ask questions. The resulting product will be a class generated Brain Encyclopedia!

7. To respond to continued student interest and questions, consider inviting a professor from an Education department in a nearby college or university to talk about learning differences, the theory of multiple intelligences, or other new ideas in education.

8. Ask a neurologist to come to class and talk about what recent brain research reveals about the learning process and/or about the structure and workings of the brain. The neurologist could bring samples of MRI's or other visual "maps" showing brain structure and activity.

One group of Marian Diamond's college students made a model of the brain and related anatomical structures using cauliflower and other vegetables.

Behind the Scenes

This background section is intended to provide the teacher with additional information that may prove helpful in presenting these activities and in responding to student's questions. It is **not** meant to be read out loud to students or duplicated for them to read. Please refer to materials listed in the "Resources" section in this guide for more in-depth information.

Activity 1: Learning a Maze

What is learning and where in the brain does it occur?

Learning is the acquisition of knowledge or skill through experience. The experience can be something you do for the first time, like taking your first step, or an activity in which you make an improvement, such as repeating the multiplication tables faster. Learning occurs in many parts of the brain depending upon what kinds of sensory stimuli provide the input and where interactions with that input occur. Scientists think that most learning is processed in the *cerebral cortex*, an area of the brain which demonstrates the most plasticity (changeability).

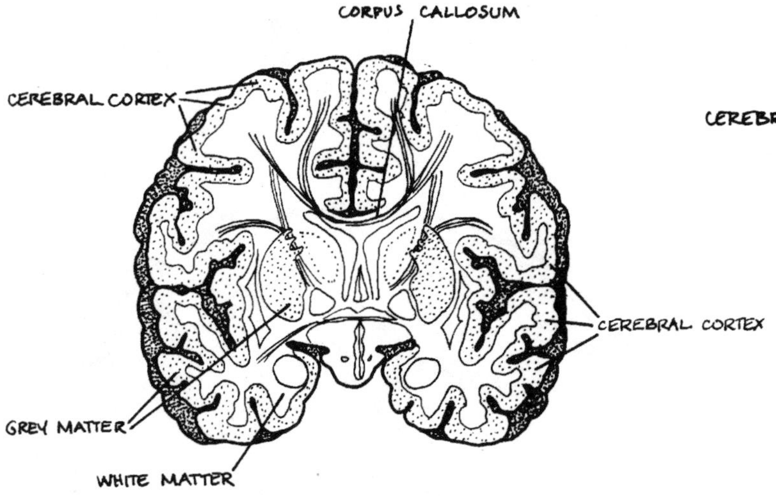

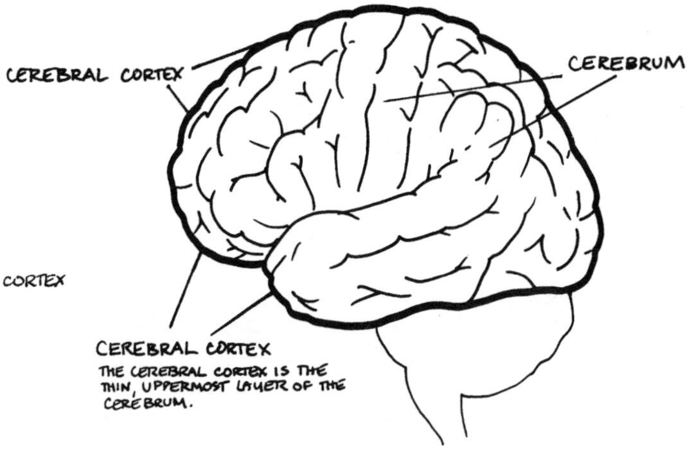

The cerebral cortex, sometimes referred to as the *cerebrum*, is the folded area of the brain that is responsible for higher functions like planning, decision-making, creativity, language, memory, and complex actions. It, like the rest of the brain, is composed of only two basic kinds of cells—*neurons* and *glial cells* (that support and feed the neurons). (See page 172 for more about these kinds of cells.)

What's happening in the brain each time you practice a maze?

When you learn, changes occur in the nerve cells (or neurons) in your brain. The neurons increase both their size and level of activity. Larger nerve cells offer more surface area with which other nerve cells can communicate, allowing for a greater variety of responses. These changes occur in your brain whether you are learning to read, to snap your fingers, to remember the words to your favorite song, or to improve your ability to shoot baskets in basketball.

How does the brain get information from our fingers!?

Actually, the brain receives no information directly—all of the information that the brain receives comes from the senses. Beneath the outer layers of the skin are *touch receptors* consisting of nerve endings with connective tissue coverings. When you touch something, you stimulate these touch receptors, generating a nerve impulse. This nerve impulse travels along the nerve through your finger, up your arm, to your spinal cord inside your vertebral column ("backbone"), to the brain. The impulse then travels through the brain to an area within the cerebral cortex called the *parietal lobe.* Your brain recognizes that impulse, received in the parietal lobe, as the sensation of touch.

A nerve *is a collection of neurons. It carries the impulses between the brain and muscles, glands, and organs of the body to give them sensation and movement.* Nerve impulses *are an electro-chemical way that neurons transmit messages.*

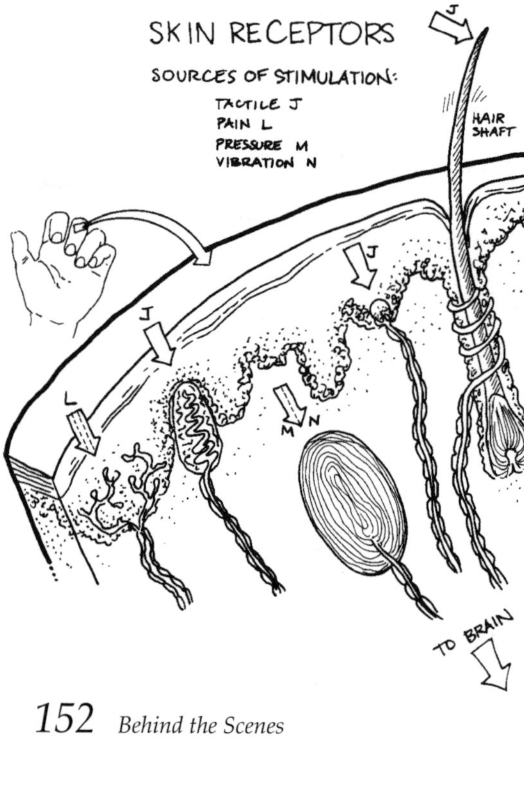

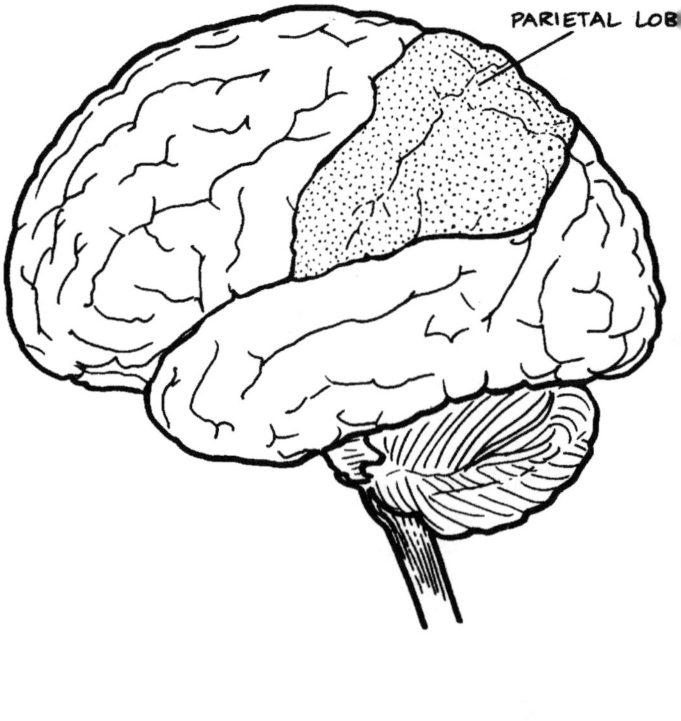

Activity 2: Good Teachers, Good Learners

What are the "multiple intelligences" referred to by Howard Gardner?

Harvard psychologist Howard Gardner first put forward his theory of "multiple intelligences" in his influential book *Frames of Mind*, published in 1983. Since then, the ideas he expressed have been widely discussed and proven to be of great practical interest to educators. He has written a number of subsequent books on this topic. These and related books are listed in the "Resources" section and we recommend them highly.

Framed in response to narrow conceptions of "intelligence," such as those derived from IQ tests and the like, Gardner proposed that in fact all human beings possess *at least* seven intelligences. He questioned the validity of determining intelligence by taking a person out of their natural learning environment and asking them to do isolated tasks they'd never done before—and probably would never choose to do again. Instead, Gardner contends that intelligence has more to do with the capacity for solving problems and the human ability to fashion products or creations in a complex real-life setting. In attempting to integrate both the findings of modern brain science and psychology, Gardner sees "intelligence" as a **biological and psychological potential**—a potential that is capable of being realized to a greater or lesser extent depending on the experiential, cultural, and motivational factors that affect a person. The seven intelligences described by Gardner, very briefly summarized are:

- **Lingustic Intelligence:** The capacity to use words effectively, whether orally or in writing. This intelligence includes the ability to manipulate the structure and syntax of language, the sounds of language, semantics or the meanings of language, and the practical uses of language, such as for explaining, remembering, persuading, etc.

- **Logical-Mathematical Intelligence:** The capacity to use numbers effectively and to reason well. This includes awareness of and sensitivity to logical patterns and relationships, functions, and cause and effect statements.

- **Spatial Intelligence:** The ability to perceive the visual and spatial world accurately and to engage in processes based on those perceptions, including sensitivity to color, line, shape, form, space, and the relationships between them. Includes the capacity to visualize, make graphic representations, and orient oneself in spatial surroundings.

- **Bodily-Kinesthetic Intelligence:** The ability to use one's whole body to express ideas and feelings, and the ability to fashion or transform with one's hands. Includes skills such as coordination, balance, dexterity, strength, flexibility, speed, and other physical skills.

- **Musical Intelligence:** The ability to perceive, distinguish between, transform, and express oneself in musical forms. Includes sensitivities to rhythm, pitch or melody, timbre and tone color. Can include either an intuitive grasp of music, an analytic or technical understanding of it, or both.

- **Interpersonal Intelligence:** The capacity to perceive and distinguish differences in the moods, intentions, motivations, and feelings of others. Includes sensitivity to facial expressions, gestures, and body language. This intelligence also includes the ability to respond to these interpersonal cues effectively, to work well with others, and to lead.

- **Intrapersonal Intelligence:** The capacity for self-knowledge and understanding, and the ability to act adaptively on the basis of that knowledge. Includes having an accurate picture of one's own strengths and limitations, inner moods, intentions, feelings, motivations, needs, desires, and a capacity for self-discipline and self-esteem.

It is imperative to stress, as soon as these seven are described, that all of us possess all seven intelligences, and that each of us possesses them in different degrees and combinations. As Gardner says, "It is of the utmost importance that we recognize and nurture all of the varied human intelligences, and all of the combinations of intelligences. We are all so different largely because we all have different combinations of intelligences. If we recognize this, I think we will have at least a better chance of dealing appropriately with the many problems that we face in the world."

It's also interesting that Gardner and others emphasize the "at least" when they describe seven intelligences. In more recent articles, Gardner discusses what he calls the "Naturalist Intelligence," and says that were he to rewrite *Frames of Mind* today he would probably include it. He writes, "It seems to me that the individual who is able readily to recognize flora and fauna, to make other consequential distinctions in the natural world, and to use this ability productively...is exercising an important intelligence and one that is not adequately encompassed on the current list." He adds that he heard the idea mentioned of what some have called a "Spiritual Intelligence" and hopes to learn more and write about what is meant by "spirituality" and being a "spiritual person" but is not certain whether or not it will be considered one of the "intelligences." Obviously—the human mind being what it is—there are a number of other potential candidates, including perhaps the "Synthetic Intelligence" or ability to bring all of the other "intelligences" into harmonious play with each other! Whether seven, eight, or more "intelligences" are detailed, the most revolutionary part of Gardner's work is simply that there are **multiple intelligences.** What is most important is not the specific definition of all these "intelligences," but the clear recognition that human intelligence is not confined to the more narrow linguistic and mathematical abilities measured by most standardized tests and traditionally described in school as being "smart." As Gardner has been quoted as saying, "It's not how smart you are, but *how* you are smart!"

Clearly these ideas can have a profoundly liberating impact on education. A number of schools around the country are seeking to put these ideas into practice. While these ideas, like all new ideas, have also been misrepresented and oversimplified, many of the schools that have emphasized them have made great strides. The implications for assessment of student progress are particularly powerful, as more and more teachers find ways for students to work within their areas of strength to demonstrate what they have learned. In assessing how his ideas have been applied in education, Gardner points out three directions he considers most positive. First, that schools should cultivate skills and capacities that are valued in the community and society—including some of the intelligences that have previously not been emphasized in schools. If the community places a high value on learning a musical instrument, for example, then schools in that community should cultivate that intelligence. If the community desires young people and citizens who can respect and take into

Each healthy human brain, irrespective of a person's age, sex, nationality, or cultural background, comes equipped with a set of exceptional features:

- *the ability to detect patterns and to make approximations,*
- *a phenomenal capacity for various types of memory,*
- *the ability to self-correct and learn from experience by way of analysis of external data and self-reflection, and*
- *an inexhaustible capacity to create.*

from Making Connections: Teaching and the Human Brain

account the feelings of others, then interpersonal intelligence should be emphasized. Second, he believes these emphases can and should be explored in a variety of ways, allowing there to be "multiple windows leading to the same room," thereby speaking to the different ways that people learn. Third, he supports what he calls the "personalization of education," meaning that human differences are taken seriously and that education works most effectively if the differences in the way people learn, think, and feel are taken into account.

How does fear shut down learning? How does pleasure facilitate learning?

Responses to these questions may be suggested by one way of looking at the brain, as described by Dr. Paul MacLean, and often referred to as the Triune Brain. (See the "Resources" section for references to his work.) He describes three distinct functional areas of the brain that constantly interact: as the "reptilian" brain, the limbic system, and the "thinking" brain.

The first level of the Triune Brain is referred to as the "reptilian" or "dinosaur" brain. This area controls the body's vital functions such as respiration and heart rate. It keeps the body alive in life-threatening situations by increasing blood pressure, pumping adrenaline, etc. This is the area of the brain related to instinctive behaviors such as food gathering, grooming, establishing social groups, etc.

The second level of the Triune Brain is the limbic system. The limbic system is an interconnected group of brain structures involved in emotions as well as playfulness, nurturing, and various hormonal drives.

The third level of the Triune Brain is the cerebral cortex, sometimes referred to as the "thinking" brain. This is where much learning is thought to occur. As we have experiences, the cerebral cortex develops dendrites and neural highways. The quality and density of the neural network is a result of environmental stimulation and multiple experiences. According to MacLean, when the cerebral cortex perceives a threat (either real or imagined) there is a "downshifting" to the limbic system and/or the reptilian brain. In this "downshifted" state, researchers believe that no learning can take place. This addresses the vivid experience many students have had of being afraid of taking tests or of standing in front of a group to perform, and how that fear inhibits our abilities. Both fear

TRIUNE BRAIN MODEL

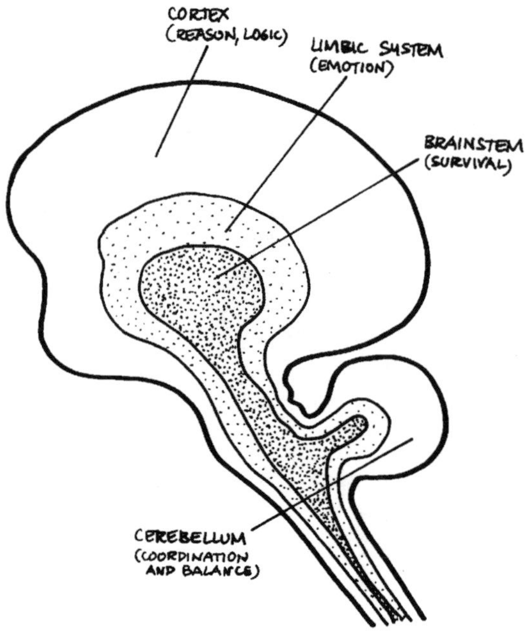

BRAINSTEM AND LIMBIC SYSTEM MODEL

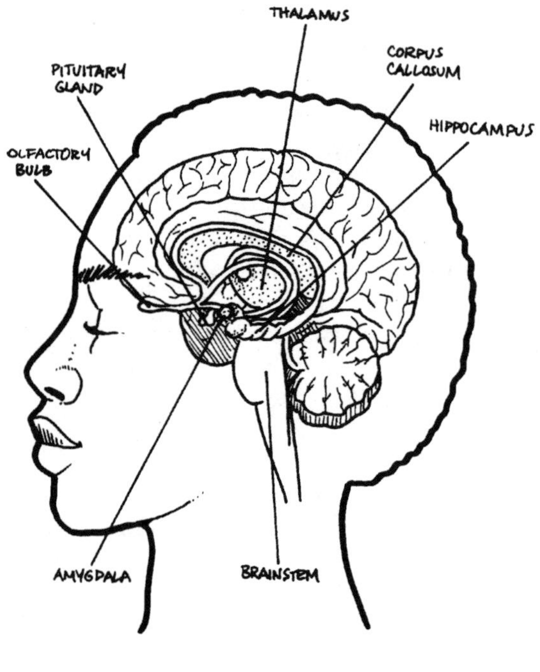

and stress can involve the release of hormones from our adrenal glands. These hormones enter our bloodstream and then the brain. The amount of these hormones makes a difference in the response from the brain. We know a little fear accompanied by adrenaline is stimulating to the brain and can enhance performance, while too much can be restrictive. The cerebral cortex is constantly being bathed in different amounts of hormones and chemicals—it is the proper balance that provides optimum conditions for learning.

Some believe that involving the limbic system (play, emotion, enthusiasm, pleasure) is key to improving memory and learning. Good teachers know that learning experiences which are also fun are particularly memorable. However, if the limbic system's response is overly dominant, memory and learning may be hampered.

What are the limitations of this model?

While MacLean's Triune Brain can provide some insight into the basic organization and orientation of the brain, it's important to recognize that this model is considered too simplistic by some. For one thing, the description of three separate divisions of the brain does not accurately depict the overlap among the functions of these three divisions. For instance, the hypothalamus (classified as part of the limbic system) plays a strong role in instinctual behavior (which in the Triune Brain is considered the domain of the reptilian brain). Also, the cerebral cortex (thinking brain) influences the hypothalamus (limbic system) to modify emotions. Further, the limbic system and the cerebral cortex (thinking brain) both deal with memory and learning.

The shortcomings of such simplistic categorization are further discussed in *Making Connections: Teaching and the Human Brain* (see "Resources" for reference listing). The book comments, for example, that "the brain does not naturally separate emotions from cognition, either anatomically or perceptually. Hence, brain research challenges the belief that teaching can be separated into cognitive, affective, or psychomotor domains. Such artificial categorizations may be helpful in designing research projects, but it can actually distort our understanding of learning." While the triune model is helpful in understanding some of the basic ways the brain reacts and operates, it is also a good demonstration of one of the important concepts in science—the limitations of models!

Whether it be the triune model, or Freud's early division of human consciousness into id, ego, and superego, or the inaccurate and misleading left brain/right brain dichotomy popularized some years ago and still influential, people seem to want to be able to sum up and simplify this most complex of human organs. Such models may provide some helpful insights and get people thinking about thinking, but all of these models fail to place on center stage perhaps the most important power of the brain—its ability to make an incredibly complex, virtually infinite array of electrochemical connections. These connections are transformed into messages that run through the nervous system, and may be variously translated into speech, visualized in shape and color, evolved into concepts and theories. Even modern computers, for all their marvels, have not yet approached the complexity of the brain.

A more flexible model or metaphor may be helpful. *Making Connections: Teaching and the Human Brain*, for example, compares the brain to a modern city. While this model may relate less to specific anatomical features of the brain, it does succeed in helping us understand the connectivity and complexity in intriguing ways. The book asks us to imagine a group of scientists from a distant planet observing a city on Earth. They might notice the large physical structures first. Analyzing further, they might observe functions and figure out that the structures are schools, factories, banks, malls, offices, etc. These large buildings are connected by streets, rails, wires, including computer networks. These distant scientists could also see that people, millions of them, are vital to the city's operation—they are the agents that make everything "work." Other observations might include how cities are divided into neighborhoods and how people tend to work in groups or clusters. Groups relate to each other in diverse ways. People with special skills are employed for specific tasks. Not all people are part of easily-defined groups and not all functions are easy to define.

Importantly, the outer space observers see lots of different functions and operations going on at the same time. Large companies are chugging along at the same time as schools are open, banks transfer funds, bakeries bake, welders repair ships, and libraries lend books. The operation of one does not detract from the working of another. In this way the city, like the brain, serves as a "parallel processor." In the brain, many things happen simultaneously—monitoring of hormone levels, digestion, and temperature goes on while we are writing a poem and worrying about the family budget! In the city and the brain, the processes and functions are interdependent and connected. Schools require food for the cafeteria, gas, electricity, water, sewage, hands-on math and science materials, and lots more. Every specialized institution is highly dependent on many others. Economic, social, political, and cultural forces can have a profound impact. Organizational complexity goes further, as every process involves decision-making, priority-setting, and adjustment for the constant changes resulting from the creative and productive labors and recreations going on apace. After making this analogy, the authors conclude, "Because this parallel and interrelated processing is typical of the brain, as of the city, the brain is described as *holographic* or *global* or *interconnected*. It is very busy. And because every element influences every other element, an understanding of this complexity is paramount for education."

Activity 3: Silent Smell Tracking

What part of the brain is involved with smelling?

There are several parts of the brain concerned with smell. The *olfactory nerves*, the shortest nerves in the nervous system, are found in the roof of the nasal cavity. You sniff something to bring the substance you are smelling to the top of your nasal cavity. The olfactory nerves enter the *olfactory bulb* (about the size of a large grain of rice) which sits on the bones inside the skull forming the roof of the nasal cavity. Scientists think that a great deal of selective processing of information related to our sense of smell takes place in the olfactory bulbs themselves. From the bulbs, nerve fibers continue, sending signals onward toward the brain, reaching parts of the upper brain stem and cerebral cortex where the different kinds of smells are interpreted.

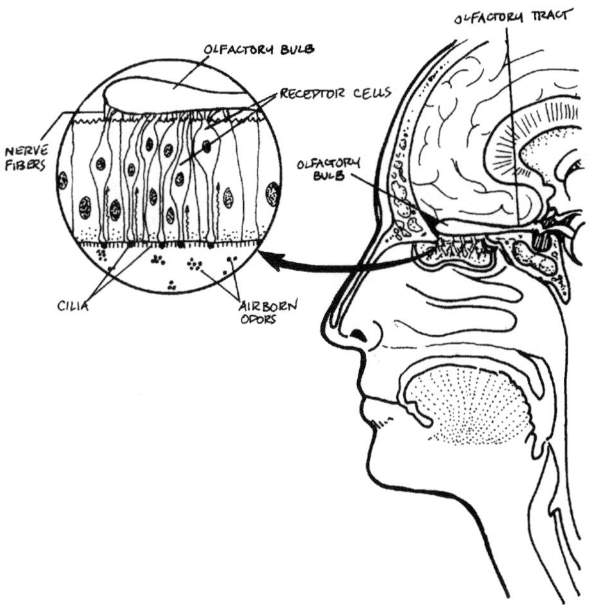

How are wolf brains different from human brains?

Wolf brains are very similar to dog brains. The main sensory difference between the human brain and the wolf/dog brain is that the olfactory system of the wolf/dog is far more developed than that of the human. This helps explain why the sense of smell plays such an important role in survival and communication of wolves (see below for more on scent marking and other smell-related behaviors). The other major difference between wolf and human brains is that the cerebral cortex is much more developed in humans.

The excellent book *A Celebration of Neurons: An Educator's Guide to the Human Brain* (see "Resources" for full reference) contains an interesting if highly speculative comment on how species adjust their sensory systems to their environment. It notes that most four-legged animals have a much stronger sense of smell than humans, while humans generally have a more powerful visual system. It then theorizes that odor molecules are heavy and tend to settle near the ground, where four-legged animals often sniff. The book adds, "When early humans stood up on two legs and so moved their head several feet from the ground, where the view was less obstructed, smell became less useful and vision became more useful. Over evolutionary time, the relative strength of the two systems reversed." Of course, this is only one theory, and the variety of adaptations of organisms to their environment, which sometimes differ greatly even among related species, casts some doubt on such a facile explanation. It is nonetheless interesting as one way to start thinking about the comparative functions played by the sense of smell in wolves and humans.

What are the first days of a wolf pup like?

The Canadian Center for Wolf Research in Nova Scotia has a large, fenced research area, where a captive wolf pack lives in a simulated natural setting, fairly undisturbed by humans. While working on her doctoral thesis, Elizabeth Coscia (with whom we consulted when preparing this information) was able to make detailed observations of wolf pup behavior by observing a mother wolf and her pups in an underground den that had hidden video cameras. The pups' eyes don't open until the second week, at which time they begin to explore the den and each other. They are very vocal, using squeaks, yips, and howls as they play and tumble.

How might lost pups behave?

Sometimes a mother wolf will transfer her pups to a new and presumably safer den when they are about three weeks old. She carries the pups using her mouth, one at a time. If some pups attempt to follow the mother, they risk losing their way. They would tend to stay close together as they searched, sniffing for the trail and the den.

When wolf pups are about five weeks old, their mother often leads them from the den to a rendezvous site to meet with other members of the pack. If some pups became separated along the way, they would tend to stay close together and attempt to follow the scent to catch up with the others. The pups would probably be very vocal, squeaking and howling in an attempt to attract their mother.

What is scent marking in wolves?

We're all familiar with scent marking, having seen dogs sniff and urinate at every tree and bush along their path. Scientists from the Canadian Center for Wolf Research have been curious about the urine messages that wolves use to communicate with each other. Studies are showing that a wolf's scent mark can mean a lot more than just "I was here!" These are some of the findings that have come from observing wolf behavior:

- High urine marks on a tree are probably made by a dominant wolf.
- Urine puddles are usually made by subdominant wolves that squat.
- Dominant wolves tend to conserve their urine, letting out only a few drops at a time, doing so periodically as they travel through an area.
- Each animal has its own distinctive urine odor, so wolves can distinguish intruders from pack members.
- Wolves can tell how "fresh" the urine is, and tend to be less interested in "old" marks.
- Wolves can tell when successive wolves have urinated on top of the scent marks.
- The age, gender, and sexual condition of the wolf is broadcast in its urine.
- Urine can convey the health of the animal, and the food it has recently eaten.

Activity 4: The Hexacarbon Solvent Mystery

What is "glue" sniffing?

For generations, people have inhaled various substances to achieve a "high." Inhalants are usually cheap and easily available. Some people, adolescents in particular, knowingly risk life-threatening effects in an attempt to bolster self-esteem or gain peer approval. In the sprawling city slums of some nations, the problem is epidemic among poverty-stricken urban youth.

Although often called "glue" sniffing, sniffers inhale much more than glue. There are many different solvents, in both liquid and gas form, that have been "sniffed" or "huffed" to create a "high." Lacquer thinners, household cements, paint and varnish removers, wax removers, spot removers, fingernail polish removers, are just a very partial list.

The effect of inhaling these substances can include feelings of dizziness, euphoria, weightlessness, distortion of senses and perceptions, awkward movement, muscle weakness, altered speech, slowed reactions, ringing in the ears, drowsiness, sleep, anesthesia, depressions, hallucinations, delirium, or disorientation. In most cases inhalants depress the central nervous system. They can interrupt and increase heart rate and alter breathing.

Inhalant abuse has reached serious proportions among young people in some locations around the world and in the United States. Newspaper articles have cited it as the leading cause of death of eighth graders in the United States.

Toxic effects of inhalation can include pains in the chest, muscles, and joints, amnesia, coma, seizures, brain damage, nerve damage, liver and kidney damage, respiratory tract damage, "glue sniffer's rash," nosebleeds, nausea, diarrhea, eye/nose irritation, glaucoma, and more. Inhalation can cause death from "SSD" (sudden sniffing death), suffocation, poisoning, respiratory depression, and suicide.

FACT: Small amounts of certain inhalants can be instantly fatal.

What are hexacarbons?

Chemicals in the hexacarbon family all contain six carbon atoms. Because of their properties, many other substances dissolve easily in them, so they are often used as solvents in industrial and research processes, as well as in products used in both work and home environments. There are a large number of chemicals in the hexacarbon family. Only some of them have been shown to cause neuropathy with repetitive exposure.

How can one chemical make another "stronger"?

There are a variety of mechanisms that result in one chemical amplifying the effect of another. In the situation of the Hexacarbon Solvent Mystery, the presence of MEK (methyl-ethyl-ketone) was found to potentiate or increase the nerve damaging effects of *n*-hexane and M*n*BK (methyl-*n*-butyl ketone). Here's why. When *n*-hexane and/or M*n*BK are inhaled or absorbed through the skin, they enter the bloodstream. The body breaks down (metabolizes) these chemicals to 2,5 HD (2,5-hexanedione)—it is 2,5 HD that causes the damage to nerves. The 2,5 HD remains in the bloodstream for a certain period of time before the body clears it from the blood. MEK blocks the body from clearing the 2,5 HD. This results in 2,5 HD staying in the bloodstream longer, thereby having more time to cause nerve damage.

What causes neuropathy? Is it reversible?

Neuropathy can happen in many different ways. Spinal injury through accident can cause damage that leads to neuropathy and paralysis. The actor Christopher Reeves, who fell off a jumping horse, is a case in point. While he has regained some very limited function, so far the effects of the damage have not been able to be reversed. Many automobile accidents and athletic injuries, especially diving accidents, damage the spinal cord and cause neuropathies. Severe injury to the neck, resulting in compression of the spinal cord, can affect the function of all nerves below it, so arms and legs can become paralyzed. In these cases, the ability to recover depends on how severe the original injury was, and on many other aspects of the individual case.

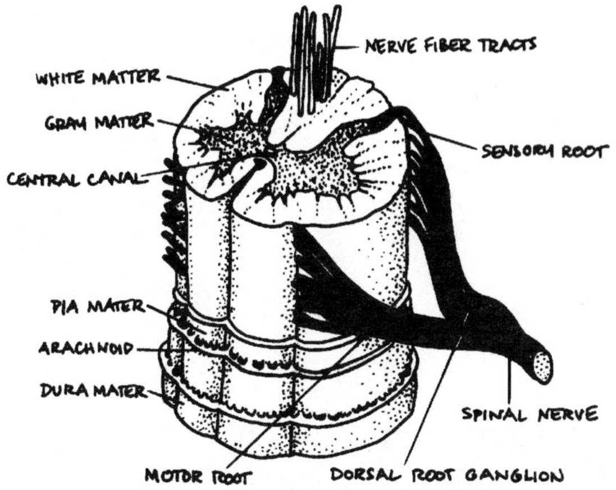

STRUCTURE OF THE SPINAL CORD

Neuropathy can also be the result of diseases and degenerative conditions, among them multiple sclerosis and amytrophic lateral sclerosis (Lou Gehrig's disease), and bony growths or calcification of the spine (or other skeletal areas) that can enlarge to compress the spinal cord or damage nerves. Some of these, such as Lou Gehrig's disease, are progressive and, with rare exceptions, lead to death in relatively few years. New treatments for multiple sclerosis have enabled many with this disease to retain more function and live much longer. Skeletal growths and related conditions can often be treated successfully by surgery, with the amount of function regained varying from patient to patient. Less systemic neuropathies involving only the peripheral nerves (e.g., conditions in the arms like "carpal tunnel" or ulnar neuropathy) can be extremely painful. Increasing numbers of workers in the modern computerized office suffer from such conditions. In many cases, these are caused by compression of the nerve at the elbow by working for long periods of time in positions that put unusual pressure on the nerve or nerves involved. Some vitamin and other non-invasive treatments improve many patients with conditions like carpal tunnel; other patients require surgery. In many of these cases, function is not lost and pain can be lessened considerably.

Your students may ask more about why the people at the printing plant and the men who sniffed "glue" had weakness in or lost the function of their limbs completely. You may want to explain that the damaged nerves cannot send their usual messages and nourishment to the muscles so the muscles begin to atrophy, or "waste." Unless the situation is remedied, the wasting continues, leading to paralysis. Unfortunately, this is what happened to several of the "glue" sniffers.

Do other "recreational drugs" cause damage to the nervous system? Can the damage be reversed?

Yes, many other drugs can and do cause damage. The ad campaign that showed a frying egg and said, "this is your brain on drugs" may not have been a particularly apt metaphor for the brain (which does *not* resemble an egg, fried or not!). But the ad did get a message across, namely that drug abuse can damage and even destroy the brain, which is the control center of the entire nervous system.

Cocaine and methamphetamines (including the designer drug called "Ecstasy") can have many severe negative impacts, up to and including death. Some of these impacts result from effects of over-stimulation on the heart and circulatory system and can also lead to stroke, paralysis, palsies, and other impairments of the nervous system. Overdoses of other drugs, including heroin, barbiturates, animal tranquilizers like PCP, etc., can also cause severe damage and death.

Hallucinogenic or "psychedelic" drugs, such as LSD, while less likely to cause this direct sort of physical damage, can cause severe psychiatric disturbance, including psychosis and suicide. In the sense that the brain is the hub of the nervous system, its misfunction during mental illness triggered by psychedelic drugs (or sometimes as a side-effect of medically prescribed drugs) can definitely be considered "damage to the nervous system." It is unfortunately also true that some medications that doctors find it necessary to use, such as the anti-psychotic Haldol (also used for other conditions) can have, especially in elderly patients, "side-effects" that damage the nervous system, such as the palsy-like disturbance known as tardive dyskinesia.

As for whether or not these effects can be reversed, the only accurate answer is that each case and situation is unique—in some cases of drug side-effects, when the patient is withdrawn from the medication, some or all of the impaired nerve function can be regained. Even in some very severe cases, such as those involving stroke, the human organism and brain have shown an incredible capacity to adapt, and some recovery of function can be gained. In many cases, however, nerve damage is not reversible, or the amount of recovery is minimal, and the individual is extremely disabled. Direct and scientific education to students about the actual damage that so-called "recreational drugs" may cause to their brains and entire bodies is seen as one important way to help defeat the tragic epidemic of drug abuse.

Activity 5: Learning What is Safe

What are some of the ways that wolves communicate?

For the time of birth on, vocalization is extremely important in facilitating the social behavior and communication of wolves. The sense of smell and use of scents is also extremely important. Scent is used to mark trails, dens, food, etc. Sight is important for receiving messages from the postures and actions of other wolves. For example, tail up, ears up, or fur bristling signify dominance, while rolling on the back, crouching to the side, tail down, or ears and/or fur flattened are submissive behaviors. Observation of den behavior also indicates that wolves use the sense of touch in communication between mother and young; wolves are very affectionate and use a lot of close bodily contact during friendly play and when just lounging around.

How might a wolf pack approach strange food?

Wolves tend to repeat the same general patterns of behavior when encountering new food. If the food is moving, it will trigger more predatory responses, and less hesitation. One researcher at the Canadian Center for Wolf Research prepared a variety of gelatin cubes flavored with different foods, then observed which cubes the wolves selected first, so in a sense these wolves did a very similar activity to the one your students do in Activity 5! The following is a possible wolf pack response to the case of the "strange" macaroni food: The dominant or "alpha" male alone would approach cautiously, hesitating, backing away, then approaching again. His lips and tongue might curl as he tried to direct the food smell into the nasal cavity. If the food smell is totally new, he might jump back and leave the area. If the food smell is similar to known prey and food odors, the wolf would first poke at the food, then pull at it, and perhaps toss it in the air. The other pack members would remain on the sidelines until the dominant wolf started to eat. The alpha male might roll on or urinate on strange items of food that he did not eat. Other members of the pack would tend to eat the food selected by their leader.

What are the basic legal regulations and ethical standards in current use for foods, drugs, and cosmetics?

Today many countries around the world, including the United States, have consumer, worker, and environmental safety regulations requiring product safety information. In the United States, the safety of different types of products and chemical ingredients is regulated by different government agencies under different laws.

Most people would agree that manufacturers also have a very clear ethical responsibility to assure that their products are safe for the workers who make and transport them, consumers who use them, and the general public exposed to them through normal or accidental contact.

It is not enough for a product to be safe only for its recommended or most obvious use. When evaluating the safety of a new chemical or product, manufacturers also must consider possible ways people may misuse a product and common types of accidental exposures, such as splashing a material in the eye. Another goal is to avoid introduction of chemicals into our environment that could have damaging effects on the health of people years from now.

What are the government agencies in the United States concerned with product safety?

The Food and Drug Administration (FDA) regulates the safety of prescription and over-the-counter drugs, medical devices, food additives, and cosmetics through the Food, Drug, and Cosmetic Act. The Environmental Protection Agency (EPA) enforces laws related to protecting human health and the environment. The Federal Insecticide, Fungicide, and Rodenticide Act covers the registration of all pesticidal products used in the United States, including some common household disinfectant cleaners and insect repellents as well as lawn and food crop chemicals. The Toxic Substances Control Act regulates all chemical substances manufactured or imported into the United States, except for those already covered under other laws. Chemicals in consumer products that are not foods, drugs, cosmetics, or pesticides are regulated under this act. The Occupational Safety and Health Administration (OSHA) is concerned with worker health and safety, including inspection of workplaces and enforcement of safety and environmental standards. The Consumer Product Safety Commissions (CPSC) enforces safety labeling regulations for common household and office products under the Federal Hazardous Substances Act. This law requires that a manufacturer determine if a product should be labeled "harmful or fatal if swallowed" or "is a skin or eye irritant."

Do the product safety laws and regulations specifically require information from animal tests on new products such as drugs, pesticides, and cosmetics?

The answer depends on whether we talk only about the specific-wording of the regulations or also look at the *intent* of these rules. For example, some regulations or guidelines specifically require information from animal tests on new products such as drugs and pesticides. Other laws, such as the one regulating cosmetics, require a manufacturer to demonstrate product safety, but do not specify the exact test procedures to be used. Government authorities expect a manufacturer to conduct any test considered scientifically necessary to *ensure* the safety of brand new materials.

What is the process used to determine the safety of a product?

The first step in any safety evaluation is to research all existing safety information on the ingredients or product mixture in question and on similar materials. This "historical" data includes both non-animal and animal test results from previous studies and human data from clinical safety studies or consumer or worker experiences. The computer age has made this task much easier! This information-gathering step is important because it prevents unnecessary re-testing of materials.

Scientists also investigate what kind of potential health effects can be predicted from information on the chemical structure and other physical or chemical properties of a new ingredient. For example, if a material is corrosive, then scientists can assume that it will damage eyes or skin without having to conduct eye or skin irritation testing.

Students are naturally very concerned about the conditions of laboratory animals. As your students discuss these issues, it may be helpful for them to be aware that scientists place a strong emphasis on humane care and treatment of lab animals. In addition, the Federal Animal Welfare Act mandates standards for veterinary care, housing, handling, treatment, feeding, watering, sanitation, ventilation, and shelter of laboratory animals. All research facilities covered under this Act must be regularly inspected, including unannounced visits. The Act also requires each institution to have an Institutional Animal Care and Use Committee to review and approve all research plans before any study involving animals can begin. Many labs also maintain approval from the American Association for the Accreditation of Laboratory Animal Care. There is currently considerable controversy in our society surrounding the issues raised by the use of animals in scientific/medical testing. Students of today will have many complex decisions to make in the future regarding these and related issues.

The careful use of existing information, computer models, and tests that use cell or tissue cultures has greatly reduced the use of animals in product safety testing. Animals are used only when the existing safety information is insufficient and non-animals tests cannot provide the necessary information. In many cases, no new animal testing is needed to approve minor changes in products or for combinations of ingredients previously shown to be safe for the intended use.

When animal testing is needed, the species used depends upon the type of safety question under investigation. Rats, mice, and other rodents account for about 90% of the animals used in research.

Activity 6: The Story of Genie

What are some of the theories about why Genie had so much difficulty putting sentences together?

One of the ongoing questions raised by the story of Genie and by other cases involving "wild children" or other extraordinary circumstances, concerns how language develops in the human brain. As our knowledge of the brain and its development advances, new theories about how humans are "wired" for language have also arisen. One of the leading thinkers in this arena is Noam Chomsky, whose revolutionary contributions to linguistics have been widely recognized. Chomsky believes (and has marshalled considerable evidence) that the human brain, as it has evolved, is already equipped with the complex and interacting powers that allow it to put words together grammatically, that is to recognize syntax, structure, and the underlying assumptions and logic of language and verbal communication. In this sense then, he and many other scientists and psychologists believe that the human is already "wired" for complex linguistic learning. This "wiring" has evolved as the human species did, and is with us at birth.

It is certainly true that the ways that young children are able to assimilate complex linguistic usage and recognize the appropriate order of words in a sentence suggests that this "wiring" exists. How then are we to explain cases such as Genie? While she could acquire many words and would often attempt to put them together in sequences, she was usually unable to do so in customary and clearly understandable ways. Nor was she able to be consistent in her limited grammatical efforts. It was exceedingly difficult for her, rather than being almost-natural and very rapid, as it happens ordinarily in young children. Didn't she already have the wiring? If so, then why couldn't she express herself with grammatical complexity?

Given the tragic circumstances, it is quite possible that Genie's brain was damaged, *in utero* and/or in early childhood. Genie may have been developmentally disabled. At the same time, Genie's situation may also provide some insight into more recent theories about human speech development. This was one of the reasons why scientists were so interested in working with her. As a further and "friendly amendment" to the ideas put forward by Chomsky and others, many scientists now believe that, while the human brain is indeed "wired" for linguistic complexity, there is a key "window of opportunity" in early childhood that also must be opened for these abilities to be put into practice. The abuse and malnutrition Genie suffered, especially the fact that she was all by herself, and hardly heard another person speak for so many years, may have deprived her developing brain of the experiences which open that "window of opportunity." This suggests that both "nature" and "nurture" play a role in our ability to develop the complex use of language.

Activity 7: Learning and Environment (Part I)

Are all neurons (nerve cells) the same?

No, there are different types of neurons. The type of neuron that is found in the cerebral cortex, which the students measured in this activity, are called *pyramidal neurons*. Pyramidal neurons do not multiply after birth.

Every neuron, no matter what type, has a *cell body, dendrites* (that receive impulses and deliver them to the cell body), and an *axon* (the long part of a neuron, through which an impulse travels away from the cell body to a new neuron). The longest axons in the body can be three feet in length and stretch from the brain to the base of the spine. Others can be quite short.

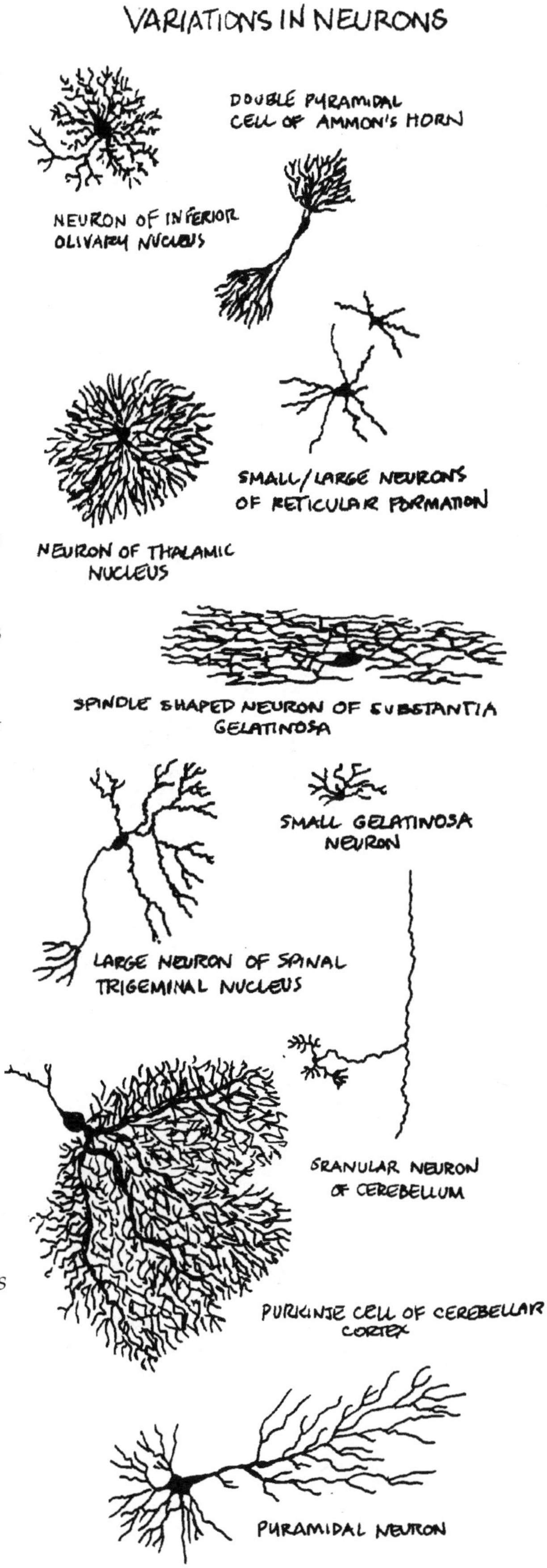

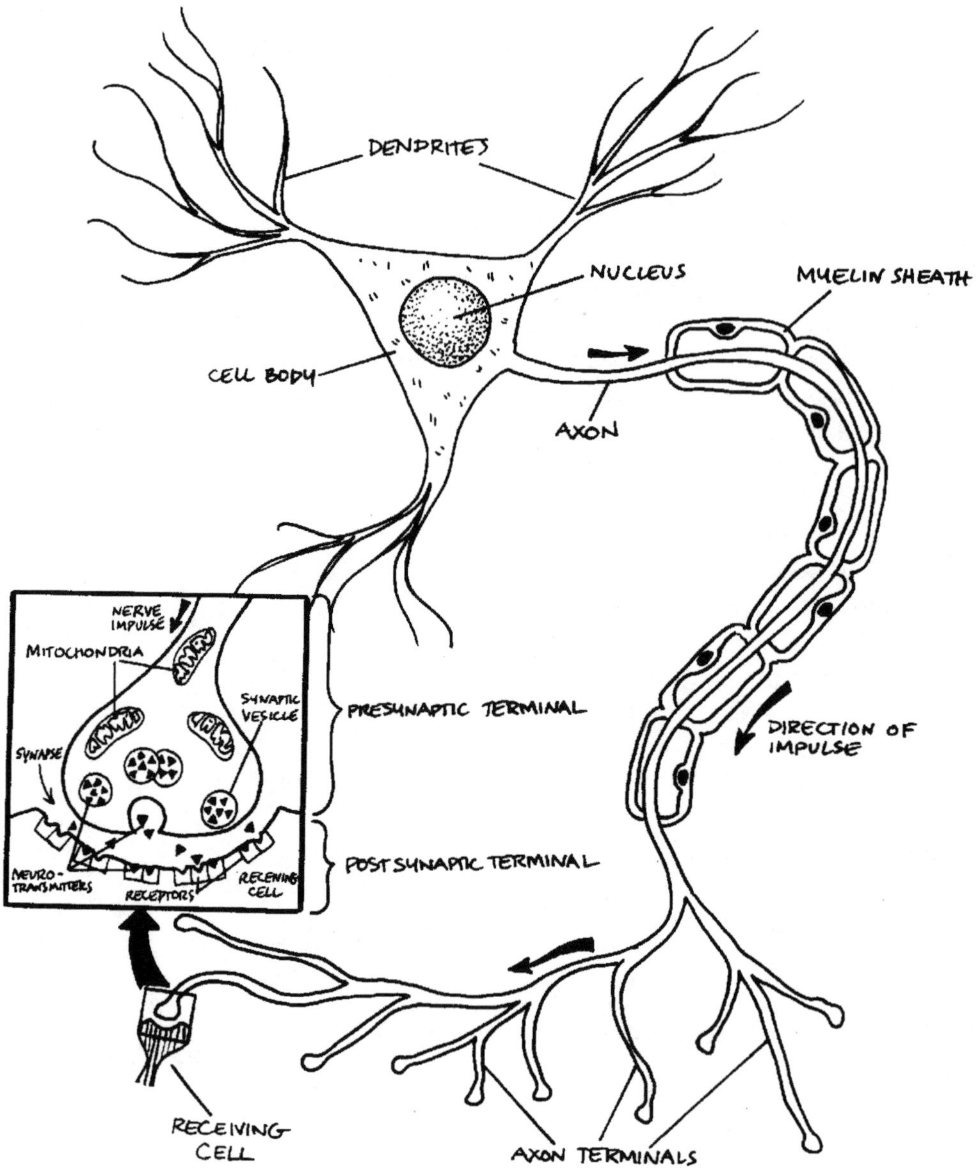

Why did Marian Diamond and her research team choose rats to study?

Rats are highly intelligent, social animals, like humans, so research findings have implications for people as well. Rats are well-studied, so a lot is known about them. Rats are easily raised and maintained in highly controlled laboratory conditions. Strains of rats have been bred for genetic similarity. Rats have a rapid life cycle so that learning behaviors of adults and old individuals may be easily studied. Another important reason rats were selected as the experimental subjects is that unlike the very folded human cerebral cortex, the rat's cortex is smooth and changes in it can be measured more easily.

How was the procedure used in this activity for measuring neurons different from that used by Diamond and her colleagues?

In the early days, when Diamond and her colleagues conducted their original research, they used the concentric circles to measure dendritic growth, just as students do in the activity. Today Diamond's group uses something called a *camera lucida,* which projects the neuron from the microscopic field directly onto a "bit pad" where the outlines of the nerve cell are traced directly into a computer.

Activity 8: Learning and Environment (Part II)

If most nerve cells do not multiply throughout life, then how does enrichment promote growth?

When comparing the brains of environmentally enriched rats with those of environmentally impoverished rats, scientists have discovered nerve cell development in *all* parts of the cell that were measured: the size of the nerve cell body, the size of the nucleus, the number and length of dendrites, the number of *dendritic spines* (lollipop-looking projections on the dendrites where synapses can occur), and the size of the *synaptic membranes* (where one nerve fiber communicates with another). In other words, every part of the nerve cell that is measured increases its dimensions with enrichment and decreases them with lack of stimulation.

How does increased use stimulate dendrites to grow?

When a nerve cell is stimulated, an impulse travels down its axon toward its target dendrite. The end of the axon is called a ***presynaptic terminal.*** When the impulse reaches the presynaptic terminal, a chemical (called a ***neurotransmitter***), is released into the gap between the axon and the dendrite. The receiving end of the dendrite is called the ***postsynaptic terminal.*** It has receptors for the neurotransmitter so that the impulse can continue. The transmission of the impulse across this gap is called a ***synapse.***

Dendrites can grow with use. When the neurotransmitter reacts with its receptor on the postsynaptic membrane, this opens channels, allowing certain chemicals (ions) to enter.

These ions influence enzymes to alter proteins directly or to activate genes to direct more protein formation. This formation of new protein is the process of growth.

What does this research mean for humans?

While these exact studies were obviously not performed on humans, the results of environmental enrichment on rats have been supported by human studies. (See the "Resources" section.) If the brain of environmentally enriched rats shows more nerve cell development, then one can infer that an enriched environment should increase human nerve cell development. Even a single activity, such as walking through a maze, might cause the extension of new dendritic branches and spines—another manner in which your brain adapts to suit your environment.

How do these changes in brain cells help a person think better?

As mentioned earlier, larger nerve cells offer more surface area with which other nerve cells can communicate, allowing for a greater variety of responses. Likewise, a greater number of dendrites, longer dendrites, more dendritic spines, and larger synaptic membranes increase the number of possible connections and therefore increase the communication between brain cells. This all leads to the development of a greater brain capacity.

Each neuron in your cerebral cortex may have more than twenty thousand connections with other neurons. The more connections that are formed, the greater brain capacity you will have.

Can you increase the size of your brain as a body builder increases the size of his or her muscles?

__Glial cells__ are the support cells of the nervous system. Glial means "glue." Glial cells can multiply to serve the additional work load of nerve cells. The multiplication of glial cells is considered beneficial, though interestingly, most brain tumors are formed from glial cells. Einstein had an extraordinarily large number of glial cells. See the "Resources" section for more information on brain anatomy and an article by Marian Diamond and others on Einstein's brain.

In muscles, each cell increases in size with use, making the overall muscle tissue more massive. Similarly, in the brain of rats experiencing an enriched environment, the cerebral cortex becomes more massive through use. In the brain, one of the contributing factors of mass is due not just to enlarged nerve cells (neurons), but also to an increased number of support cells (glial cells). A unique aspect of enrichment is that it primarily affects the cerebral cortex, the top layers of the brain. The cerebral cortex is responsible for higher order tasks, such as thinking. Because rats show growth of new glial cells with use, we suspect that the same occurs in humans when we exercise and use our brains. So when you exercise your muscles, you can also "exercise" your brain by thinking about what you are doing and thus providing yourself with one form of enrichment.

How long does it take for changes in the brain to occur?

Scientists have shown that in an interesting, interactive environment, changes in a rat's brain can occur within a very short time. Over a period of a month, as little as two hours per day of challenging activity is sufficient experience to produce a rat brain with measurable enriched characteristics. Continuous living in an enriched environment can produce measurable brain changes in four days. If a rat's brain can show characteristics of enrichment after a short time in a stimulating environment, then the human brain may also display similar characteristics when exposed to an enriched environment. Physical activity is an enriching activity that promotes changes in the brain. In addition, the physical activity in sports can involve partners and teams, thus promoting social interaction which is also enriching.

Activity 9: Ethics of Learning

What are some examples of research methods which do not use animals?

Scientists are seeking better ways to assure the safety of new products using alternative methods that replace specific animal methods, reduce the number of animals needed in particular tests, or refine test procedures to minimize or eliminate any discomfort for the animals. Cell and tissue culture methods, computer and mathematical models, use of chemical structure activity relationships, and new analytical methods in chemistry and biology are helping to replace or reduce animal use. In some cases, these alternative methods are faster, cheaper, or provide better information than traditional animal methods.

Why can't current non-animal methods replace all animal tests now? First of all, scientists don't know enough about the complex workings of a living being to reproduce certain effects outside the body in artificial environments such as cells growing in test tubes. Many safety questions, such as what happens when a chemical is absorbed internally, still require the study of complex interactions of inter-related tissues and organs—events that for now can only be studied in a living, intact animal.

Also, many different types of alternative methods must be developed to answer different kinds of safety questions. For example, a test used to predict eye irritation doesn't predict the potential of a chemical to cause birth defects. Even for a specific concern such as eye safety, a single test method often cannot reliably predict a response for all different kinds of ingredients used across the wide range of consumer products. For instance, you can't test an oily ingredient that won't "mix" with water with a method that requires the test material to be dissolved in water.

The use of animals in research goes beyond product safety testing. Basic research, designed to help us learn more about human physiology and health, in order to seek treatments and cures for the wide variety of human illness and diseases (such as cancers, AIDS, heart disease, etc.), as well as to learn more about appropriate nutrition to enable us to stay healthy, is done in humans when possible, but currently requires animal testing. It is difficult to imagine making progress in uncovering these mysteries without some use of animals.

Why are ethical issues important in science?

This is of course a huge question and many books have been written about it. Ethical issues related to science have also been explored in literature, from works like *Frankenstein* and *Dr. Jekyll and Mr. Hyde* to the early 20th century Sinclair Lewis novel *Arrowsmith* (which is listed in "Literature Connections" for this guide) as well as countless science fiction books, films, and Star Trek episodes. In the modern era, with the advent of nuclear weapons, genetic engineering, and other new medical advances and medicines, as well as increasing environmental awareness and concerns about animal and plant life, ethical issues have increasingly come to the fore.

As the content of this guide amply demonstrates, science and society are inextricably intertwined. Even abstract and complex mathematical manipulations can turn out to have great practical significance and enormous consequences. Einstein's Theory of Relativity, conceived in the realm of theoretical physics, provided the flash of insight that led to nuclear energy. The growing awareness by scientists that their work could be used in both destructive and constructive ways contributed to a wider awareness of ethical issues. With astounding breakthroughs in our understanding of DNA and genetics, numerous legal and ethical questions arise and continue to be debated. From the universally-condemned Hitlerian experiments to the wonderful advances in determining possible genetic defects, this is another part of science that has major and controversial societal repercussions. Fierce debate continues on topics such as whether or not to treat certain neurological disorders with tissue transplants—the list is long and growing. Topics such as abortion, organ donation, and the patenting of human genetic material also provoke intense debate with major ethical, moral, and religious overtones. More and more, citizens and scientists have become deeply concerned about the global environment—from the destruction of the rainforest and global warming to pollution of many kinds, population pressures, the endangerment and extinction of large numbers of plant and animal species, and the treatment of animals in nature, in captivity, and in scientific experimentation. In fact, specialized professional categories in law and medicine have developed to help facilitate discussion of and decisions on questions that have ethical consequences. Increasingly, scientific research institutions and committees have recognized the need to provide funding for and place high on the agenda environmental impacts, ethical and moral concerns, and, in general, to pay increased attention to the complex and changing interface between science and society.

For the purposes of this unit, the ethics of experimentation is discussed openly by students, and they can bring information from the unit as well as their own background knowledge to the discussion. The discussion is intended as a way for students to better understand the issues, make their own further investigations, and, most of all, make up their own minds. From Lash-Lure, hexacarbon solvents, and drug abuse to Marian Diamond's experiments with rats and general scientific and psychological interest in "wild" and "closet" children, numerous issues and connections arise. In the realm of learning, multiple intelligences, and the organization of our school systems, ethical concerns (such as the widely held belief that children of all backgrounds and cultures are entitled to an equal education) are far from absent! In the world that your students are already an important part of, where they will soon be decision-makers and leaders, there will be no shortage of ethical issues. It is hoped that their experience with this unit may contribute in some small way to their future decision-making wisdom.

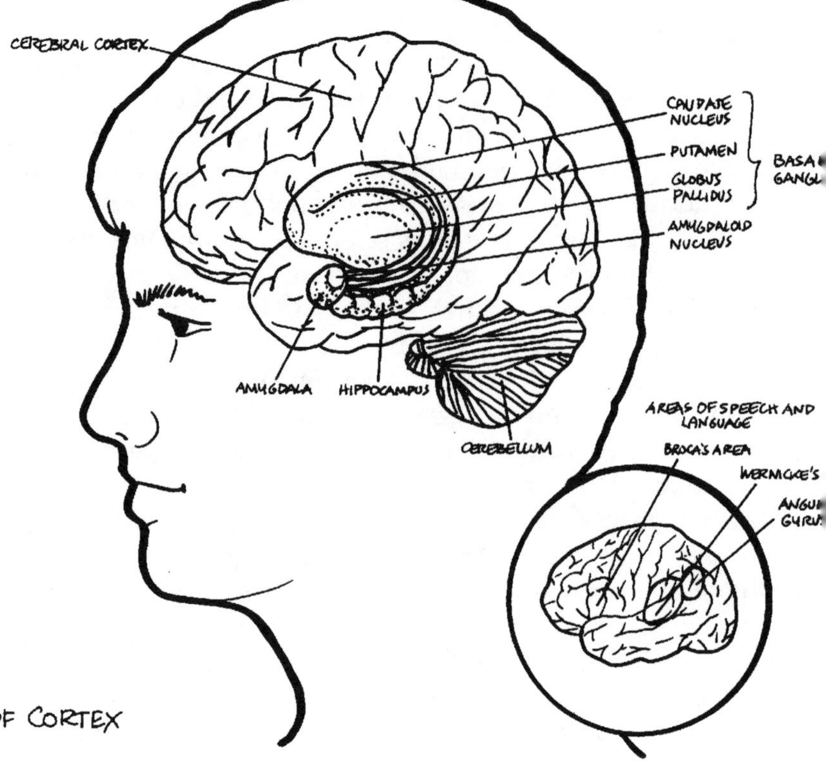

SCHEMATIC TOP VIEW OF CORTEX

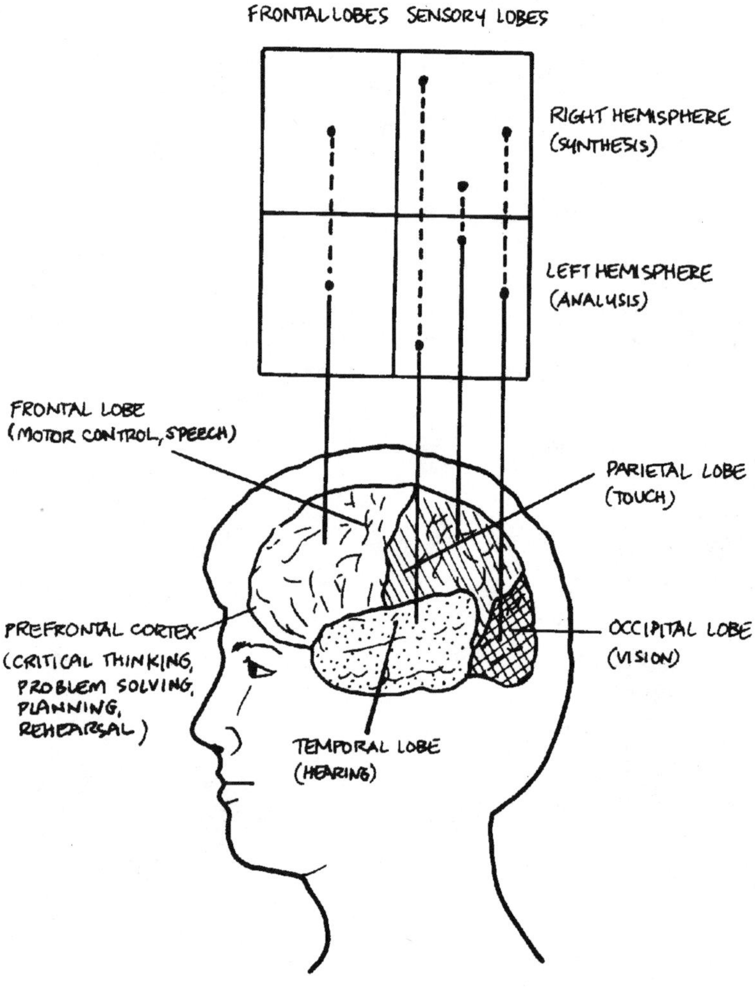

Resources

Brain Anatomy and Function

The Amazing Brain, Robert Ornstein and Richard Thompson, Houghton-Mifflin, Boston, 1984.

An Anthropologist on Mars: Seven Paradoxical Tales, Oliver Sacks, Knopf, New York, 1995. A book of case studies on autism.

Awakenings, Oliver Sacks, Summit Books, New York, 1987. The feature film, *Awakenings,* which is based on the book, is available from RCA/ Columbia Pictures Home Video, Burbank, California, 1991 VHS.

The Brain, Richard M. Restak, Bantam Books, New York, 1984.

"Brain Basics" by the National Institute of Neurological Disorders and Stroke, National Institutes of Health. NIH Publication No. 92-3440-a. Available from:

> Neurological Institute
> P.O. Box 5810
> Bethesda, MD 20824
> (800) 352-9424
> (301) 402-2186 (fax)

"Brain Calisthenics," Daniel Golden, *Life* magazine, July 1994. This article includes the information on the nuns from Mankato, Minnesota, who are volunteers in a study to examine the effects of stimulation on brain growth. It also contains an excellent summary of recent research on the human brain's ability to change and adapt throughout life.

"Brain Changes in Response to Experience," M. Rosenzweig, R. Bennett, and M. Diamond, *Scientific American,* volume 226, pages 22–29, 1972.

"Brain Facts: A Primer on the Brain and Nervous System" by the Society for Neuroscience, 1990. Available from:

> Society for Neuroscience
> 11 Dupont Circle, N.W., Suite 500
> Washington, D.C. 20036
> (202) 462-6688

*BrainLink*SM is a series of multidisciplinary activity-based units designed to teach elementary and early middle school students about the brain and nervous system. In addition to strong neuroscience content, the units aim to promote healthy behaviors and foster awareness of science and health careers. Four main units developed so far include many interesting and accessible hands-on activities, a mini-magazine, and stories about a group of children who call themselves the "Neuroexplorers." The four units are: "Brain Comparisons," "Motor Highways," "Sensory Systems," and

"Memory and Learning." The materials can be used at home, as well as in classrooms, museums, or community settings. The *BrainLink*[SM] project is headquartered at Baylor College of Medicine, Division of School-Based Programs, 1709 Dryden, Suite 545, Houston, TX 77030, and the phone number is (800) 798-8244. There are also regional *BrainLink*[SM] Centers at Boston University, University of Kentucky Medical Center, and the University of California, San Francisco (Science and Health Education Partnership). For more information, materials, or training, contact Baylor College of Medicine.

A Celebration of Neurons: An Educator's Guide to the Human Brain, Robert Sylwester, Association for Supervision and Curriculum Development, Alexandria, Virginia, 1995.

"Cerebral Changes in Rats Exposed Individually to an Enriched Environment," M. Rosenzweig and R. Bennett, *Journal of Comparative and Physical Psychology,* volume 80, pages 304–313, 1972.

de Bono's Thinking Course: Revised Edition, Edward de Bono, Facts on File, New York, 1994. An instruction manual for adults that contains a series of challenging intellectual exercises that children of most ages could learn to do, with strong emphasis on bringing creativity and problem-solving to the classroom. It is offered to provide ways to encourage students to really think. The final chapter suggests starting a "thinking club," aimed at improving thinking ability, with lots of fun happening in the process.

Emotional Intelligence: Why it can matter more than IQ, Daniel Goleman, Bantam Books, Doubleday Dell Publishing Group, New York, 1995. This best-seller focuses on the ways human brain structure and function contribute to our "emotional intelligence." It argues that this "emotional intelligence" (which includes much about how we relate to others in the family, the workplace, and the community) can often be far more decisive in a person's accomplishments and successes than the kind of intelligence presumably measured by IQ tests.

Enriching Heredity: The Impact of Our Environment on the Anatomy of the Brain, Marian C. Diamond, Free Press, New York, 1988. This book, by the leading brain scientist whose work forms the basis for the data simulations students analyze in Activities 7 and 8 of this guide, summarizes Dr. Diamond's research findings, with emphasis on the effects of impoverished and enriched environments.

"Gray Matters," Sharon Begley, *Newsweek,* volume CXXV, number 13, pages 48–54, 1995.

The Human Brain Coloring Book, Marian C. Diamond, Arnold B. Scheibel, and Lawrence M. Elson, HarperCollins, New York, 1985. Here's a great way to learn more about the basic anatomy of the brain—color it in! As with the other books in this series, concise, detailed, and accurate anatomical and physiological information and terminology accompanies the illustrations.

Inside the Brain: An Enthralling Account of the Structure and Workings of the Human Brain, William H. Calvin and George A. Ojemann, New American Library, New York, 1980. Though somewhat dated, this book remains one of the most accessible (and enthralling!) general treatments of the brain, peppered with intriguing stories and medical anecdotes.

"The Lost Art of Ginny Ruffner," Ann Japenga, *Health,* March/April, 1995.

Making Connections: Teaching and the Human Brain, Renate Nummela Caine and Geoffrey Caine, Addison-Wesley, Menlo Park, California, 1994. An excellent and up-to-date discussion connecting modern knowledge of brain structure and function to classroom practice and an improved understanding of the process of human learning. Highly recommended.

The Man Who Mistook His Wife for a Hat and Other Clinical Tales, Oliver Sacks, Summit Books, New York, 1985.

"A Mind of Three Minds: Educating the Triune Brain," P. D. MacLean, in Education and the Brain, *77th National Society for the Study of Education Yearbook,* edited by J. Chall and A. Mirsky, University of Chicago Press, Chicago, 1978.

The Mind, Richard M. Restak, Bantam Books, New York, 1988.

"A Neurologist's Notebook: Prodigies," Oliver Sacks, *New Yorker* magazine, volume LXX, No. 43, January 9, 1995. Also earlier article on an autistic woman who is a highly successful and innovative veterinarian.

"On the Brain of a Scientist: Albert Einstein," M. Diamond, A. Scheibel, G. Murphy, and T. Harvey, *Experimental Neurology,* volume 88, pages 198–204, 1985. The upshot (Dr. Diamond tells us) is that Einstein had an extraordinarily large number of glial cells. These are cells which provide support to the neurons. We are constantly creating glial cells as our brain functions and is stimulated (as opposed to neurons, of which we have only so many).

Origins of Neuroscience: A History of Explorations into Brain Function, Stanley Finger, Oxford University Press, New York, 1994. This detailed book surveys theories about many aspects of the human brain. It is written, with technical terminology, at an adult (or advanced high school) level, with emphasis on the historical development of current knowledge. It includes interesting details about the personalities involved in early explorations, with in-depth documentation of the thought processes that led to modern theories and understandings of brain functions.

"Plasticity in the 904-day-old Rat," M.C. Diamond, R.E. Johnson, A.M. Protti, C. Ott, and L. Kajisa, *Experimental Neurology*, volume 87, pages 309–317, 1985.

"Quiet Miracles of the Brain," Joel L. Swerdlow, *National Geographic*, volume 187, number 6, pages 2–41, 1995.

Rain Man, MGM/UA Home Video, Culver City, California. 1989 VHS

Your Child's Brain, ABC News Video Collection, Prime Time Special, 1994.

"Genie" and other Case Studies of "Wild Children"

The Forbidden Experiment: The Story of the Wild Boy of Aveyron, Roger Shattuck, Kodansha, New York, 1994.

Genie: A Linguistic Study of a Modern-Day "Wild Child," Susan Curtiss, Academic Press, San Diego, 1977. Dr. Curtiss worked with Genie for many years, especially on language.

Genie: A Scientific Tragedy, Russ Rymer, HarperCollins Publishers, New York, 1994.

Genie: An Abused Child's Flight From Silence, Russ Rymer, HarperCollins Publishers, New York, 1993.

NOVA: The Secret of the Wild Child, Linda Garmon, 1990. Videotape is available from:

WGBH
P. O. Box 2284
South Burlington, VT 05407
(800) 255-9424
item #WG2112

or from Blockbuster Video, item #21329. (If your local Blockbuster store doesn't carry it for rental, they can order it for purchase.)

The Wild Boy of Aveyron, Jean Itard, Appleton-Century-Crofts, New York, 1962. Details Itard's association with Victor.

The Wild Boy of Aveyron, Harlan Lane, Harvard University Press, Cambridge, Massachusetts, 1976. The opening chapters develop a remarkable picture of Victor's life before he came to Itard.

The Wild Child, Les Films du Carrosse, Warner Home Video, Culver City, California, 1991 VHS. This is the Truffaut film on Itard's work with Victor mentioned in Activity 6 of this guide.

Wolf Child and Human Child, Arnold Gesell, Harper, New York, 1941.

Wolf Children and the Problem of Human Nature, Lucien Malson, Monthly Review Press, New York, 1972.

Wolf Children and Feral Man, J.A.L Singh and R. M. Zingg, Harper, New York, 1942.

Howard Gardner's Theory of Multiple Intelligences

7 Kinds of Smart: Discovering and Using Your Natural Intelligence, Thomas Armstrong, Plume/Penguin, New York, 1993.

Common Miracles, ABC News Special with Peter Jennings, on education in the United States and theory of multiple intelligences.

Frames of Mind: The Theory of Multiple Intelligences, Howard Gardner, HarperCollins Publishers, New York, 1983.

In Their Own Way: Discovering and Encouraging Your Child's Personal Learning Style, Thomas Armstrong, Jeremy P. Tarcher Publishers, Los Angeles, 1987.

Multiple Intelligences in the Classroom, Thomas Armstrong, Association for Supervision and Curriculum Development, Alexandria, Virginia, 1994. This excellent and accessible summary is available from:

Association for Supervision and Curriculum Development
1250 N. Pitt St.
Alexandria, Virginia 22314
(703) 549-9110
(703) 549-3891 (fax)

Multiple Intelligences: The Theory in Practice, Howard Gardner, HarperCollins Publishers, New York, 1993.

"Reflections on Multiple Intelligences: Myths and Messages," Howard Gardner, *Phi Delta Kappan*, November, 1995.

The Unschooled Mind: How Children Think and How Schools Should Teach, Howard Gardner, HarperCollins Publishers, New York, 1992.

Braille Information

Information on Braille is available from:
American Foundation for the Blind
11 Penn Plaza, Suite 300
New York, NY 10001
(212) 502-7660
Teachers can request a free Braille card.

Biographies of the Blind

Mathematician and Computer Scientist, Caryn Navy, Mary Ellen Verheyden-Hilliard, Equity Institute, Bethesda, Maryland, 1988.

Ray Charles, Sharon Bell Mathis, Crowell, New York, 1973.

The Story of Stevie Wonder, James Haskins, Lothrop, Lee & Shepard, New York, 1976.

Please also see the "Literature Connections" section.

Product Testing

American Chamber of Horrors: The Truth About Food and Drugs, Ruth deForest Lamb, Ayer, Salem, New Hampshire, 1976.

Animals and Alternatives in Testing: History, Science, and Ethics by Joanne Zurlo, Deborah Rudacille, and Alan Goldberg, Mary Ann Liebert, Inc., Publishers, New York, 1994.

Consumer Product Safety: Why We Need It; How We Achieve It
Join Hands, the Health and Safety Educational Alliance
818 18th St. N.W., Suite 630
Washington, D.C. 20006-3513
(800) 933-8228

Wolf Behavior

Gray Wolf Web, the new Internet information system of Wolf Awareness, Inc. can be accessed on the Worldwide Web by connecting with the address: **http//publix.empath.on.ca/clupus**

Scent Marking in Wolves and Dogs. HOWLINGS, Wolf Awareness, Inc. volume 5, issue 3, Winter/Spring, 1995. Copies available from:

Wolf Awareness, Inc.
Ailsa Craig
G-2 Farms, R.R. #3
Ontario, Canada, N0M 1A0.

The Wolf: The Ecology and Behavior of an Endangered Species, L. David Mech, University of Minnesota Press, Minneapolis, 1981. A comprehensive and well-researched compendium of wolf biology written by the field's leading wolf biologist.

Of Wolves and Men, Barry Holstun Lopez, Charles Scribner's Sons, New York, 1978. Barry Lopez is the author of many children's books, as well as books on the environment and Native Americans. In this book, he draws the reader into the world of the wolf and explores diverse cultural images of this much-maligned animal: the wolf of the scientist/naturalist who collects biological data; the wolf perceived by the Eskimo people as, like themselves, a hunter and provider. For other Native peoples the wolf is a spiritual symbol of strength, both individual and collective. For the wolf killer, the wolf is seen as a frenzied predator to be annihilated. The author also explores the wolf of the human imagination—werewolves, feral children, the wolf of folklore and fable. As the book jacket puts it, "in reading *Of Wolves and Men* we not only learn a great deal about wolves, but we come face to face with ourselves."

Assessment Suggestions

Selected Student Outcomes

1. Students increase their understanding that learning relies on information from the world that we receive through our senses, and that learning is important to our survival.

2. Students describe factors that help and hinder learning and increase their understanding of their own learning strengths.

3. Students gain knowledge of the methods scientists use to test product safety and improve environmental and occupational health and safety, thereby increasing student understanding of how, as a community of humans, we learn things that are important for our survival and well-being.

4. Students improve their ability to collect and interpret data.

5. Students measure and compare diagrams of brain cells (neurons). They can describe the parts of a neuron.

6. Students are able to express and discuss relationships between enriched environments, increased learning, and increased growth of brain cells, thereby increasing their understanding of how learning enables organisms to thrive.

7. Students are able to articulate the potential benefits and disadvantages of various research methods.

Built-In Assessment Activities

- **Reflecting on Tactile Mazes.** At the conclusion of Activity 1, students discuss their experience learning mazes, their attempts to measure that learning, and the effects that limiting sensory information may have on their learning. Teachers can observe their students' progress in understanding how learning occurs. (Outcome 1)

- **What Helps and Hinders Learning.** In Activity 2, students generate two lists: things that help their learning, and things that hinder their learning. Teachers can note the quality of these class-generated lists. (Outcome 2)

- **Reflecting on the Lost Wolf Pup Simulation.** At the conclusion of Activity 3, students discuss their experience of doing the silent scent tracking activity and what was challenging about it. Teachers can observe their students' progress in understanding how learning occurs. (Outcome 1)

- **Solving the Hexacarbon Solvent Mystery.** In Activity 4, each medical research team comes to their own conclusion about what they think caused the problem in the two medical mysteries. Their conclusions and the reasoning behind them will demonstrate their ability to interpret data and make inferences from evidence. The teacher can assess this as she circulates among the groups and again when each group makes its report to the class. (Outcomes 3, 4, 7)

- **Reflecting on the Hungry Wolves Simulation.** In Activity 5, students reflect on their experience of watching themselves as wolves checking out "strange foods." They discuss what and how they learned about the foods. Through this discussion, the teacher can observe students' progress in understanding how learning occurs and how it is important to survival. (Outcome 1)

- **Letter to the Editor.** As a homework assignment after Activity 5, students write a letter to the editor discussing the importance of protecting people by testing products, and/or the controversy of using animals to test food, drugs, and cosmetics. Depending on his particular assessment goals, a teacher may choose to further focus this assignment. (Outcomes 3, 7)

- **Reflecting on The Story of Genie.** At the conclusion of Activity 6, students reflect on The Story of Genie and discuss the concept of enriched and impoverished environments and the ethics of conducting research with humans. (Outcomes 6, 7)

- **Parts of a Neuron.** In Activity 7, the teacher introduces students to neurons with her hand as a model and later asks students to identify the parts of a neuron in a diagram. The teacher can observe students' ability to use the terms axon, dendrite, and cell body accurately and comfortably throughout Activities 7 and 8 as they measure and compare neurons. (Outcome 5)

- **Measuring and Comparing Neurons.** In Activity 7, students measure neurons using a circle grid. The teacher can observe students' ability to do this as she circulates around the class and by observing the graphs students produce. (Outcome 5)

- **Drawing Conclusions.** In Activity 8, student research teams draw conclusions and make inferences about the data collected from Diamond's experiments. The teacher can observe abilities to interpret data as she circulates among the groups and when student groups present some of their findings. (Outcome 4)

- **Learning from Diamond's Research.** At the conclusion of Activity 8, students make inferences about Diamond's research and consider various questions regarding enrichment and brain growth. The discussion and student responses to questions provide insight into students' grasp of the relationship between enrichment, learning, and brain growth. Some teachers choose to assign the "provocative questions" listed in this section as an individual homework assignment, after they have been discussed in class. (Outcome 6)

- **Benefits and Problems of Research.** In Activity 9, students discuss the benefits and ethics of learning by conducting research of various kinds. This rich discussion provides the teacher with good insight about students' ability to articulate the issues involved. Some teachers choose to have students follow-up by writing both their personal viewpoint and the counter-arguments to it. (Outcome 7)

- **Reflecting on the Entire Unit.** At the conclusion of Activity 10, students reflect on the entire *Learning About Learning* unit and what they have learned. (Outcomes 1–7)

Additional Assessment Ideas

- **Reflecting on Learning with Limited Sensory Information.** As Going Further activities at the conclusion of Activity 1, students experience 10–15 minutes of class time blindfolded or watch a video with the sound off. They then write about their experience of learning with limited sensory information. The teacher may choose to further focus the writing. (Outcome 1)

- **What Kind of a Learner Am I?** Students can individually describe to the teacher what they have learned about their own learning and what learning modes seem most conducive to their learning. What were the things that really helped them learn? What factors seemed to strongly interfere with their learning? (Outcome 2)

- **Applying Learning Strategies.** As a Going Further activity at the conclusion of Activity 2, students apply some of the learning methods they discussed in class as they coach someone at home in learning their maze. Also, as a sidebar suggestion in Activity 2, students are challenged to find a new partner and use some of the best learning strategies that were mentioned to see if the rate of maze learning can be increased. Teachers may want to ask students to report which methods they tried and which were most successful. (Outcome 2)

- **Dramatize the Hexacarbon Solvent Mystery.** As a Going Further activity at the conclusion of Activity 4, students dramatize the story of the Hexacarbon Solvent Mystery for another class. Teachers may ask students to be sure to depict the methods scientists use to determine environmental and occupational health and safety. (Outcome 3)

- **Write a Letter.** As a Going Further activity at the conclusion of Activity 7, students are challenged to write a letter to someone telling about Diamond's research findings and how they relate to choice of lifestyle. (Outcome 6)

Literature Connections

In selecting literature connections for this diverse and complex guide, we sought books that reflected upon and deepened the context for one or more of the main activities. A number of the books focus on the process of scientific research; others delve into the experience of blindness; some examine the behavior of wolves. There are also books that focus on the importance of learning and sensory information for survival. We have included several books that, while technically non-fiction, connect strongly to the guide and are written in a literature-like narrative style. Several biographies are also included. Other resource books can be found in the "Resources" section. We welcome literature suggestions from you and your students. Your nominations will be considered when this teacher's guide is revised and may also be included in the GEMS handbook entitled *Once Upon A GEMS Guide: Connecting Young People's Literature to Great Explorations in Math and Science.*

Abel's Island
by William Steig
Farrar, Straus and Giroux, New York. 1976
Grades: 3–5

Abel is an urban mouse who suddenly finds himself stranded on a river island. Longing to return to the comforts of his home, Abel attempts to cross the river. Each time he comes up with a new method and is met with failure, he analyzes the situation and builds on his idea to devise a new method. Thus, he learns from his own experience—as students do in Activities 1 and 2 with tactile mazes. Through trial and error, Abel solves the problems of daily survival and the ultimate river crossing. This book also illustrates a valuable lesson from Activity 3—the importance of learning and sensory information to survival. Newbery honor book.

Arrowsmith
by Sinclair Lewis
P.F. Collier & Son, New York. 1925
Grades: 7–Adult

This book, by the noted American novelist, derives from the same historical period as the Lash-Lure story, and relates to both the Hexacarbon Solvent activities and the discussion of the ethics of experimentation in Activity 9. The novel tells the story of Martin Arrowsmith, who begins as a doctor, then becomes a researcher against disease at a large medical institute. The author tells us, "With all his amateurish fumbling, Martin had one characteristic without which there can be no science: a wide-ranging, sniffing, snuffling, undignified, unselfdramatizing curiosity, and it drove him on." For Martin, life is a constant learning process, both positive and negative, as he encounters great scientists with principles and integrity, as well as corruption, bribery, and deliberate experimental falsification. A major ethical issue (among many) arises in the latter part of the book, as Martin, supposed to be testing a vaccine on a Caribbean island, finds himself in the midst of a deadly epidemic and abandons his controlled experiments to give his vaccine freely to the population. Although the spread of the epidemic is halted and he is hailed as a savior, the vaccine's effectiveness is still unproved. Other preventative measures, such as the eradication of rodents who spread the disease, may have been responsible. Pondering the ethics of his actions, he thinks to himself, "Men who have never had the experience of trying, in the midst of an epidemic, to remain calm and keep experimental conditions, do not realize in the security of their laboratories what one has to contend with." The book ends on a note that echoes the trial and error joy of scientific investigation, as Martin chats with a fellow researcher: "I feel as if I were really beginning to work now...This new quinine stuff may prove pretty good. We'll plug along on it for two or three years, and maybe we'll get something permanent—and probably we'll fail!" The author acknowledges his debt to Dr. Paul H. DeKruif, the scientist and author of the classic book, *Microbe Hunters*, for creative collaboration, realistic detail about how large laboratories function, and bacteriological/medical information.

Better Mousetraps:
Product Improvements That Led to Success
by Nathan Aaseng
Lerner Publications, Minneapolis. 1990
Grades: 5–10

The book's focus is on "improvers, refiners, and polishers" and not on pioneers or trailblazers. To dramatize the results of safety testing, Elisha Otis set up an elevator at a big exposition in New York and had an assistant intentionally cut the cable with Otis aboard! The safety device brought the elevator to a halt in midfall. Getting heavy machinery to travel over muddy ground was the challenge faced by Caterpillar Tractor Company—what was learned in product development was applied to tank technology in World War I. The chapter on Eastman Kodak introduces the concept of a brand name, showing how Eastman promoted the names "Kodak" and "Brownie." This book illustrates how learning can be built up in a long-term way and that one person's idea can be developed by others. It also shows the development of knowledge in society.

The Cay
by Theodore Taylor
Doubleday, Garden City, New York. 1969
Grades: 5–9

When the freighter on which they are traveling is torpedoed by a German submarine during World War II, Phillip, an eleven-year-old white boy, blinded by a blow on the head during the explosion, and an old West Indian named Timothy are cast up on a very small Caribbean island—a cay. This is the story of their struggle for survival and of Phillip's efforts to adjust to his blindness and to understand the dignified, wise, and loving old man. Phillip soon begins to use his other senses to perceive what his eyes no longer do—he says, "I was learning to do things all over again, by touch and feel." Ties in well with Activities 1–3. See also *Timothy of the Cay*, the sequel to this book.

Dear Dr. Bell... Your Friend, Helen Keller
by Judith St. George
Putnam's Sons, New York. 1992
Grades: 4–6

This book outlines Helen Keller's life and gives additional information about the life-long influence that Alexander Graham Bell had on Helen. When Helen's father took her to a famous eye doctor hoping the doctor could help, the eye doctor recommended that Mr. Keller talk to Alexander Graham Bell, a well-known and well-respected teacher of the deaf. It was through Bell that Anne Sullivan came into, and forever altered, Helen's life. As with the autobiography, students will gain insight from this book into how Helen learned through her other senses (as the students themselves experience in Activities 1–3) and how the ingenuity and inventiveness of her teacher and herself allowed them to solve learning problems that had stymied others.

The Disease Fighters
The Nobel Prize in Medicine
by Nathan Aaseng
Lerner Publications, Minneapolis. 1987
Grades: 6–12

In Activities 4–8 of the guide, students learn how humankind, as a community, learns what is important for our survival and what foods, cosmetics, and medicines are safe. This book describes some of the major medical discoveries, such as the cure for tuberculosis and the cause of malaria, made by scientific researchers who were eventually awarded the Nobel Prize for medicine. For example: frustrated by his inability to treat his patients, Dr. Robert Koch, a country doctor in mid-1800s Prussia, focused his attention on research rather than the practice of medicine. He knew of Anton van Leeuwenhoek's discovery of bacteria nearly 200 years earlier, and of Louis Pasteur's theory that diseases are caused by bacteria and other microorganisms. Koch began to investigate the disease anthrax in sheep and discovered that a rod-shaped bacterium appeared in the blood of every sick sheep. After much research, he was able to isolate the anthrax bacterium and prove that it caused the disease. The laboratory procedures that Koch developed were adopted by many other scientists and advanced the study of microbiology, research, and medicine.

Eleven Blue Men
and Other Narratives of Medical Detection
by Berton Roueché
Little, Brown & Co., Boston. 1953
Grades: Adult

Though this is an older book, and therefore may be hard to find, it is worth tracking down (call around to several libraries; you'll find it). The book is a collection of articles originally published in *The New Yorker* magazine between 1947 and 1953; quite a while ago, so some of the medical information may be seriously out of date. But the unfolding of clues in each of the cases is the important part. This is a collection of epidemiological mysteries, much like the Legionnaire's disease outbreak of 1976 in Philadelphia. The intriguing title of the book comes from one of the cases presented—a case in which eleven men are all affected by sodium nitrite poisoning. Each of the men suffers from cyanosis—a bluing of the skin resulting from an insufficient supply of oxygen in the blood. Each of the cases in the book stands alone and could be read to the class by the teacher or assigned as homework. The investigative style through which each of the cases is solved closely parallels the hexacarbon solvent mystery of Activity 4 in *Learning About Learning*.

Flowers for Algernon
by Daniel Keyes
Harcourt Brace Jovanovich, San Diego. 1966
Grades: 7–Adult

Through his own "progris riports," this book chronicles the experiences of Charlie Gordon, a developmentally disabled adult who participates in an experiment designed to increase his intelligence. From his early child-like writing through his eloquent insights into human behavior and thought, the reader can follow Charlie's emotional and intellectual development. The experiment does work—it turns Charlie into a genius—but only temporarily. Many features of the book make it an excellent literature connection to *Learning About Learning*: the fact that Charlie is learning more and more, and at an accelerated rate; the ethics of animal experimentation; the use of mazes to demonstrate learning; and the implication that the results of the experiment on Charlie may help others with learning disabilities.

Follow My Leader
by James B. Garfield; illustrated by Robert Greiner
Viking Press, New York. 1957
Grades: 5–8

After a tragic accident with a firecracker, eleven-year-old Jimmy is blinded. Angry and certain he'll never be able to do anything again, Jimmy learns the importance of his other senses. As his rehabilitation teacher tells him, "You have an eye on the tip of each finger, one at the end of your white cane, one more on the point of each shoe, and the one great eye in the center of your brain. People don't see with their eyes; they see with their brains. They don't feel with their fingers or hear with their ears. When you touch something with your hand, or when you hear a sound, the brain tells you what it is." Connects well to Activities 1–3. Sexist attitudes and stereotypical depictions of females seriously detract and must be noted, but the book does effectively portray how Jimmy learns to use his other senses.

Hatchet
by Gary Paulsen
Bradbury Press/Macmillan, New York. 1987
Puffin/Viking Penguin, New York. 1988
Grades: 6–12

After the pilot of a single-engine plane dies of a heart attack, the sole passenger, thirteen-year-old Brian, is left to land the plane then survive alone in the forested Canadian wilderness. With nothing but the clothes on his back and a hatchet to help him, he slowly learns how to provide fire, shelter, and food for himself. Much of what he learns is from observing the animals, birds, and fish with whom he shares the forest. In all, he spends 54 days in the wilderness. In the ways Brian becomes more observant and learns from the world around him, this book connects to Activities 1–3 of *Learning About Learning*, and as Brian learns skills for survival, it also connects to Activities 4 and 5.

Julie of the Wolves
by Jean Craighead George; illustrations by John Schoenherr
HarperCollins, New York. 1974
Grades: 6–9

Thirteen-year-old Miyax runs away from her terrifying husband to walk across the Arctic tundra to the sea, intending to board a ship bound for the modern world of her San Francisco pen pal who calls her Julie. Close to starvation when she encounters a pack of wolves, she remembers her father's important lessons of the old ways and carefully observes the wolves, learns and copies their nonverbal language, and is eventually accepted as a member of the pack. The opening section of the book is rich with descriptions of wolf behavior as well as details about the tundra and its life, thus connecting strongly with Activities 3 and 5 of *Learning About Learning*. Newbery medal winner.

Louis Braille: The inventor of a way to read and write that has helped millions of blind people communicate with the world
by Beverley Birch
Gareth Stevens Children's Books, Milwaukee. 1989
(part of the "People Who Have Helped the World" series)
Grades: 5–9

In Activities 1 and 2, the students make tactile mazes and talk about how limited sensory input makes learning more difficult. But due to the invention of the raised-dot alphabet by Louis Braille, the world of books, and therefore learning and knowledge, became available to people with impaired vision. This book tells the life story of the 19th-century Frenchman, blinded at age 3, who was determined not to accept the idea that blindness must be a prison without books. Braille's invention was based on a system for printing books containing embossed letters developed by Valentin Haüy and a system using dots and dashes to express whole sounds developed by Captain Barbier for secret night writing by soldiers. Braille's lifelong dedication to perfecting his "little system" enabled millions of people with impaired vision to enter a different life because they could read, write, communicate, learn, and create—they could take their rightful place in society as cultured and educated human beings.

Lyddie
by Katherine Paterson
Penguin Books, New York. 1991
Grades: 6–10

This is the story of Lyddie, a poor farm girl in 1840s Vermont who, in search of a better life, is forced to work in a textile mill. There she makes many friends and is exposed to new ideas and new ways of life. One of her friends introduces Lyddie to reading and the joy of learning. From the lint-filled air of the mill, her friends and then her sister, who all work in the mill, develop bad coughs and other health problems. There are labor protests for better working conditions at the mill and many of Lyddie's friends leave their jobs because of health problems. Lyddie herself loses her job from defending one of her friends from the improper advances of their lecherous overseer. Unsure where she fits in the world, Lyddie goes on to college. A good literature connection for discussions of health and working conditions in factories (the hexacarbon solvent mystery in Activity 4), how earlier labor movements shaped today's working conditions, the need for health and safety regulations (as in Activity 5), and the impact of technology on societal change.

Mrs. Frisby and the Rats of NIMH
by Robert C. O'Brien; illustrated by Zena Bernstein
Atheneum, New York. 1971
Grades: 4–12

In this well-known book, a mother mouse named Mrs. Frisby learns that the rat colony near her home is actually a group of escapees from a NIMH research institute. She also discovers that her husband, recently killed by a cat, was also part of the NIMH experiment. The rats, injected with DNA and other substances, have acquired great intelligence, both from the injections and through increased stimulation. They have learned to read and write, and are planning to develop their own civilization. Many of their earlier research experiences and the escape are described in detail. This book presents an opportunity for reflection about the benefits and costs of learning by conducting research with animals, as in Activity 9 of *Learning About Learning,* and touches briefly on learning from environmental stimuli as in Activities 7 and 8. Newbery medal winner.

The Music of Dolphins
By Karen Hesse
Scholastic/Apple 1996, 1998
Grades: 6-12

Tells the story of a child thought to be lost at sea who is raised by dolphins. She is found by the Coast Guard and taken to Boston where she tells her story and longs to return to her dolphin family. Strong connection to the story of Genie.

Never Cry Wolf
by Farley Mowat
Atlantic Monthly Press/Little, Brown & Co., Boston. 1963
Bantam, New York. 1984
Grades: 6–Adult

Wolves are said to be killing too many of the Arctic caribou, so the Canadian Wildlife Service assigns a naturalist to investigate these changes. Farley Mowat is dropped alone onto the frozen tundra of Canada's Keewatin Barrens to live among the wolf packs and study their ways. This story of Mowat, his interactions with the wolf packs, and his growing respect and understanding for the wild wolf, will help students expand their knowledge of wolves beyond that given in the wolf simulations of Activities 3 and 5.

The Problem Solvers
by Nathan Aaseng
Lerner Publications, Minneapolis. 1987
Grades: 6–12

Insight and curiosity, the willingness to try something new, and using all one's senses are all valuable qualities to possess for learning. In Activities 1–3 of the guide, students learn how individuals learn. In Activities 4–8, the students discover ways in which the scientific community learns. This book discusses how individuals with insight and curiosity were able to form successful companies by finding creative solutions to problems. The names of these companies and the products they started are now famous—Evinrude, Kitchen-Aid dishwasher, Prudential Insurance, Polaroid, John Deere, and others. It is hard to imagine a time during which these familiar products did not exist, but as the introduction of the book states "a person with a creative, inventive mind might discover a new product where someone else just sees an annoyance."

Seeing in Special Ways: Children Living with Blindness
by Thomas Bergman
Gareth Stevens Children's Books, Milwaukee. 1989
Grades: 6–Adult

Interviews with a group of blind and partially sighted children in Sweden reveal their feelings about their disability and the ways they use their other senses to help them "see." Large black and white photos of the children accompany the interview text. The book also contains frequently asked questions about blindness, one of which debunks the myth that the other senses are automatically better in persons with vision impairments. It explains that instead the other senses must be developed because they are more necessary. Connects well to Activities 1–3 and is unique because it discusses blindness from the children's perspective.

The Seeing Stick
by Jane Yolen; illustrated by Remy Charlip and Demetra Maraslis
Thomas Y. Crowell, New York. 1977
Grades: K–6

This story, set in ancient Peking, relates how an old man teaches the Emperor's blind daughter to see. With the old man's carved seeing stick the princess learns how to use the "eyes" in her fingertips. Although this book is best suited for a younger reader, it is included here for its central message that although a person may be deprived of one sense, life can still be rewarding when they learn to use their other senses. This importance of senses is discussed in Activities 1–3 of *Learning About Learning*.

The Story of My Life
by Helen Keller and John Albert Macy
Doubleday, Garden City, New York. 1905
Grades: 8–Adult

As described in the preface, the book is divided into three parts: the story of Helen Keller; her letters (1887–1901); and a supplementary account of her education, including passages from the reports and letters of her teacher, Anne Mansfield Sullivan. By assimilating all three parts, the reader gets a full picture of Helen's life from several different points of view. While only a few students would read this book from cover to cover, essential passages could be assigned as homework or read to students to help them see that even though Helen was, at first, impaired from learning by physical barriers, she had an active mind. With caring, loving, and patient instruction from Anne Sullivan, Helen was able to learn volumes of information through her senses of touch, smell, and vibration (just as students experience learning through other senses in Activities 1–3).

Timothy of the Cay
by Theodore Taylor
Harcourt Brace, San Diego. 1993
Grades: 5–9

Having survived being blinded and shipwrecked on a tiny Caribbean island—a cay—for four months with an old West Indian man named Timothy, eleven-year-old white Phillip is rescued and hopes to regain his sight with a delicate operation. Alternate chapters follow the life of Timothy from his days as a young cabin boy to the days when his dream comes true and he is the captain of his own ship. Though not as closely connected to Activities 1–3 of *Learning About Learning* as *The Cay*, *Timothy of the Cay* does discuss learning through sensory input, visual impairment, survival, and wisdom. It also "fills in" *The Cay* as it tells the further story of Phillip—showing how his life changed after meeting Timothy—as well as telling the previous story of Timothy—how he became what he was when Phillip met him.

The Wild Boy
By Mordecai Gerstein
Farrar, Straus, and Giroux, 1998
Grades 6-9

Based on the true story of the "wild boy of Aveyron," who grew up wild in the forests of France and was later captured and studied by doctors in Paris. Strong connection to the story of Genie.

Note: On the internet, at book-related locations (such as Amazon.com) you can search under the category "feral children" and find a number of fictional and non-fictional works.

The Wise Woman and Her Secret
by Eve Merriam; illustrated by Linda Graves
Simon & Schuster, New York. 1991
Grades: K–3

A wise woman is sought out by many people for her wisdom. They look for the secret of her wisdom in the barn and in her house, but only little Jenny who lags and lingers and loiters and wanders finds it. The wise woman tells her, "...the secret of wisdom is to be curious—to take the time to look closely, to use all your senses to see and touch and taste and smell and hear. To keep on wandering and wondering." Though this book is intended for a younger reader, it is listed here because it captures the essence of what is meant by discovery, student-centered, use-your-senses learning, and, as such, serves as a fine accompaniment to *Learning About Learning*.

An "Electronic" book (available on the Internet)

Maze
by Christopher Manson
Henry Holt & Co., Inc., New York. 1995
Grades: 5–Adult

Based on the book *Maze: A Riddle in Words and Pictures* by Christopher Manson (Henry Holt & Co., Inc., New York. 1985), this new dimension in literature can be found on the Internet! The Uniform Resource Locator (URL) is

http://www.obs-us.com:80/obs/english/books/holt/books/maze/index.htm

As the Maze Directions say, "This is not really a book. This is a virtual space in the shape of a book...a maze. Each numbered page depicts a room in the Maze. The doors in each room lead to other rooms. Your challenge is to find your way from room 1 to room 45 and then back to room 1 using the shortest possible path. There are any number of clues in the drawings and in the story to help you choose the right door in each room." The reader goes into a room simply by clicking on one of the doors in the drawing. While not highly imaginative, this book is engaging, represents a new direction for books, and invites the reader to "use your head." Connects well to Activities 1–3 where students discover that learning relies on information from the world around us that we perceive through our senses.

There is an excellent website called "Neuroscience for Kids" which provides a regular e-newsletter free to those who sign up. The site is maintained by Eric H. Chudler, Ph.D. and supported by a Science Education Partnership Award (SEPA) from the National Center of Research Resources. It describes itself as created "for elementary and secondary school students and teachers who would like to learn more about the nervous system" and urges students to "enjoy the activities and experiments." It is highly recommended! Find it at:

http://faculty.washington.edu/chudler/neurok.html

Summary Outlines

Activity 1: Learning a Maze

Getting Ready Before the Day of the Activity

1. Acquire materials.
2. Duplicate student sheets and make overhead transparency.
3. Cut stick-on strips from mailing labels.
4. *(Optional)* Place stick-on strips and stickers in envelopes for easy distribution.

Getting Ready the Day of the Activity

1. Set up overhead projector.
2. Have materials for demonstration and distribution on hand.
3. If students don't have watches, set up a clock with a second hand.

Learning About Learning

1. Ask students, "How do you think we learn?" Accept all responses. Record ideas on the board.
2. Tell students this is the first session of a unit called *Learning About Learning*. Summarize what they will be learning about.

Introducing the Tactile Maze Activity

1. Tell students they'll be challenged to learn a maze, without using sense of sight. First, they design the maze.
2. Second, they'll work in pairs to learn each other's mazes. One partner will do the other's maze, blindfolded, several times, while partner times them. Then they'll switch roles. By timing maze runs, they can measure learning.
3. Model how to make tactile maze on overhead. Talk about your decisions as you make your maze. When students design their mazes, they'll do it behind a barrier.
4. Model how to conduct maze-learning trials with a volunteer partner. Students will conduct three timed trials of each maze.
5. Address issues of competition and judging each other. The main goal is *not* to do the maze as quickly as possible, but rather to see *how* they learn the maze and whether they can *measure* that process.

Making Mazes and Measuring Learning

1. Assign partners, distribute materials, and have students begin making their mazes.
2. Circulate, encouraging students. Have them finish within about ten minutes.
3. When each pair has made their mazes, begin maze-learning trials. Help them pace themselves so there is time to conduct three trials on each maze.
4. Ten minutes before end of class, focus students' attention.

Reflecting on the Experience

1. Conduct brief discussion about the experience of learning mazes. Could they tell they were learning? Ask questions to encourage discussion.
2. Ask if timing the trials was a good way to measure learning. Was it possible to learn without improving your time?
3. Conduct brief discussion about learning maze without their sense of sight. Did they use other senses? Was it harder?
4. Point out that **the more multi-sensory information we receive, the easier learning is.**
5. Collect mazes and student sheets or have students save them.

Activity 2: Good Teachers, Good Learners

Getting Ready

1. Have completed mazes and student sheets on hand.
2. Write "Helps Learning" and "Hinders Learning" on top of two large pieces of paper. Post at front of room. Have marker nearby.
3. If students don't have watches, set up clock with a second hand.

Learn How You Learn

1. Tell class that their job as students is to learn—they are professional learners! It is important for us to be aware of how we learn best so we can become better learners.
2. This session is also on tactile mazes, but this time they'll focus on **things that help or hinder their learning.**

Coaching Each Other

1. Tell students they will work with a new partner. As before, they take turns learning each other's mazes, but, in addition to timing, they are also their partner's teacher or coach. **The goal is to help partner learn maze.**
2. Ask for several suggestions of good teaching techniques.
3. Emphasize that goal is not to complete maze quickly, but to learn the maze. As teachers, they are responsible for their partners' learning.
4. Perhaps set up some parameters as they coach each other (e.g., no touching your partner's hand while he does the maze; no telling specific ways to go).
5. Tell students they'll have 15 minutes to coach each other—they'll need to conduct three timed trials for each maze and record their results on the student sheet.
6. Distribute mazes and student sheets. Have students choose partner, get a blindfold, and begin.
7. Circulate as students teach and learn mazes. Remind coaches their role is to help partners learn. Help students articulate strategies they're using.
8. Help students stay on task by reminding them of time limits.

What Helps and Hinders Learning

1. Refocus students' attention. Assist them to make two lists: things they discovered that helped their learning; things that hindered their learning.
2. As you call on students, help them articulate specific experiences as general statements.
3. To add to list, ask students to think beyond today's maze experience to their general experiences as learners.
4. Add some things to the list yourself (e.g., take notes, get your hands on it, use a highlighter, devise memory tricks, teach somebody else).
5. Summarize by saying these lists represent good ideas about ways humans tend to learn best and things that interfere with learning. Remind class that every learner is different—some people tend to be visual learners, others are more auditory, others kinesthetic. **All of us reflect different combinations of ways of learning.**
6. Bring up learning differences. Ask them to imagine their brains couldn't: see letters and words in order, tell left from right, remember auditory instructions.
7. Ask how these differences might affect their learning. How might they compensate? Explain that many people encounter challenges in the ways they learn. Most of us tend to learn best in a particular way or ways. **This has nothing to do with intelligence, but does affect the kind of sensory information people need to learn most effectively.**

Activity 3: Silent Smell Tracking

Getting Ready Before the Day of the Activity

1. Acquire materials.
2. Decide how many film canisters you will need for each extract.
3. *(Optional)* Label each film canister with a secret code.
4. Add some extract to each film canister.
5. Duplicate student sheets and overhead transparency.

Getting Ready the Day of the Activity

Decide where you want to conduct the activity.

Introducing the Activity

1. Remind class of how the unit so far has focused on how humans learn. Ask, "What are situations in which wolves need to learn in order to survive?"
2. Say that wolves, like people, rely for learning on information they perceive through their senses—they rely heavily on their very sensitive sense of smell.
3. Ask students to imagine they are lost wolf pups. Each pair of lost "wolf pups" will receive a "secret scent" in a film canister. Their challenge is to find all the other pups from their own pack, then together to find their home den.

4. Explain procedure:
a. Take whiff of scent and roam around room looking for other wolf pups from their pack by comparing smells in each other's canisters.
b. When they've located all in their pack, together they find home den.
c. This should be a silent smell tracking activity.
d. Point out orphan area for wolves who cannot find their packs.
e. If you labeled canisters, tell them not to look at bottoms of canisters.

Lost Wolf Pups Simulation

1. Have students begin simulation.
2. Circulate, reminding students not to speak. Packs should seek out dens.
3. Assist orphans.
4. When almost all have located their pack and den, collect canisters and have students sit down.

Reflect on the Wolf Simulation

1. Lead discussion about what it was like to do scent tracking activity.
2. Relate simulation to reality—in real life, each wolf pack does have its own smell. Tell how wolves generate and share their pack scent.
3. Close wolf discussion by saying that **this is an example of how learning is crucial to wolf survival.**

Humans as Sensory Beings

1. Point out that human beings use sense of smell for learning and protection, too. Give example of odor of rotten meat.
2. Ask class to brainstorm other odors that tip us off to potential danger.
3. Explain that not all things that smell bad are dangerous, but a bad smell can be a clue that a substance is in some way hazardous.
4. Distribute Nervous System Diagram. Show how information from our senses travels through our nerves to brain.
5. Summarize by saying that our senses, the **nerves that carry sensory information to the brain, and our brains are all involved in learning. Whether we are wolves or humans, learning is crucial for survival.**

Activity 4: The Hexacarbon Solvent Mystery

Getting Ready Before the Day of the Activity

1. Prepare medical research packets.
2. Prepare Chemical Suspect statements.
3. Duplicate copies of What Really Happened.
4. Prepare name tags.
5. Prepare yourself to play role of two neuropathy victims.

Getting Ready the Day of the Activity

1. Assemble materials needed for demonstration.
2. Have medical research packets and other student sheets ready for distribution.

3. Have chemical name tags and chemical statements on hand. *(Optional)* Attach statements to back of each of the name tags.
4. Set up overhead projector with nervous system transparency (from previous session).

Revisiting the Nervous System

1. Remind students that you previously talked about **the value of learning for survival.** Today they'll learn about actual events that show how scientists solved **two mysteries that threatened the lives and well being of many people.**
2. Present dollar bill challenge. Demonstrate catching it yourself. Then instruct them to watch your fingers, and, as you drop the bill, catch it with their fingers.
3. Invite a few volunteers to try, one at a time.
4. Ask students why they think you could catch the bill and they couldn't. Explain that our brains communicate with our bodies through the nervous system.
5. Show overhead transparency of nervous system. Point out central nervous system (brain and spinal cord) and peripheral nervous system (cranial and spinal nerves).
6. Explain pathway that begins with fingers letting go of dollar and ending with signaling muscles to catch it. The reason they couldn't catch the bill is that these messages don't travel fast enough. If we drop it ourselves, our own brain can *anticipate* the release time and instantly send the catch response.
7. Have students balance on one foot. This demonstrates that their nervous system is working. Explain how their brains initiated this action.
8. Have students sit down and circle their right foot in a clockwise direction on the floor while writing the number "6" in the air with their right index finger. Explain why this is difficult. Brains have to learn and remember the patterns they send through nerves.
9. Make comparison of learning to hitting a ball with a bat. This is a difficult task, too, until it is learned.
10. Instruct your students to sneeze, then have them try to hiccup. Explain difference between *voluntary* and *involuntary* brain messages.
11. **When the nervous system is damaged, these messages, both voluntary and involuntary, get messed up.** The results can be subtle or great.
12. Have students close eyes, stretch out right arm, then bring in arm and, with one finger, touch their noses. This is one test a doctor might use to test for *damage* to a part of a person's nervous system.

Introduce the Mysteries

1. Tell students they're going to attempt to solve two real medical mysteries about damage to the nervous system. They'll work in teams of four, and will receive similar evidence to that analyzed by real medical research teams.
2. Explain that in both mysteries, people were discovered to have nerve damage (what doctors call neuropathy). These people could no longer

do some of the activities students just did using their nervous systems.
3. Tell students you'll be playing the role of two neuropathy victims—one from each mystery. Their job is to be "medical detectives" or researchers and interview you to find out what's wrong and what might have caused it.
4. Mention that they'll soon have access to lists and other information that contain some important clues, but first they get a chance to interview. Suggest they may wish to take notes.
5. Emphasize you will be answering their questions **not** as yourself, but as the characters would probably answer. Mention again that they'll question you as one of the victims in Mystery #1 first, and then as a victim in Mystery #2. Point out that information about one is on white paper; the other on colored paper.

Conduct the Interviews

1. Put on Luis Marquez name tag and assume his character. Write his name and Mystery #1 on board. Introduce yourself and have students ask questions. Conduct interview standing. Ask students to limit questions to two or three minutes—there will be time for more questions later. Be careful to keep critical answers vague enough so that you don't give away the "answer." Don't volunteer information.
2. After you finish Luis Marquez interview, put on Steve Billings name tag and assume his character. Write Mystery #2 and his name on board. Introduce yourself and have students ask questions. Conduct interview sitting. Again, keep responses short.

Students Conduct Medical Research

1. Show students contents of packets teams will receive.
2. Information relating to Mystery #1 is on white paper; Mystery #2 on colored paper.
3. Tell students more information may become available later.
4. Students may continue to ask "victims" questions as they analyze information and you circulate.
5. Distribute research packets and have students begin.
6. Circulate, carrying the two name tags and victim information sheets. When students want to question Luis or Steve, put on name tag to clarify who is answering.
7. Spend some time with each team. Ask questions to challenge more rapid groups; drop hints to groups having difficulty.
8. After about ten minutes, announce that Tim Watkins (17-year-old on artificial respirator) has unfortunately just died of asthmatic complications.
9. Pass out two additional sheets to groups at appropriate times. Make sure every group eventually receives both sheets.
10. Teams work until they draw conclusions or you sense loss of interest.
11. Give five-minute warning before ending activity. Tell students to write down what they think caused nerve damage in each mystery on two pieces of paper, white and colored.

Reveal the Suspects

1. Ask member of each team to announce what they think caused the problem in Mystery #1, then in Mystery #2—r ecord on chalkboard.
2. Tell students you will divulge findings of medical research teams that worked on these mysteries in real life.
3. Ask three volunteers to come forward and face the class. Give each a chemical name tag and chemical suspect statement. Have them read statements to themselves.
4. Explain that these three will play the part of three chemicals suspected of causing the neuropathies in the two mysteries.
5. Read aloud teacher and student statements to create this mini-drama.
6. Thank volunteers and have them return to their seats.
7. Point out that all of these chemical suspects are in same family of solvents—they are all hexacarbon solvents. Some types of solvents, such as certain ones in the hexacarbon family, can cause nerve damage in people. This hazard was first discovered through these historic cases.
8. Point out that, unlike in the drama, chemicals are not guilty or bad. There are good and bad *uses* of chemicals, not good and bad chemicals. **Dangerous chemicals can be safely used with proper safety precautions—however, these precautions were not known at the time, because product testing done on these solvents was limited.**
9. Conclude by saying that student research teams did a great job—working together, like professional scientists, they learned more about what was causing the health problems. Have them reflect on the process they used.

What Really Happened

As a class, read aloud What Really Happened.

Activity 5: Learning What is Safe

Getting Ready Before the Day of the Activity

1. Plan how to color and flavor five different portions of macaroni.
2. Acquire materials.
3. Prepare the "strange" food.
4. Duplicate homework article for each student.

Getting Ready the Day of the Activity

1. Place prepared macaroni in five piles on tray and cover it.
2. Decide if article is to be read as homework or in another class session.

Hungry Wolves Simulation

1. Tell students they are again going to pretend to be wolves—this time they'll investigate how wolves learn what is safe to eat.
2. Ask them to imagine they are all members of a pack. They have been without food for a while and are very hungry. Several wolves run across what appears to be food and are checking it out. Ask for several volunteers.

3. Choose four or five and have them come to the front of room. Say you will show them food items in just a moment, after you explain procedure.
4. Describe procedure: each "wolf" needs to eat one food item. They take turns choosing and eating an item. While they may not talk, they can communicate as wolves do, reacting with their bodies, facial gestures, and sounds.
5. Remind rest of wolf pack (the class) they also should not speak. Their job is to learn, by observing, what they can about whether these food items are safe to eat.
6. Uncover tray of food items; have wolf volunteers begin.
7. End simulation after a variety of learning behaviors shown by wolf volunteers—this may take one or two rounds.

What Did You Learn?

1. Thank volunteers. Ask them and rest of "pack" to become students again.
2. Ask questions to lead discussion of the activity.
3. Send volunteers back to their seats.
4. Summarize by saying that people, like wolves and other animals, learn to avoid bad smelling and tasting things through their senses, memories of bad experiences, and observations of how others respond to certain foods.
5. Give another example of survival-related learning, such as birds eating red cherries but avoiding poisonous red berries.
6. Ask for ideas about how birds might learn this.

When There Are No Sensory Clues...

1. Point out that not all hazardous things have bad taste or odor, so learning also has to occur by observing what happens when someone comes into contact with that substance. Observation of a bad reaction may have to happen many times to make the connection (as in the Hexacarbon Solvent Mystery). Proving a substance is hazardous sometimes takes generations (e.g., cigarette smoking).
2. As humans, we have more options than wolves. Ask, "What are some of the things that we, as a society of humans, do to avoid potentially dangerous substances?"
3. Mention Food and Drug Administration—the FDA. We don't have to taste everything ourselves, like the wolves, to see if there is a hazard. Laws and regulations don't eliminate all danger, but provide a certain degree of protection.

Introducing the Homework: The Case of Lash-Lure

1. Explain to students that, within the lifetime of their grandparents, there weren't federal protective regulations. For homework, they'll read an article about a true story that led to establishment of Federal Food, Drug, and Cosmetic Act of 1938.
2. Ask students to write a letter to the editor about the article. Their letter can focus on any of the issues raised, such as the importance of protecting people by testing products, or the controversy about using animals to test food, drugs, and cosmetics.

Activity 6: The Story of Genie

Getting Ready Before the Day of the Activity

1. Duplicate The Story of Genie for each student.
2. *(Optional)* Obtain a video showing Genie or one of the "wild children." Schedule time for students to view.

Enriched and Impoverished Environments

1. As humans we are driven to learn. Curiosity is a trait of humans and other animals. Whether to learn how to protect ourselves or to find out something new—we go to great lengths to learn. Learning results not just in our survival—**learning causes us to thrive.**
2. Our **environment makes a huge difference** in how well we learn. Ask students to imagine trying to learn how to count in two different situations: an "enriched" environment or an "impoverished" environment. Expand on what these two environments might be like.
3. Ask, "In which environment would you learn to count best, an enriched or an impoverished one?"
4. Explain that, over the centuries, people learned a lot about learning through cases of children raised in strange circumstances—"wild children" and "closet children." Briefly describe some of the well known cases.
5. Explain that both "wild children" and "closet children" were exposed to extremely impoverished environments.
6. Say that when these children have been discovered, many different kinds of scientists have been very interested. Scientists wanted to know what would happen if these children were put in an enriched environment—would they now be able to learn language and other things they had been unable to learn in their impoverished environments? Or had their brains been permanently affected by having been in impoverished environments?

Reading and Discussing The Story of Genie

1. Tell students they are going to read a story about Genie—one of the most studied of these children.
2. Distribute copies of story and have students read, either silently or aloud as a group.
3. Allow time for open-ended discussion.
4. Steer discussion to concept of impoverished and enriched environments and whether the environment in which humans are raised can affect how a person's brain develops.
5. Ask class if they think it was wrong for scientists to study Genie. Ask, "Is it possible for scientists to learn about learning without studying humans?"
6. Tell students that a scientist named Dr. Marian Cleeves Diamond wondered about some of these same questions, including—does learning change the structure of our brains? She conducted studies on rats to see if being in impoverished environments (where little learning occurs)

caused the brain to grow differently than in enriched environments (where lots of learning occurs).
7. In the next two sessions, students will learn more about Diamond's research as they conduct simulated experiments based on her work.

Activity 7: Learning and Environment (Part I)

Getting Ready Before the Day of the Activity

1. Duplicate one copy each of the Rats in Cages diagrams and color code.
2. Duplicate one Rat Brain Cell—Control Group diagram for each student and yourself. Make overhead transparency of it.
3. Duplicate set of four Rat Brain Cell diagrams from other Experimental Groups for each team of students, and an extra set for yourself.
4. Using blank transparencies, make a Circle Grid for each student and one for yourself.
5. Duplicate Dendrite Graphing Sheet for each student and make an overhead transparency of it.
6. Make overhead transparency of Instructions for Dendrite Graphing.
7. Set up folders for each team, with student sheets and circle grids.

Getting Ready the Day of the Activity

1. Set up overhead projector. Put Rat Brain Cell—Control Group diagram on overhead, with other transparencies and masking tape nearby.
2. Tape up five Rats in Cages diagrams with five corresponding Rat Brain Cell diagrams.
3. Have materials on hand for distribution.

Marian Diamond's Experiment

1. Tell class they are going to do "brain research" similar to that done by Dr. Marian Diamond. Diamond investigated if spending time in "enriched" environments causes the brain of rats to grow in different ways than in "impoverished" environments.
2. Diamond compared rats in a standard cage environment with rats in impoverished and enriched environments.
3. Focus attention on five Rats in Cages diagrams, representing cage environments Diamond used in her experiments.
4. Start with the Rats in Cages—Control Group diagram. Explain this is the standard environment for rats used by research labs around the nation. It is called the "control group" because the other groups are compared to it.
5. Introduce diagrams of the other four experimental groups and point out the features of each cage environment. Ask, "What might make these environments impoverished from a rat's point of view? enriched?"
6. Students will collect and compare data from some experiments that Diamond and her team did, using similar methods.

Introducing Neurons

1. Explain that at first it was hard for Diamond and her group to decide how to compare the rats' brains. They tried many different ways, including comparing individual brain cells.
2. Introduce brain cells (neurons) to your students using your hand as a model. Point out the cell body, the axon, and the dendrites. Mention that real neurons are very tiny.
3. Show diagram of the Rat Brain Cell—Control Group on the overhead. Ask students to point out cell body, axon, and dendrites.
4. Re-emphasize that Diamond's research focused on comparing individual brain cells from brains of rats in impoverished environments to those in enriched environments. That is just what students are going to do.

Comparing Neurons

1. Point out the posted Rat Brain Cell diagrams from brains of rats that spent time in the different cage environments. Students will measure differences between these brain cells.
2. Ask, "What are some of the ways we could measure the differences in brain cells?" Explain that Diamond and her team tried a variety of ways before they arrived at the measurement technique they used. You'll show students the circle grid method Diamond used so they can use it too.

Demonstrate How to Count Dendrite Crossings

1. Focus on overhead of Rat Brain Cell—Control Group diagram. Put Circle Grid on overhead for class to see.
2. Model procedure for counting and graphing the number of dendrite crossings until students understand the process.
3. Four students are a research team. Each person in the team counts and graphs the dendrite crossings for a rat brain cell from the Control Group. Then each student will count and graph one of the four Experimental Groups. When done, each team will have a complete set of graphs that compare the brain cells of rats from all of the cage environments.
4. Point out the "tag" in upper corner of each graphing sheet. Tell them they will each need to record information about the Control Group and the Experimental Group on their graphing sheet.

"Research Teams" Measure Brain Cells

1. After class understands what to do, put transparency of Instructions for Dendrite Graphing on overhead. Distribute file folders with student materials and lengths of masking tape. Have them begin.
2. As they work, circulate, checking progress, clarifying procedures, and encouraging them to make and share observations.
3. As they finish, have them replace their materials in the folder, label the folder with team member's names, and return folders to you.
4. In next activity, they'll work in teams to interpret graphs.

Activity 8: Learning and Environment (Part II)

Getting Ready Before the Day of the Activity
1. Make overhead transparency of Completed Dendrite Graphing Sheet.
2. Make overhead transparency of Questions to Consider.

Getting Ready the Day of the Activity
1. Post five Rats in Cages diagrams and corresponding five Rat Brain Cell diagrams.
2. Set up overhead projector and place transparency of Completed Dendrite Graphing Sheet on it.
3. Have file folders and blank paper ready to distribute.
4. *(Optional)* Duplicate copies of What's Really Going On In There? for homework.

Delving Into Data
1. Students will work in their teams to draw conclusions about data. Explain that this is one of the most enjoyable parts of research. After weeks, months, or years of conducting an experiment and collecting data, scientists finally get to see if initial questions were answered, make new discoveries, and generate new questions.
2. Remind students of the Diamond team's question: Are brains of rats raised in impoverished environments different from brains of rats raised in enriched environments? They wanted to know if there was an effect on the brain related to these variables: living with other rats ("friends"), in different-sized cages, with or without "toys."
3. Model process of drawing conclusions based on this data:
a. Focus class on Experimental Group 1 compared to the Control Group. Ask, "What is the difference between these two experimental groups?"
b. Show transparency of Completed Dendrite Graphing Sheet. Ask, "What can you say about the brain cells in these two groups based on the data in these graphs?"
c. Ask, "What conclusions could you draw from the data?" Record statements on board.
4. Tell class to work in their research teams to draw further conclusions based on their results. Ask them to consider these questions—display Questions to Consider on the overhead.
5. Have student generate conclusions statements and record them on sheet of paper.

Drawing Conclusions—the Fun Part!
1. Have students begin. Circulate as they work, asking questions to encourage logical thinking and stimulate curious minds.
2. After about 15–20 minutes, invite research teams to share one conclusion they made about the data.
3. After students present some findings, share some of Diamond's findings.

Learning from this Research

1. Stimulate students to make inferences from the Diamond research by asking provocative questions such as:

- "Do you think this research would hold true for humans—that neurons will lose some of their dendrites if a person goes from an enriched environment to an impoverished one?"
- "What would an enriched environment for humans be like—an impoverished environment?"
- "What advice would you give to the parents of a new baby? to a friend? to your grandparents?"
- "What does this research say about the old proverb 'It's never too late to change?'"

2. Explain that while such research could never be performed on humans, there has been other research conducted on human brains. Results indicate some of the same positive effects of stimulation and enrichment on brain health.

Activity 9: Ethics of Learning

Benefits and Problems of Research

1. Tell class that in this unit they've learned about some research done by scientists: The Hexacarbon Solvent Mystery, the story of Lash-Lure, the research done with Genie, and Marian Diamond's brain research.
2. Ask them to think of the **benefits of this research.** What was discovered? How did this help humans? List their ideas on the board under heading "Benefits of Conducting Research."
3. Ask them to think about the **problems of conducting research using humans.** Make a list on the board under heading "Problems of Conducting Research on Humans."
4. Ask them to think about the **problems of conducting research using live animals.** Make a list of their ideas on the board under heading "Problems of Conducting Research on Animals."
5. Ask them to think about the **problems of conducting *in vitro* research.** Make a list of their ideas on the board under heading "Problems of Conducting *In Vitro* Research."
6. Summarize by saying that we saw what happened in situations where people died and/or were damaged by products that weren't tested adequately. Protecting ourselves in these cases requires learning as much as we can about these products through testing. However, each of these testing types has its problems or issues—there is rarely a perfect solution. Scientists are working to develop alternatives to animal testing whenever possible.
7. Stimulate further discussion by asking questions that bring out complexity of the issues.

Activity 10: Learning About Learning—The Play

Getting Ready Before the Day of the Activity

1. Duplicate seven copies of Common Sense: The GEMS Learning About Learning Play. *(Optional)* Duplicate enough so "audience" can read along.
2. Write name of one character on one copy of the play and highlight the lines that character says. Do this for the other five characters. *(Optional)* Highlight stage directions in different color.
3. Make name tags for each character.
4. *(Optional)* Decide about costumes and props.

Getting Ready the Day of the Activity

1. Put name tag and script for each character together, for distribution.
2. Decide who you would like to play each character.
3. Decide if you want to gather actors together for a few minutes, to alert them to the stage directions, point out difficult words, etc.

What Have We Learned About Learning?

1. Tell students they'll reflect on the *Learning About Learning* unit in a fun way—by putting on a play.
2. Choose six volunteers and have them come to front of room. Give each a name tag and script. Organize them in the order in which they appear.
3. Describe the characters in the play.
4. Start the play by reading the narrator's paragraph. Have characters read their parts and prompt stage directions as necessary.
5. After the play, facilitate a discussion to help summarize and wrap up the unit. Encourage students to keep discovering the ways each of them learns best, to keep exploring how people learn with their senses and their amazing brains—in short, to keep learning about learning!